Roads Taken

HASIA R. DINER

Roads Taken

The Great Jewish Migrations to the New World and the Peddlers Who Forged the Way

Yale

UNIVERSITY PRESS

New Haven & London

Published with assistance from the Annie Burr Lewis Fund.

Yale University Press books may be purchased in quantity for
educational, business, or promotional use. For information, please e-mail
sales.press@yale.edu (U.S. office) or sales@yaleup.co.uk (U.K. office).

Set in Times Roman and Perpetua display type by IDS Infotech, Ltd.
Printed in the United States of America.

The Library of Congress has cataloged the hardcover edition as follows:
Diner, Hasia R. author.
Roads taken : The great Jewish migrations to the new world and
the peddlers who forged the way / Hasia R. Diner.
p.   cm.
Includes bibliographical references and index.
ISBN 978-0-300-17864-7 (cloth : alk. paper)   1. Jews—Economic
conditions—History.   2. Jewish peddlers—History.   3. Jewish
businesspeople—History.   4. Jews—Migrations—History. I. Title.
DS140.D56 2015
381'.108992407—dc23
2014022369

ISBN 978-0-300-23439-8 (pbk.)

A catalogue record for this book is available from the British Library.

To Hannah and Abraham
To Anh
To Emmanuel

Welcome to my world!

You road I enter upon and look around, I believe you are not all that is here,
I believe that much unseen is also here
—Walt Whitman, "Song of the Open Road"

Contents

Preface

Roads Taken tells a story about a mass of ordinary people who in their or-dinariness made history. The immigrant Jewish peddlers and the non-Jewish women to whom they sold come across here as actors in a vast historical drama which transformed both the Jewish people and the countries to which they immigrated by means of this prosaic, indeed pedestrian, occupation. A nearly ubiquitous figure on multiple continents around the "new world," the itinerant Jew, weighed down by a pack on his back or sitting behind a horse—no doubt as exhausted as himself—went house to house, farmstead to farmstead, mining camp to mining camp, and plantation to plantation, selling consumer goods to customers, one by one. These peddlers, newcomers from Europe, the Ottoman Empire, and North Africa, envisioned their peddling as a transitional phase in their lives, one that linked their lives in the homes they had just left and settling down in some new place.

Roads Taken may take as its subject a not particularly heroic or glorious chapter in history, but it allows its subject, peddling, to do some heavy work. It challenges the overwhelming tendency in Jewish history to emphasize antipathy to the Jews as the most powerful engine, which drove all develop-ments. The migrations to all these new lands cannot be explained fully by the conventional and worn-out explanation of anti-Semitism, anti-Jewish violence, or pogroms. Rather, the beckoning of newly opened territory for commerce in widely scattered places more powerfully pulled them out of their old homes than did persecution push them out.

"My" Jewish peddlers did not fall back on this classic Jewish occupation because the hostility of the larger world precluded engaging in other pursuits. They opted for it because they calculated that it provided them with the shortest and most efficient path to fulfilling the goals of their migration, namely economic advancement, marriage, family reunification, and achieving what they considered a good life. They did not turn to other Jews for credit because banks and other lending institutions harbored negative views of Jews. While bank presidents in fact might have not liked Jews, the Jewish peddlers had no interest in going to non-Jewish credit sources. They preferred to turn only to other Jews.

The experiences of the peddlers also chips away at some of the prevalent ideas in the scholarship and Jewish collective memory about peddlers. Jewish peddlers did not lack skill. Although they did not run machinery, make tools from iron, or build furniture, they knew or learned languages, developed accounting systems, and figured out where the best opportunities existed. They developed interpersonal communication skills, mastering the art of how to approach a variety of customers. The peddlers had to sharpen what the twenty-first century has defined as their "people skills."

So, too, new-world Jewish peddlers had more in common with one another than they differed based on where they came from. The notion that "German" and "eastern European" Jews underwent essentially different experiences falls by the wayside in the face of their shared peddler histories. The division of world Jewry into Ashkenazic—that is, European—and Sephardic, or Spanish-derived, halves fades on recognizing how peddling brought both to the Americas, the British Isles, and southern Africa. While they may have formed separate synagogues and communal bodies in Atlanta or in Havana, their new-world experiences took their shape from the fact that both took their first footsteps in these places as peddlers.

Finally, *Roads Taken* asks scholars of the many places to which Jews went through the aegis of peddling, to think about Jewish history as crucial to the histories of the United States, Canada, Mexico, Cuba, Wales, Jamaica, Argentina, Australia, Ireland, and so on. The experience of Jews in these places merits more than a paragraph or two, at the most, nor should it be considered to have been independent of or tangential to local and national developments. Rather, despite the relatively small number of Jews who may have migrated to these countries, and the various regions within, Jews furthered colonial developments and the exploitation of land for European expansion. The material goods that Jews brought to the women and men who did the basic work of the society—farming for themselves or laboring on the plantations of others, mining, logging, fishing—made a profound difference in their lives. The peddlers, young Jewish men drawn from the far reaches of Europe and the Islamic world, including the Ottoman Empire and North Africa, clothed, furnished, and decorated the homes of the people whose labor made possible the development of so many national treasures. The peddlers participated in a process which broke down class barriers in the places where they sold, and they spread the gospel of consumption as a matter of individual choice and personal enhancement. In many places they blunted the social isolation of farmers and their families living in remote regions, starving for company and news of the outside world. The story of the peddlers does not stand outside of the story of those countries and its people. Rather, the immigrant Jewish peddlers' story forms an integral element of these histories.[1]

In *Roads Taken* I look at the entirety of the new world, obviously offering only a bird's-eye view. But despite my global focus, much of my attention centers on the United States. Of the Jews who made up the foot soldiers of the great Jewish migration, more than 80 percent came to America. Of the 20 percent who did not, many wanted to, and some eventually did. The United States, more than any other place, matters in this history of peddling and the history of Jewish migration in the modern period. It offered Jewish immigrants a bundle of rights, political and economic, which could not be matched anyplace in the new world. The level of civic integration and religious innovation exhibited by the former peddlers who chose America had no new-world equivalent. Indeed, the experience of Jewish immigrant peddlers in America provides ringing endorsement of American exceptionalism, a concept much discredited by American historians, but one that reclaims its vitality when we investigate the experiences of the Jews.

The road functions as the central metaphor of this book, providing its intellectual core as well as its title and those of its chapters. That metaphor takes readers on a journey back to the points where and when Jewish peddlers got on the road, and down political, communal, and personal paths to where those roads took them. It evokes life on the road, with each vignette or narrative, each story about an individual or a place, a paving stone on the path toward the ultimate goal, which for the peddler meant crossing the road and getting off of it for good. The roads here connected Jewish peddlers to the homes of potential customers and led them to hubs of Jewish life.

Whom do I consider to be a peddler and whom not? The peddlers here went out on the road and crossed the thresholds of their customers' homes. The pushcart vendors who plied their goods in New York, London, Buenos Aires, Montreal, Johannesburg, and elsewhere are not here. They have a story that cries out to be told, but not in this book. They did not perform the one act which unites all the peddlers of this book. They did not go into their customers' domestic spaces. They carried on their business in the city streets, not going through the intensive process of cross-cultural engagement that on-the-road peddlers did, the ones who had to knock on the door, enter the abodes of those to whom they wanted to sell. These street merchants either stood in one place so that potential customers could come to them or they walked up and down the streets and alleyways singing out the nature of their wares. Women and men, adults and children rushed out to them and bought, and that constituted the entirety of their face-to-face engagement. They faced their own challenges, different from those of the on-the-road peddlers. In some places, at various times, urban peddlers did knock on doors of houses and apartment buildings and did cross over into their customers' spaces. These men, referred to often in Yiddish as *kloppers*—literally knockers—do, however, fit in this narrative, inasmuch as they traversed the boundary that separated seller and buyer.

Traveling salesmen also had an experience that put them in a different category from peddlers, and therefore their histories do not appear here.[2] Employees of a company, they carried a fixed set of goods to sell, and they had to follow a set record-keeping procedure. They could not, unlike the peddlers of this book, improvise; nor could they decide, based on either their own sense or the requests of customers, to offer new products. From the point of view of research, corporate archives of companies like Fuller Brush or the Singer Sewing Machine Company document the activities of the traveling salesman. Drummers also worked for manufacturers or distributors, and they sold not house by house, farm by farm, but rather store to store. They sold to shopkeepers, and therefore the drummers did not come into competition with the local business community. The Jewish peddlers who journeyed all over the new world worked for themselves, and no formal archives document their histories. Their stories emerged only as needles in the proverbial haystack.

Roads Taken tells the story of the male Jewish peddlers who trudged on and got off the road, but their story cannot be told without that of women, Jewish and non-Jewish. My narrative makes much of Jewish women, particularly those whom the peddlers married and whom they left in order to go out on the road. Men's peddling enabled Jewish women to take up communal roles they had not had before, and while they may have considered this a burden rather than an opportunity, as a new-world reality, the men's absence on a weekly basis allowed women to play key roles in shaping the modern Jewish experience. *Roads Taken* puts the Jewish male peddlers on center stage, but it makes clear that without the actions and aspirations of their female customers their journeys would have been roads to nowhere. Without the cooperation of the millions of women around the world to whom the Jewish peddlers wanted to sell, and without their ability to control some of their families' money, the peddlers would, in Israel Abrahams's words, have had to stay at home. While I take men to be my primary subjects, my narrative validates one of the central contentions of the field of women's history as it emerged in the latter part of the twentieth century. Leaving women out of the analysis, women's historians have contended, renders the narrative not only thinner and monochromatic but also wrong. You cannot study the activities of men independent of those of women.

I make no claim that this book is exhaustive. In national archives, the local historical societies in North, South, and Central America, in the British Isles and Ireland, in Sweden and elsewhere in Scandinavia, in Australia, New Zealand, South Africa, and Namibia, and in the official censuses of all those places, the details of the Jewish peddlers' experiences can be found. I saw some of these holdings and know how rich they are. Yet however many years I put into this project and regardless of the number of libraries and other repositories I went to, I know that the material I found, a fraction of which appears in these pages, represents the small tip of a veritable mountain range of what could be mined. Jewish peddler history is global history, but a global history made up of thousands of local histories, and no one can see everything. Indeed no one could actually say what everything means.

So this telling of the peddlers' tale involves posing a question which glides over time and space, perhaps promiscuously. How did the nature of the occupation of peddling, its ubiquitous knocking on the door of someone's home whose language the peddler did not know and whose culture he could not comprehend, help shape three phenomena of historic proportion: the great Jewish migration that lies at the heart of Jewish modernity, the integration of the Jews into the lands to which they went and in which they sold and then settled, and a new iteration of Jewish life?

This larger question raises numerous more. What did it mean for a woman to open the door of her home to a strange man, someone she had no reason to trust? What did it mean to the immigrant Jewish peddler to be moving in and out and about some strange new world? Did he define it as fundamentally hostile or as something within his power to comprehend and triumph over? How, given the scattered nature of the sources and the peripatetic nature of the peddlers' lives, particularly during the years they peddled, can we write with accuracy about their experiences? How reliably do memoirs, autobiographies, oral histories, family narratives, and the like record the details of life on the road? How can censuses, tax records, license applications, and police investigations be taken to have been accurate, given the fundamentally peripatetic nature of these men's lives?

This book tells the history of no single place or time. Rather, using the concepts of trade and migration, *Roads Taken* moves from place to place and time to time seeking comparisons, connections, and differences in trying to answer questions about the nature and legacies of Jewish peddling. Regardless of geography or chronology, the roads along which the Jewish peddlers traveled, out of the old world and into the new, shaped them, shaped Jewish history, and shaped the societies whose women and men in invited the peddlers into their homes.

Acknowledgments

The longer one works on a project, the more debts one incurs. The longer one works on a project, however, the more friends one makes, and the more one gets a chance to witness and enjoy the generosity of others, people who have made their time and resources available. I offer these few pages to them.

As always, funding must come first, and I begin with Alex Goren and the Goldstein-Goren Foundation, which created its center at New York University for the study of American Jewish history, which in turn provided generous assistance in multiple forms for this book. The book actually began at Princeton University's Shelby Cullom Davis Center for Historical Studies, directed by Tony Grafton. I had set out to write something on the Jews of Ireland, and everyplace I turned in that aborted research project I confronted the reality that so many of the Lithuanian Jewish men who immigrated there in the late nineteenth century came as peddlers. That piqued my interest in the occupation and its connection to Jewish migrations. I benefited tremendously from a year's fellowship at New York University's Humanities Institute, ably led by Jane Tylus and administered by Asya Berger. They and my fellow fellows provided a wonderful springboard for my ideas and valuable release time from teaching and committee work. Finally, I am grateful to the Guggenheim Foundation for a year's fellowship. I had applied previously for a Guggenheim and somehow never got it. But maybe the fact that Meyer Guggenheim got his start in America as an immigrant on-the-road peddler pushed my application to the top of the pile.

Rightly, librarians and archivists come next. If the money bought me the time to research and write, these repositories provided the material that made this all possible. The archivists and librarians at the Center for Jewish History, including YIVO, the American Jewish Historical Society, the Leo Baeck Institute, and the American Sephardi Federation, know that they serve as the custodians of probably the greatest repository of materials in modern Jewish history, and they all helped me tremendously. The fact that Jewish immigrant peddlers showed up in all their separate libraries and archives bears witness to the connectedness between those institutions, linages which transcend geography or institutional histories. Kevin Proffitt and his team at the American Jewish Archives in Cincinnati surely know how to treat researchers well, and they extended themselves for me, once again. The staff at New York University's Bobst Library, particularly Evelyn Ehrlich, did more than their job when it came to working with me on this project and indeed on all the ones that came before it.

Over the course of the years that I worked on this book I went to numerous archives around the United States and the bigger world, and I will name some here. Others can be gleaned from the footnotes. In Ireland I spent days on end at the Irish Jewish Museum, crowded with boxes galore full of rich material, watched over by the late Asher Siev. I found Jewish peddlers in the archives of Trinity College, the Limerick City Archives, and the Cork Historical and Archaeological Society, as well as the Central Archives for the History of the Jewish People in Jerusalem and the State Library of Victoria, which houses the papers of the Australian Jewish Historical Society of Victoria. I am in debt to the staffs of all those places.

Closer to home the Baker Library at Harvard University, the Maine Historical Society, the Bangor Public Library, the Wisconsin State Historical Society, Emory University, Tulane University, the Oregon Jewish Museum, the Jewish Museum of Maryland, the New-York Historical Society, the Jewish Heritage Collection at the College of Charleston, the South Carolina State Archives, the Rocky Mountain Jewish Historical Society, the Upper Midwest Jewish Archives at the University of Minnesota–Twin Cities, the Urbana (Illinois) Free Library, and the William Breman Jewish Heritage Museum in Atlanta all allowed me access to their holdings, which in turn led me to the worlds that the peddlers and their customers made. I want to give particular thanks to a few of the specific individuals who could not have been more generous, and they include Jeanne Abrams at the Rocky Mountain Jewish Historical Society, Deborah Weiner at the Jewish Museum of Maryland, Bill Barry at the Maine Historical Society, and Dale Rosengarten at the College of Charleston.

I went to some of these archives and libraries in conjunction with lectures I gave, some of them about peddlers and peddling, and I frankly cannot list all the names of the colleges, universities, and Jewish community centers which brought me to speak. My attentive audiences concurred with me that the peddlers had made history, and in fact nearly every time I spoke, whether in Fairfield, Connecticut, or Melbourne, Australia, numerous individuals got up and shared with me details of their family peddling stories, providing me with even more details. Their tales and their excitement about the project influenced me tremendously. Sometimes, in fact, before or after the talk, someone handed me a document, a photograph, a memoir, or a beloved grand-father's peddler license, material I would never have seen if I had merely stuck to the archives. I thank each and every one of them for their gifts and for their enthusiasm, a reaction that led me to consider even more strongly that the very ordinary immigrants whose stories I tell in this book functioned as actors in a great historic drama.

On the publishing end of this project, special thanks to my agent, Don Fehr, and to Jennifer Banks and Heather Gold at Yale University Press. They articulated real enthusiasm for the project and showed great faith in me.

One of the best parts of working on this book involved spending time with two wonderful women, both former students (and current friends) who approached me and asked if they could help as research assistants. I had to tell them that I had no money to pay them, but if they still wanted to work on the book, I had plenty for them to do. Jerri Sherman and Harriet Yassky did vast amounts of work in a variety of libraries, and they allowed me to see a range of documents that far exceeded what I could have done on my own. They were both meticulous in their research as they combed journals and magazines. Harriet went with me on several out-of-town archival expeditions, and eve-nings spent with her in the hours after the libraries closed made my time in Baltimore and Cincinnati pure fun. I thank them from the bottom of my heart and want them to know how much I appreciate what they did. They should, however, beware. I might ask them again.

The longest list comes next and is probably the one that will be most incom-plete. These are the many scholars and colleagues who over the years let me ramble on and on about "my" peddlers and who provided me with pointed questions, great insights, and unbounded enthusiasm. They include, first, nearly all of my colleagues in the Skirball Department of Hebrew and Judaic Studies at New York University, particularly Gennady Estraikh, my Yiddish reading partner. From the History Department at NYU, I want to shout out in particular to Barbra Weinstein, who alerted me to the fact that Jewish peddlers sold to workers in the Amazon rubber plantations, and to Lauren Benton and Andrew Needham, who never failed to ask me how the peddlers were coming along. Our conversations taught me much. Beyond NYU, Mitchell Hart provided a constant ear and sent me references galore. Tony Michels, Diane Vecchio, Ira Berlin, Tavolia Glymph, Steven Zipperstein, Louis Schmier, Leonard Rogoff, Sarah Stein, Ann Kirchner, Mark Bauman, Riva Krut, Lee Shai Weissbach, Anton Heike, Stuart Rakoff, Eric Goldstein, Josh Teplitzky, Natalia Aleksiun, and Stephen Whitfield, as well as Paula Eisenstein Baker, Jonathan Karp, Adam Teller, Milton Shain, Marsha Rozenblit, David Sorkin, Tobias Brinkman, Gur Alroey, Jerry Muller, and David Friedenreich, all listened and reacted. Derek Penslar, Sander Gilman, and Sarah Stein wrote letters on my behalf, and without their labors the process of birthing this book would have been delayed. Donna Gabaccia generously offered to read a draft of the cumbersome and bulky first manuscript, as did Diane Ashton, and I thank them heartily. Similarly, several of my students worked with me on this undertaking in various research and editorial capacities, and they include Amy Weiss, Shira Klein, Allan Amanik, and Yigal Sklarin. Three other individuals, one a high school student, Isabelle Singer, another a college student, Hannah Blume, and yet another a midcareer professional between jobs, Yehuda (Jason) Arenstein, emerged, as it were, out of the blue and asked to help me with my research, just for the experience, and they did fine work for me. No doubt I left off some very important names, and I am so sorry about that.

Marion Kaplan, however, deserves a paragraph of her own. She listened and listened as the project evolved. She asked probing questions, and in the end invested a great deal of time reading the manuscript, marking it up with queries and comments, and revealed that even I—the great enemy of the passive formulation—allowed a few of them to creep in. She blurs the line between professional associate and deep personal friend.

Three other individuals fall into two discrete categories, making it difficult for me to know where to include them. Should I thank them for their scholarly contributions to this book or for their emotional ones? I consider Eugene Sheppard, my son-in-law, and my husband, Steve Diner, to be both scholars whose ideas and insights shaped my work and, obviously, beloved family members. Steve once again read the manuscript, edited it with a vicious red pencil, trimming it, removing repetitions, and finding many—hopefully all—logical inconsistencies which plagued the early drafts. Eli Diner, with his sharp intellect, wide reading, and fine historical training, also played a part in making this book, from penetrating questions to editorial assistance and everything in between.

They, like my other immediate family members—my children Shira and Matan and the four newcomers to the Diner family circle to whom I dedicated this book—make life meaningful. On some imaginary scale which might be invoked to judge the relative value of writing another book versus being part of this family, the latter far outweighs the former. But having said that, I am thrilled to have had a chance to produce *Roads Taken*, which let me do what I love, namely, to take something fairly obvious and to invest it with historical meaning.

Roads Taken

Road Maps

An Introduction

"The Jewish peddler of recent centuries," wrote Israel Abrahams, a distinguished British Jewish scholar, "was no coward; had he lacked courage he must have remained at home." Abrahams's few words—delivered in 1896 as a rebuke to Anatole Leroy-Beaulieu, a French Catholic historian and writer who had recently claimed that Jews shunned "arduous physical undertakings" because they tended to be "averse to dangerous occupations"—not only revealed an element in the strategy Jews employed in their quest for rights and respectability at the end of the nineteenth century, but it focused attention on the most humble and, literally, most pedestrian segment of world Jewry, the peddler, making his way on the new world's many roads.[1]

Abrahams could have seized on other, more heroic images of contemporary Jews to prove their willingness to assume physical challenges, citing perhaps the Jewish men who had donned the military uniforms of their respective countries—France, Germany, England, and the United States, among others—and gone off to war. He also might have marshaled images of the groups of young Jews, men and women, embarking for Palestine, ready to conquer the soil and transform themselves into healthy tillers of the land. Willing to tackle the challenges of a hostile environment, these pioneers surely presented a stirring example of Jews who needed to be courageous. But instead Abrahams personified his claim of Jewish noble action in the figure of the more mundane, and much maligned, peddler "of recent centuries."

Those Jews, men who did not remain at home but rather went out to a variety of new worlds, launched their migrations by means of an occupation long associated with Jews. Whether the peddler was moving along the roads and plying his itinerant trade in Alsace or in Bavaria, in Lithuania or Galicia, in Morocco or Rhodes, places from which Jews emigrated, or in New York's Adirondack mountains, the cotton plantations of Georgia both in the ante- and postbellum eras, the foothills of the Andes in Peru, the Transvaal of southern Africa, the Swedish borderlands, the Irish Midlands, the vast prairies of Manitoba, the mining towns of Wales, or, for that matter, the mining camps of New South Wales, a smattering of the places to which Jews migrated, peddling mattered. This occupation, linked with the Jews for centuries, had shaped Jewish life before migration, but, as Abrahams pointed out, it also served as the engine which fostered the great Jewish migration, a mass movement which gave modern Jewish history much of its shape. Peddling also changed the multitude of places to which the Jews went, altering the material lives of men and women around the world.

That vast movement of people spanned nearly a century and a half, from the end of the eighteenth century, as the first batches of Jews left Poland and Morocco, making their way to the small provincial towns of England, through the 1920s, when for the most part large-scale Jewish migration ground to a halt in the face of restrictive legislation.[2] In that span of time, the long nineteenth century, more than three million Jews, about one-third of world Jewry, left their countries of origin, crossed some national border, in most cases got themselves across an ocean, or two, and set off on unfamiliar roads in a wide array of unfamiliar places which together constituted their new world.[3]

Their journeys altered the map of world Jewry. One Jewish writer in the second decade of the twentieth century proclaimed that this migration had "only one parallel in the whole of Jewish history, namely, those in the times of Jesus Christ, when multitudes of Jews were uprooted from Palestine to be planted along the coast of the Mediterranean." The newest dispersion of the Jews brought them to lands and continents unknown when they commenced.[4]

Some of the new places, such as England, Ireland, Wales, Scotland, and Sweden, do not properly fit the "new world" category. Europeans did not have to "discover" them in their colonial expansion of the world, and their indigenous population did not have to be subdued, enslaved, or displaced.[5] But for the Jews, the British Isles and Scandinavia constituted new lands. Hardly any Jews lived there, and the Jewish immigrant peddlers came as strangers, strikingly different in religion and language from the core populations. They earned their bread through occupations, namely commercial ones, that distinguished them from almost everyone else. Their experiences as peddlers differed little from those of Jews who went to, for example, Northern Rhodesia or New Zealand. There too, peddling defined Jewish settlement patterns and enabled the distribution of material goods.[6]

The great Jewish migration of the modern era created new Jewish communities all over the colonized world, with the United States as the most significant and the largest, by far. It left an indelible mark on Jewish history, creating new enclaves of Jews, women and men who, while sharing much with those who remained at home, forged new identities and modes of living. How they lived and constructed their Jewishness, influenced deeply by their time on the road, reflected much about their destination societies, including the political and cultural opportunities open to them as Jewish newcomers.

Peddling does not, by any measure, provide the only way to understand Jewish modernity, but it surely contributed to it. The experiences of these Jewish peddlers, their lives on and off their roads, the relationships which developed with their customers, and their own transformations, present a dramatic, albeit quotidian narrative. Ordinary men, they made strategic decisions that affected not just themselves but their families and communities back home and helped, one by one, to alter the places to which they went. They faced dangers. They lived with loneliness, week in and week out on the road. For most, the tribulations paid off, and they fulfilled the goals of the migration.[7]

This tale starts with millions of young Jewish men, who by themselves and in groups of brothers, cousins, and friends, decided that circumstances in their familiar homes held out few options, feelings sharpened by information trickling into their communities about possibilities elsewhere. Letters and remittances sent from abroad by their kin and friends who had already left convinced them that those other places around in the world offered so much more. Acting upon the discontent they felt and the knowledge they had acquired, they resolved to go far away and, in those new places, to take to the road as peddlers. The peddlers' story brings us into their homes and intimate lives as they negotiated with parents, wives, and sweethearts over the details and implications of leaving home and going off, probably for years, to barely known faraway lands, to be separated from each other by thousands of miles, across bodies of salt water, for some period of time, or maybe even forever.

The plot line of the peddlers' story, no matter which region they left and regardless of where they went, tracks their strategies as they, speakers of Yiddish or Ladino, as well as Polish, German, Ukrainian, Greek, Arabic, and Russian, immersed themselves, by necessity almost immediately, in the worlds of their customers, who communicated in English, French, Spanish, Mayan, Gaelic, Afrikaans, Cherokee, Swedish, Welsh, and a Babel of other languages. Into the dwelling places of those who spoke these unfamiliar tongues the newly

arrived Jewish immigrants had to go and sell. Their customers not only communicated in unfamiliar words but practiced cultures unknown to the central
and eastern European Jews and the Jews of the Muslim world who now found
themselves in Scotland, Quebec, Chile, Mexico, the Cape colony, Sweden, or
South Dakota. To sell their wares, the peddlers had no choice but to acquire
literally and figuratively new languages, to learn the details of the cultural
systems in which they found themselves.

The peddler's story, whether or not his specific name has survived in some
written source, whether he or his daughter or son someday became famous,
repeated itself, by the millions, all over the world. In this new-world Jewish
story the newcomer, laden with a pack of goods on his back, walked the roads
and knocked on doors of farmsteads in remote regions or in working-class
homes of settled neighborhoods on the edges of cities. Often lonely and miserable, enduring stifling heat and bitter cold, battling the elements, he began
his new-world road trip by striding through mining and logging camps, and
into laborers' homes on cotton, sugar, coffee, and rubber plantations.

In a way it did not matter where he went. The Jewish peddler experience
proved remarkably consistent around the world and across time. He knocked,
introduced himself to, almost always, a woman who opened the door. He asked
her to look in his bag, or box, or pack. He had to figure out how to ingratiate
himself to her, as every sale mattered, and to do so he had to guess what she
might want, what message to deploy in talking with her, and how best to charm
her into buying this or that. In this little drama played out on multiple continents,
in multiple languages, he proffered a range of goods which represented a new,
higher, and actually better, standard of living. He did not carry food or fuel, life's
basic necessities. Rather, from the depths of his pack he brought out for display
sheets and pillowcases, pictures and picture frames, clothing and cloth, needles,
threads, buttons, lace, bedspreads and tablecloths, eyeglasses, suspenders. The
list went on and on, as this paradigmatic peddler moved up the ladder and managed to acquire a horse and wagon. Then the goods got bigger and heavier,
stoves and bathtubs, still representing a cosmopolitan standard of consumption,
associated with cities, modernity, and the lifestyles of the better-off classes. The
Jewish immigrant peddler educated the farmers, miners, loggers, plantation
laborers, millworkers, and working-class families to crave these finer things in
life, goods associated with their social betters. The peddlers brought these goods
within reach of the more humble women whose homes they entered.

Few of the women to whom they sold, or their husbands, had had any previous contact with or exposure to Jews. They probably knew about the Israelites
of the Hebrew Bible and those who in Christian theology had betrayed Jesus,

crucified him, and continuously rejected his divinity. But until that first knock on the door, Jews did not exist as flesh-and-blood human beings. The young man who spoke a few halting heavily accented words in the local language became for the customers the bearers of Judaism, the exemplars of the Jewish people. As they went about the task of selling their jumble of goods, the peddlers exposed people to Jews as real people, the men who often slept in their homes, ate at their tables, chatted with them, with increasing fluency about the weather, religion, politics, family, whatever. Jewish peddlers immersed themselves in the new and previously unknown culture, and conversely the customers came to know Jews on an intensely personal basis. Each customer's home in each new-world setting functioned as a lived-learning laboratory in cultural contact, with the peddler teaching the customers about both cosmopolitan consumption and the Jewish tradition, and the customers teaching the Jewish peddler the basics of local life. Both the peddler and the customer benefited and changed through this exchange.

This trade created a cultural bridge between people who seemingly had so little else in common. The buying and selling of goods, conducted person to person, helped foster exchanges across otherwise deep divisions between people. The idea of trade as a positive force in forging human interactions has been a trope of liberal thinking since the eighteenth century. Tom Paine, in his revolutionary tract *The Rights of Man* (1791), declared it to be "a pacific system, operating to cordialise mankind, by rendering nations as well as individuals, useful to each other."

However useful or pacific, trade in general and immigrant Jewish peddling in particular also involved conflicts and enmities. One place after another witnessed acts of violence and resounded with ugly words, directed at the immigrant Jewish peddler. All around the peddlers' world danger rode with them along the roads. Wherever they went they had to be prepared to dodge snarling dogs and flee jeering young pranksters who found it amusing to hurl insults, snowballs, and sharp-edged stones at the strange-looking men with funny accents, loaded down by their heavy packs. Stories in local newspapers reported on robberies, beatings, and murders of hopeful Jewish peddlers. Unarmed men walking or riding the roads with goods and cash, the Jews attracted the unwanted attention of lawless individuals who considered them easy marks. Politically, local merchants had no love for the peddlers. As competitors who went into the women's homes, selling goods on the spot, on the installment plan and at lower prices than the owners of stores charged, the peddlers raised the ire of shopkeepers who wanted to capture the women's dollars, pounds, or pesos. The shopkeepers and their representatives pressed for political action, whether on the local or national level, to make life difficult for the peddlers. These actions in turn stimulated public debates about the Jewish peddlers and the danger they posed to the local order of things.

Their detractors argued that Jewish peddlers had other unfair advantages as well. They operated within a closed economic network, accessible only to Jews. They got goods and credit from Jewish shopkeepers, wholesalers, or owners of peddler warehouses. These in turn got their goods and their credit from Jewish wholesalers who sold on a larger scale and who themselves acquired stock and financial assistance from Jewish manufacturers and importers. In this worldwide story the individual peddler stood on the bottom rung of an integrated Jewish economy. Those at the higher rungs needed him to get those goods out directly to customers; he, in turn, needed those above him for the merchandise to sell. The peddlers functioned as the foot soldiers of a vast army of Jewish economic activity.

As in all ethnic niches, a culture of trust within the group underlay these business transactions. Because all players shared their Jewishness and all maintained connections to and through local Jewish communities, often sustained by family ties and common premigration hometowns, they, whether the peddlers or the suppliers, risked social exclusion and censure if they betrayed the confidence the others had placed in them. While disputes and conflicts flared within the Jewish niche, with arguments breaking up partnerships or splitting peddlers from their suppliers, for the most part Jews, from the peddlers on up to the highest levels, adhered to unwritten but deeply felt contracts that underlay the intricately articulated Jewish economic system.[8]

One peddler recruited another. Jewish shopkeepers relied on Jewish peddlers to get goods to customers who lived beyond easy access to the physical store. Jewish wholesalers needed the shopkeepers and the peddlers, while Jewish manufacturers, particularly in the clothing field, used wholesalers, warehouse owners, shopkeepers, and peddlers to move their products. Warehouse owners, fellow Jews and often former peddlers who had set themselves up in strategic regional locations, created larger or smaller entrepôts, nerve centers for this highly developed and ubiquitously replicated Jewish chain. Additionally, peddlers, once they graduated to distribution by horse and wagon, expanded their operation, buying up scrap, metal, paper, rags, and bones, and these items then ended up in the junkyards owned by Jews, former peddlers, now liberated from life on the road. Credit and money flowed along this circuit, an economic web which the Jews could call their own.[9]

Like other immigrants in a variety of countries around the world, Jewish peddlers fell into the category of middlemen, the stranger-trader, who linked the goods produced in the cities and imported from abroad to the millions of scattered potential customers who might want such items. These traders influenced deeply the development of new modes of consumption, which involved more than just one set of players selling goods to another. Items purchased and their cost touched on matters of family and community, politics and power. Escalating standards of desire for material goods challenged the hegemony of religious, economic, or political elites who in the main expected the poor to remain satisfied with the little they had, fearing escalations in aspiration. Spending and consuming goods in emulation of the behavior of the better-off seemed, the elite feared, to lead the poor, the have-nots, to want to share the political rights of those above them also. John Brewer and Roy Porter, in probably the most important book on the history of consumption, began their analysis by declaring, "In the modern world the ultimate test of the viability of regimes rests in their capacity, in the literal sense, 'to deliver the goods.' " Material acquisition mattered, and those who delivered shaped history.[10]

Women, primarily poorer ones, decided which goods to buy, when, and how, and did so with their husbands absent. That too made these transactions politically fraught. That wives engaged in these business undertakings without their husbands' knowledge and in concert with strangers, Jews who came in and then left, only heightened the historical gravitas of these commercial encounters, rendering them more than simply a purchase, say, of a tablecloth or a pair of glasses on credit. That women decided what to do with those goods, whether to use them or maybe pawn them when times got tough, also made consumption a crucial factor in gender and class politics.[11]

The Jewish peddlers stood, or better, walked, between the producers and the consumers, carrying the metropolis on their backs to the hinterlands. Once they began to collect junk, they conveyed the detritus of the hinterlands to the cities. Always different from the resident populations in every way that mattered—religion, language, occupation, cultural and social life—the Jewish peddler embodied all the characteristics of the middleman.

Petty commerce, whether sedentary or ambulatory, had been the Jews' métier for centuries. Peddling in particular had consumed the energies of millions of Jews, although new-world peddling differed markedly from that pursued in the old. Jewish peddlers in their premigration settings tended to follow that trade for a lifetime, and sons followed their fathers' paths. In much of Europe Jewish peddlers sold to Jews as well as non-Jews, and the nature of Jewish settlement patterns meant that peddlers could lodge in the homes and inns of their fellow Jews. Most of the Jewish peddlers' customers knew Jews, and whatever they thought of the Jews and their religion, Jews functioned as known elements of the local scene. At times, and in a variety of places, Jewish women peddled as well as men, and perhaps most important, governments, whether in Europe or the Muslim world, limited the goods Jews could sell, and when, where, and to whom they could do so. None of these conditions prevailed in the Jews' multiple destination sites.[12]

For sure, peddling before migration and after shared some common characteristics. Most profoundly, peddling in every environment involved life on the road, going home to home, beseeching customers to buy something, perhaps on the installment plan. Peddlers everywhere functioned in a dense Jewish economic web of relationships, with each peddler having a territory to operate in, usually referred to, perhaps sarcastically, as a *medinah*, or kingdom. The peddler received his medinah, whether in Alsace or Louisiana, Lithuania or Ireland, Turkey or Amazonia, from his wholesaler, the Jewish merchant above him on the pecking order who provided goods and credit.

Whether old-world and new-world peddling differed more than they resembled each other, the vast involvement of Jews in this field marked them as quite unlike most people around them. The nexus between Jews and trade had attracted the attention of commentators for centuries. Voltaire, Marx, Kant, Keynes, and numerous others, positively sometimes, negatively for the most part, had much to say about the concentration of the Jews in trade. Both non-Jewish and Jewish notables and intellectuals squirmed at the image of the Jews as peddlers and at the reality that so many of them passed through this occupation, not only in Europe but spreading out around the world to engage in this shameful undertaking. Worldwide Jewish philanthropic bodies and the great men who stood at their helm hoped to devise schemes to wean the Jews from peddling, to civilize the Jews, clean them up, and then, they hoped, lessen anti-Jewish prejudices.

Such efforts had little impact. Those who wanted Jews to become farmers, for example, failed to see not only how well most new-world customers interacted with the peddlers but how rapidly the peddlers moved from the road to settled circumstances. When the peddlers achieved the goals of their migration, as most did, they helped sustain the global web of Jewish commerce. When they got down from behind the horses which had pulled them on the road, the erstwhile peddlers opened up shops of one kind or another, or they became the proprietors of junk yards, pawn shops, peddler warehouses, and factories. They then outfitted the newest immigrants, who arrived and became the next cadre of peddlers to go out on the road. The newest newcomers, perforce, penetrated recently opened regions whose residents yearned for, or learned to yearn for, those material goods that enhanced life, recapitulating the experiences of the earlier Jewish peddlers.

Neither before nor after migration did Jews monopolize the peddling trade. Others traversed the roads as well.[13] In the middle of the eighteenth century in Europe all sorts of peddlers crossed borders, selling as independent entrepreneurs or as agents for established, settled merchants. Like the Jews, non-Jewish peddlers often followed fixed routes which linked specific places or regions to one another. Whether they carried a range of goods or specialized in a particular type, the expansion of peddling reflected the decline of traditional agriculture in the home regions and the opening up of newer hinterlands.[14] Wherever peddlers went, wherever they came from, they brought new goods, providing customers with novelty and luxury. Laurence Fontaine, author of one of the few books to take peddling seriously, *The History of Pedlars in Europe*, described peddlers as "men from marginalized regions . . . [who] travelled into the countryside to circulate the newest articles from the town." Popular literature and folk tales depicted *all* peddlers as inherently dangerous, prone to trickery, and foisting unnecessary consumer items on unsuspecting rural naïfs.[15]

Like the Jewish peddlers in the new world whose stories will emerge in the pages that follow, non-Jewish peddlers in Europe, Christians selling among Christians, inspired fear and distrust among elements of the population, particularly guild members and settled merchants who resented the competition posed by the peddlers. Local officials eager to maintain the peace sided with the peddlers' critics. Peddlers in England went by the title of "hawkers," a word linked to the negative imagery of spying and thievery. In every region peddlers penetrated, repressive legislation flourished in an effort to keep them out. Their presence as fixtures of everyday life and the pervasive sense that society had to protect itself against them provided a lived backdrop to "stranger" theory developed by the early-twentieth-century German sociologist Georg Simmel. "In the whole history of economic activity," Simmel wrote, "the stranger makes his appearance everywhere as a trader, and the trader makes his as a stranger. . . . The trader must be a stranger."[16]

Others peddled in the places from which Jews emigrated, and so too in the places to which they immigrated. Like the Jews, non-Jews, both old-time residents and newcomers from abroad, sought their livelihoods on the road, looking for customers to sell to. For many young men, primarily although not exclusively from New England in America's early national period, peddling proved an attractive threshold occupation. Coming from large farm families struggling to succeed on increasingly depleted soil, these Yankee peddlers fanned out through their own home region, and also made their way to the South and the newly settled trans-Appalachian Midwest. They became the stuff of literature, humor, and repressive legislation that sought to limit their access to potential customers.[17] In England, the hawkers, sometimes also called "cheap jacks," flooded the countryside, coming into people's homes, enduring the reputation of being "part gipsy, part thief, part lawyer and part idiot."[18] Sweden's Vastergotland province allowed peddlers, known as *knallar*, to sell from the road. They traveled from farm to farm selling goods. Even though the itinerants shared the religion, language, and national identity of the population as a whole, local merchants and craftsmen pressured the government to legally restrict them to selling only certain goods, such as bowls, iron products, and cloth, and all these goods had to be made locally. They similarly restricted the knallar to selling only three times a year, on dates fixed by official policy.[19]

These native insider traders fared no better and no worse than did later Jewish immigrant peddlers or than the peddlers of other backgrounds with whom the Jews shared the road. Other immigrants also came to the new world and took their first footsteps as peddlers. Irish and Scotch Irish peddlers also wended their way through Pennsylvania and the South for much of the nineteenth century, as did some German Gentiles, who seized on peddling as a reasonable economic strategy. Chinese peddlers made their way to and around Cuba in the early twentieth century.

But only for one immigrant group other than Jews did peddling constitute a way of life, a formative force in launching the migration, and a fundamental institution which both structured community life and provided the mechanism by which group members integrated into their new world home. Arabs, primarily Syrian (sometimes referred to as Syrian Lebanese), mostly Christians, made peddling part and parcel of their immigrant years. Their peddling journeys took them to many of the same places Jews went, including England, Australia, southern Africa, New England, the prairie states of the Middle West, the South, and throughout Latin America. Like Jewish immigrants, they built up an intricate, highly articulated ethnic economy with importers and wholesalers in the big cities connecting through smaller merchants and shopkeepers to the peddlers on the road. They too built up a system based on internal group credit and trust born of familial and communal intimacy.[20] Be it Brazil, Colombia, Mexico, or North Dakota, Syrian peddlers quickly learned the languages and cues of their customers' culture and used them to prosper, albeit for many (as with most Jews), modestly. Like the Jews, they, according to one observer of the Syrians in Mexico, "show great aptitude for learning Spanish."[21] Those who needed to, in Mexico, also mastered Mayan and various dialects which their customers spoke. As with the Jewish peddlers, immigrant Arab peddlers responded globally to changes in the destination places, calculating quickly when hearing the news about options in some new place, that those locales might be good places to go to try their hands (or feet) at peddling. Syrian immigrants, for example, began to show up in Brazil immediately upon the end of slavery in the 1888, and they took to the road carrying small household goods to the recently freed workers on the *fazenda*, or coffee plantations.[22]

Jews alone did not take to the roads of the new world to transform their lives, nor did they by themselves change the material circumstances of the women and men who welcomed them into their homes, peered into their bags, and made a purchase or two. Others joined them, but each yoked migration and peddling in distinctive ways. The ways they peddled, the routes they took, and the communal contexts of their days on the road reflected distinctive histories. Each has a story worth telling and this one focuses on the Jews. In the world history of peddling, from the end of the eighteenth century onward, they in particular seized upon this occupation, a familiar one, as a safe bet. They calculated that migrating to some new place, especially one where they already knew someone who could get them launched, and taking up the peddler's pack offered a reasonable chance at a better, safer, and more secure existence than what they would have endured had they stayed put.

1

Road Warriors

The Migration and the Peddlers

Of the world's approximately ten million Jews in the period from the end of the eighteenth into the early twentieth century, nearly five million left their homes, the communities of their birth, and went out into the world in search of new places to make a living. They moved mostly from rural areas to cities, from places of low and declining productivity to regions shaped by the commercial and industrial revolutions, beginning at the end of the eighteenth century as they sought out environments throbbing with new opportunities. Of those five million Jewish women and men, half of world Jewry, most crossed one or more national borders, millions making transoceanic voyages. That migration constituted a vast exodus out of Europe, the Ottoman Empire, and North Africa. Those who migrated, according to a pamphlet published decades later by the World Jewish Congress, should be considered in quasi-military terms. "Not the warrior, sword in hand," but "the toiling man in search of work with tools as his only weapon," the author wrote. He might well have added, "and with a pack on his back."[1]

Not all migrating Jews crossed bodies of salt water. Larger numbers abandoned the small towns and economically declining hinterlands for larger cities in their own or neighboring countries.[2] But in this very long nineteenth century, from the 1780s through the 1920s, the Jewish people also spread out to multiple lands on faraway continents. They went to places newly "discovered" and colonized by European powers. Some migrating Jews went to countries that needed no European discovery but had never supported visible Jewish populations. Yet as women and men in these lands started to aspire to higher levels of material consumption, they welcomed the arrival of the Jews, the peddlers. Only a small handful of Jews had lived in England, Ireland, and Sweden before the great migration, and the Jews who arrived in these places in those years made possible, for all intents and purposes, the first real encounters between the Jews and the autarkic population.[3]

The great Jewish migration constituted a mass human movement which might be seen as merely an extension of a process by which Jews in the seventeenth century began to move en masse from east to west. This reversed a long, drawn-out process that began in the eleventh century of moving from west to east, and also north to south: Jews from Spain in the fifteenth and sixteenth centuries had made their way to Italy, the Balkans, Asia Minor, and North Africa. Within Europe and the Ottoman Empire, Jews, partly due to peddling, had long moved around. Every place Jews lived, their communities mixed together the long settled and the new, native-born and foreign Jews.

But the great migration of the nineteenth century had a dynamism of its own that made it something to be considered in its own right. Peddling helped facilitate this new migration. Not that all came as peddlers, but so many did—countless numbers—that their presence and activities shaped the Jews' arrivals and their encounters with the native populations. For those Jewish immigrants who set up shops, for those who opened workshops to produce various kinds of consumer goods, clothing in particular, the peddlers among them functioned as the distributors of goods, the ones who got wares into customers' homes and hands. The willingness, or indeed eagerness, of so many to peddle, enabled the flourishing of the other, sedentary, and more capitalized enterprises of their fellow Jews.

WHY PEDDLING?

Large numbers of immigrants went immediately into some other low-level form of trade, and after the 1880s those who went particularly to New York took their first footsteps not across the thresholds of their customers' homes as peddlers, but into tenement sweatshops and then factories to sew clothes. But peddling offered something that other occupations did not. Keeping a shop required capital, and most immigrants did not have the resources to go immediately into sedentary trade. The shopkeeper needed the money to get started and keep the business going. He, or she, also had to cultivate a customer base, which required local knowledge, familiarity with prevailing tastes and cultures. Newcomers probably did not have any of these, and any who did not want to peddle had to work as a clerk in an already existing enterprise owned by a relative or another Jew. Shopkeeping worked best if a male entrepreneur had a wife present to "help." But many immigrants came either as bachelors or as married men whose wives remained back home, so they lacked the essential input of a female partner that spelled the difference between success and failure.

As to factory employment, although it dominated the work lives of migrating eastern European Jews after the 1870s, it, too, lacked some of the advantages that peddling offered. The industrial garment worker, whether laboring in a small workshop or in a factory, did not have what all commentators declared Jewish immigrants yearned for, self-employment. Working in a factory meant working for someone else, following his rules, bending to his dictates, toeing the line to a schedule set by the boss.[4]

Generally, beginning a new life in the United States, England, South Africa, or Canada as the employee of a garment factory meant ending it that way too. Some workers did manage to catapult themselves into ownership of a factory or a store, but most did not. The conditions of their work did not change much from the time they started their jobs until the time they stopped. Unionization certainly improved conditions in the factories, and modern factories differed from the sweated trades, but ultimately one still labored for someone else who held the power. Although garment factories tended to be owned by other Jews, until effective labor organizing and the imposition of state-mandated restrictions on the number of hours employers could force employees to labor, most factories churned out their goods on Saturday, the Jewish Sabbath. Not all the immigrants adhered meticulously to Jewish law, but the Sabbath, *shabbes* for the millions of Yiddish speakers, retained the aura of sanctity, however they observed it, and sitting in front of sewing machine did not comport with visions of holiness. J. K. Buchner, an immigrant from eastern Europe to the United States, wrote in 1871 that "They"—the immigrants—"could work in factories; but they are loath to do so, as they are eager to observe the Sabbath." The 102 Jewish women and the men (45 Italian immigrants also perished) who worked in New York City's Triangle Shirtwaist factory, the scene of an infamous 1911 fire, met their deaths on a Saturday, a mundane work day for them.[5]

Finally, industrial employment for Jewish immigrants, particularly in New York, meant working predominantly, at times exclusively, with others just like themselves, immigrant Jews from eastern Europe. Yiddish served as the language of the shop, as Jewish immigrant workers and Jewish bosses created a Jewish world of work. Work did not bring the immigrant Jewish masses into contact with other Americans, did not teach them the language of the land or the customs, tastes, and mores of the larger society. If Jewish immigrant workers in the factories had contact with non-Jews, they tended to be with other immigrants, mostly Italians who had no more exposure to American culture than the Jewish immigrants did.

But peddling held out, for those with little means, the prospects of some kind of self-employment, regardless of how little capital they arrived with, and it gave them the chance to maintain the kind of weekly calendar they wanted. Buchner, who observed the unhappiness of the Jewish immigrants whose factory employment forced them to violate the Sabbath, noted therefore, "they become peddlers or glaziers," the latter also a peripatetic occupation, albeit an urban one.[6]

In the later years of the great age of migration in more developed economies, the Jewish immigrant peddling phase waned, although it persisted in pockets of those places that developed later and more slowly. By the late nineteenth century the masses of Jewish immigrants going to the United States gravitated directly to the factories that produced garments in New York and other large cities. By that date, the establishment of department stores, often by former Jewish peddlers, and the emergence of mail order catalogues obviated the need for peddlers. But even then and into the early twentieth century some immigrant Jews went out beyond the large cities, and they, like those who arrived earlier, turned to peddling as their initial occupation. Jewish immigrants going to places like Ireland, South Africa, Australia, and much of Central and South America and the Caribbean, with large swaths of sparsely settled land, incomplete railroad systems, fewer industrialized cities, less robust economies, and less developed commercial infrastructures, cast their lot with peddling in substantial numbers, recapitulating what had been the American norm in the early nineteenth century.

THOSE WHO PEDDLED

In these places, throughout this long era, immigrant peddlers played a critical role in the spread of wares and the creation of local, regional, and national Jewish economic infrastructures. Although immigrants and outsiders with low status, the peddlers helped make possible the planting of Jewish enclaves around the world. Peddling became for many a significant, and in some times and places, the premier weapon in the struggle to gain a foothold in new places.[7] Yet everywhere, only fairly recent Jewish immigrants peddled. They did so for a few years, after arriving in their destination homes. Life histories, communal narratives, and statistical surveys show that the vast majority commenced peddling upon disembarkation from immigrant ships but plied the roads for no more than a decade. Most peddled for even shorter periods of time, and the sons of immigrant peddlers did not follow their fathers.

Only some of the Jewish immigrants had been peddlers before leaving home. Among the Jews who came to the United States from the Russian Empire, artisans far outnumbered those with commercial backgrounds, while among the central Europeans, many of the young men had probably peddled before emigrating.[8] But even among the former manual laborers, untold numbers went into peddling in their new worlds. Even if they themselves had never peddled in their former homes, young Jewish men would have known peddling as an ordinary and ubiquitous element of Jewish life. Faced with the challenge of getting started in a new place, they turned to something familiar, something, they considered, that Jews did. For them, as for those who had in fact peddled before migration, peddling functioned as a migration strategy, a way to put their dreams of starting over in a new place into action. They opted for peddling based on the advice of those who had earlier undergone the same ordeal, who assured them that it provided the surest route to making a bit of money, learning the ways of the new land, and achieving, in the long run, economic security.

We cannot know how many of the Jews who left for the new world had once peddled, or whose fathers had, but the places they abandoned had been peddler strongholds, including but hardly limited to Alsace, Lithuania, Galicia, Romania, Bavaria, Morocco, or Syria. The emigrants knew peddling, even if through osmosis as a quotidian detail of life. As immigrants they turned to it when they landed, learning where to get goods, credit, and a route. The details of the migrations, the demographic profile and economic conditions of those who left, the patterns by which they traveled, and the kinds of places they left behind, juxtaposed with the kinds of places to which they went, rendered peddling, the Jews' long métier, a perfect way to facilitate a transition from old to new.

WHERE THEY PEDDLED

The possibility of uncovering peddling opportunities shaped the emigrants' decisions in terms of where to go. They learned through books and newspapers, through letters and community talk, sometimes through Jewish philanthropic networks, about the opening up of places where peddling might be undertaken. Geography books circulated among Jewish readers, highlighting the details of all the world's strange and faraway places, describing the topography, flora, fauna, peoples, and cultures. Among these intriguing places, the United States in particular captured the imagination of Jewish writers, publishers, and readers. From the early nineteenth century on, the idea of America as a place where a poor boy could, through peddling, make himself over into a substantial man of property, took hold. I. M. Dick, a popular early-nineteenth-century Yiddish writer, used his novels to celebrate America, the land he described as "God's wonder," and he built many of his narratives around vignettes of peddling as a means of transforming poor Jewish immigrants into men of means.[9] Joachim Kampfe's *The Discovery of America*, published in 1817, also described the achievements of Jewish peddlers; the book went through numerous editions and reached large numbers of Yiddish readers.

Earlier, decades before the emigration from central Europe to America began, the idea of America as a place for Jews and its relationship to Jewish peddling circulated in Jewish circles. In 1783, the year that the British surrendered at Yorktown to the victorious Americans, an anonymous Jewish pamphleteer published *Schreben eines deutschen Juden an den americanischen Presidenten*, a letter to the president of the Continental Congress, asking him to consider inviting Jews to the new republic. First he introduced the Jews to the president, who probably never read the letter. "You would be astonished, most mighty President," the letter began after congratulating the Americans on their defeat of the British, "at the perseverance of a German Jew, if you could witness it. The great, nay, perhaps the greatest part of them, spend almost their whole life on the highway in the pursuit of retail business, and the trader consumes for his own person nothing but a herring and a penny loaf, the nearest brook or well has to supply his drink." This miserable Jew "has to strain . . . if he wants to live by it with his family." Writing as much to inspire the Jewish youth of the German-speaking states, the author declared that these same skills and experiences could easily be put to use in America, whose newly independent people, eager to burst out of the confines of the East and move west to land newly opened for settlement, would want someone to provide them with material goods. Who better, the article implied, than the selfsame German Jew, who already knew "life on the highway."[10]

Decades later, as the migration of young Jews from the German-speaking states proceeded at full speed, others among them, not sure where to go and what to do about their futures, could read numerous articles on the subject of America and its great possibilities for the Jews, like the one which reported in the *Allgemeine Zeitung des Judentums* in 1847:

We have in this city [New York] a great number of retail merchants who own business concerns which amount to 100 or 200 thousand dollars—and these people, upon their arrival six years ago, had not a penny in their pockets. They first carried 100 to 120 pound packs on their backs all day. . . . When they had already earned this "trifle," they began to peddle goods with horse and buggy.[11]

The information that flowed to the many places back home did not falsely sing the praises of the destination societies, nor did they make short shrift of the hardships attendant upon migration and peddling. An 1874 book by Leon Horowitz of Minsk, *Romaniahva'-Americka* (Romania and America), subtitled *A Book Containing My Travels in Romania, the Goodness of the United States and a Guide for Going to America*, assured his readers that "peddlers who go about the countryside with their wares on their shoulders can . . . earn their bread in America," but warned that despite the benevolence of America toward the Jews, "the work is exceedingly hard, and every peddler can sincerely say every day, 'This is the bread of affliction.' "[12]

Knowledge of particular places in the new world spread through books, newspapers, and word of mouth, and that knowledge stimulated migration and then further migration, despite reports of hardship. Jewish men from the Bessarabian cities of Czernowitz and Novoselitsa in the province of Bukovina made their way to the Caribbean island of Curaçao in the middle of the 1920s. Their letters sped eastward across the Atlantic, stimulating more and more of their friends and family to join them there. The letters that made their way from Curaçao to Bessarabia probably contained complaints of hard work, details of the drudgery and humiliation of being a klopper, the one who goes door to door trying to make a sale. But the letters also contained money, which spoke louder than words, telling a story of success and savings.[13]

The difficulties endured by the first immigrants to any one of the new-world places, as they struggled to find a foothold, did little to dim the sense by many still in the place of origin that emigration offered them the best chance to better their circumstances and that among the places they could go, America trumped them all. Norman Salsitz, describing his boyhood on the eve of World War I in the Polish town of Kolbuszowa, a place of four thousand residents, where the Jews labored as "artisans, craftsmen, peddlers, merchants and businessmen," thought of the United States as

a magical place, the perfect object of our desire. Citizens of Kolbuszowa, still we were in love with America. Nothing could change that; nothing ever did. . . . Such unqualified affection we had for America . . . whatever the realities, it was the idea of America that captivated us. Freedom, individual wealth, abundance, possibility—such a combination we found intoxicating.

Though neither a demographer, an economist, nor a sociologist, Salsitz rightly analyzed the connection between class, religious traditionalism, and migration as he pondered who among his neighbors yearned for America: "Kolbuszowa's poor had little to lose by leaving, and by and large they were the ones most eager to go." But on the other hand, "the well-to-do, those firmly established in the economic and religious life of our town, found the prospect less attractive."[14] And for those poor, peddling made sense as literally a threshold occupation.

Visits back home, undertaken by some successful immigrants, whether in the middle of the nineteenth century in central Europe or in the early twentieth in the Ottoman Empire, also helped whet the appetite of others to leave and spread knowledge of conditions in the destination society. That those conditions included peddling did not deter young Jews facing constricted opportunities at home. Julius Weis, from a village in the Rhenish Palatinate in 1826, grew up poor. America had captured his imagination, in part because his brother had left for the United States in 1837 and peddled in and around Natchez, Mississippi. In 1844 a cousin, also an emigrant to America, came back to the village, where "his arrival created quite a stir among our people, as he was one of the first from that section who had ever returned from America." The young Weis "listened to his accounts of this country, and made up my mind to come here." He got his wish. He left in 1845 bound for the port of New Orleans, and with the help of that cousin who had fired his longing for migration, he began to peddle.[15]

TO GO OR NOT TO GO

Balancing the choices open to them—staying put; going to a big city in Europe, the Ottoman Empire, or North Africa; or emigrating to the new world—consumed the Jews in the old one. Joseph Austrian was born in 1833 in a small village, Wittelshoffen in Bavaria. His mother never emigrated, but for the sake of her son, she "began planning," he wrote in his memoir, "as to my future. The income of the fields and the cattle business had declined, and considering the large family to be provided for, did not permit of incurring much expense for my higher education. ... My mother was anxious to get me away from Wittelshoffen, as she could see no future for me there." Since an older brother already had gone to California, via Panama, "it was ... decided that I with my sister Ida should emigrate to America." Like so many of his peers, he peddled upon arrival, selling at various times in northern Michigan among "the Indians and half breeds," and to the miners. His mother's deliberations worked out well enough, and he experienced the "improvement to be gained," which staying home, she had calculated, would not have afforded him.[16]

Jewish historians, among others, have long emphasized how Jewish migrations differed from other migrations at the time, insisting that Jews migrated because of the violence directed at them in the places where they lived and suffered. Unlike the millions of other Europeans and peoples of the Islamic world, who migrated for economic reasons, Jews joined them on ocean-bound ships fleeing persecution, often subsumed under the Russian word "pogrom." The Jews' migrations, this narrative has long insisted, lacked the economic impulse and the kind of deliberate calculations of costs and benefits, the weighing of risks and opportunities, that non-Jews engaged in.[17]

Jews differed, according to conventional thinking, because persecutions pushed them out and they had no real agency in deciding whether, when, and where to go. The Jewish philosopher Martin Buber, writing in the 1920s and deeply informed by his Zionism, described those Jews who left Europe, and who continued to go to all sorts of places other than Palestine, as "those dull nearly stupefied masses, being loaded aboard ship, not knowing where to or why." He echoed a widely shared Jewish sentiment that Jews did not migrate because they affirmatively embraced the greater opportunities awaiting them elsewhere, but reacted in fright to the oppressive conditions, to the bloodlust of their anti-Jewish neighbors who drove out the "homeless, tempest tossed," in the words of another Jewish writer, Emma Lazarus, who in her poem "The New Colossus" also got it wrong. While Lazarus's words, now emblazoned on the base of the Statue of Liberty, did not refer exclusively to Jewish immigrants, her other writings, such as "Songs of a Semite," detailing the suffering of the Jews in Russia during the 1881 pogroms, and her advocacy for the Jewish newcomers gave her universalistic words a decidedly Jewish patina.[18] Both Buber and Lazarus emphasized passivity. The Jews they described left as they heard the bloodcurdling screams of the anti-Semitic mobs crushing down on them.[19]

Certainly Jews lived with the reality of severe limitations on their rights. The specter of violence and expulsion hung over their heads, and those cannot be completely discounted in charting the migrations. But the Jewish migration cannot be explained purely in terms of the horrors of harrowing scenes of slaughter. Rather, the Jewish migrations of the nineteenth century resembled those of other peoples in terms of the economic calculus, the waning of possibilities back home, and the opening up of new ones in new places. The very patterns of Jewish migration bore witness to the economic bases of this vast human movement and the deliberateness of their planning.

And for the Jews, peddling helped shape that migratory experience, from the decision-making process in the old world to their first footsteps in the new. For example, many of the migrations involved men leaving first and establishing an economic base in a new home, leaving wives and children behind. The migrant would call for those left behind once he had saved enough to pay the fare for their transportation and could provide them with a new-world home. Had the pogroms or other forms of anti-Jewish violence been the root cause of the migration, Jewish men would have hardly exposed their families to the mob while they went off to Ireland or Australia.

What *did* make them different from so many of their coimmigrants, non-Jews who left and who settled in the same places, was the Jews' long history of migration, the self-awareness of Jews that they, in the sense of being part of the Jewish people, had once lived someplace else and had left it for yet another place. While the Jews were never nomads, their past migrations assumed a deep place in their self-conception. The stories they told themselves involved these many migrations. For many Jews, previous migrations had been part of their families' experiences. Being a stranger or an outsider hardly constituted a novel and traumatic experience for them, and indeed that alien quality enhanced the quality of group life.

So, too, their long history of being, as one writer has put it, those who "cultivate people . . . not fields or herds" also set them apart. Commerce of one kind or another infused their personal and communal lives for generations. While not all non-Jewish immigrants to the United States or Canada, Australia, or elsewhere came from the ranks of those who had cultivated fields and herds, most did.[20]

Jewish and contemporary non-Jewish migrations differed in other ways as well, and these differences also underscored the importance of peddling among Jews and the near absence of peddling among other immigrants.[21] Proportionately more Jews left than non-Jews, as measured by the percentage who abandoned particular places. A larger proportion of Jews abandoned the Russian Empire, Bavaria, Posen, Alsace, and Romania than did non-Jews from those same places. While in absolute numbers Christian immigrants predominated, proportionately the Jewish migration proved to be more intense and more dismissive of the societies they came from.

In addition, the often repeated statement holds true that Jews, unlike so many other immigrants, did not go back to their homelands. Such small numbers of Jews returned to their lands of origin as to render this phenomenon analytically insignificant. In contrast, nearly one-third of the Italian men who came to the United States, Argentina, or Brazil went back. Though Jews rarely reversed their migrations, some did visit. For a central European or Ottoman Jew who had gone to the Americas as a bachelor and spent his first years peddling, the return trip to a home village offered a chance to see parents and kin, show off his American clothing, and maybe most important, find a bride to take back to the shop which he had just opened in the new land.

Many Jews made multiple country migrations, starting off in one new land and then moving on to another. Polish Jews who emigrated to Sweden and England during much of the early to mid-nineteenth century, or Turkish Jews who went to Cuba in the twentieth, eventually went on to the United States. Many Jews who came from Lithuania to Ireland then joined their fellow "Litvaks" in South Africa. But none aspired to return to Suwałki, Izmir, or Kovno, or any of the hundreds of regions and towns in their old lands. Jews as immigrants, knowing they would not go back, recognized the need to get to know the places to which they had emigrated, to master languages and the details of prevailing values and norms. They needed to go through a process of cultural immersion, investing in the learning of the ways of life of their destination countries, and no occupation facilitated this better than peddling.

MIGRATION TALES

Each Jewish immigrant had a unique story worth telling, but in fact those narratives resemble one another as an aggregate more than one differs from the next. The networks by which they emigrated and immigrated, the Jewish communal resources that allowed them to peddle and in turn facilitated their success, bear striking likeness, one to the other. The chronologies, the place names, the local vocabulary differed, but not the dense connection between Jewish peddling and migration.[22]

The Jewish migrants who took up peddling in the far reaches of the world became an entrepreneurial proletariat, which undertook its work under a variety of names. In Europe, before migration, they went by the names *Nothandlers, dorfgeyrs, tendelrs*, and *karabolniks*, but in America they became "peddlers," in England and Australia "hawkers," and in Ireland "weekly men." Their customers referred to them as *ambulantes* (walkers) and *semananiks* (weekly men) and *cuentaniks* (those with accounts) in the Spanish-speaking countries of Latin America, *clientelchiks* (those with clients) in Portuguese-speaking Brazil, and *smous* among the Afrikaner in South Africa. Those who operated in cities were called *kloppers*, particularly among the Dutch speakers in Curaçao.

Whatever name or epithet they went by, the Jewish peddlers relied, every-where, on Jewish networks, whether made up of family members, fellow townspeople from back home, or just other Jews, to get started. While the origins and initial specific economic activities of the first Jews who showed up in any particular place and established some kind of business in many cases lay shrouded in the unrecorded past, by the time the great migration commenced and swelled, the small number of Jews already present and settled linked the waves of newcomers to peddling. Each new peddler arriving in a place encountered another Jew who had already ceased his days on the road. That old-timer provided information, credit, goods, and the means to realize the goals of the migration. Knowing in advance that when he would arrive in a place another Jew, whether a relative or not, would jump-start his career, provided each erstwhile immigrant peddler with the confidence to undertake the journey. Invaluable to the new immigrant, that knowledge along with a pack of wares launched the newcomer's new-world career.

The links that stretched between places of origin and places of destination defied Buber's image of "dull masses" or Lazarus's "wretched refuse," but the newcomers to strange societies mastered the circumstances they encountered. In the main they fulfilled the dreams of their migrations, which had begun oceans and continents away. Few became fabulously wealthy, and many migrated again to other places to do better, but for the most part, they lived better and more securely than they would have had they stayed put.

WHAT PUSHED THEM OUT

What forces compelled this vast exodus of Jews from the old world to the new? The migration took place in the context of massive Jewish population growth. Though local circumstances obviously varied, much of the outmigration reflected the dramatic growth of the number of Jews in any given place, in the nineteenth century. Even if new economic developments, including but not limited to the transportation revolution of those same years, had not threatened the basis of the Jewish economy, their petty trade—the growth in the number of Jews who mostly clustered in a particular sector of the economy—would have created a crisis. Too many Jews competed for constantly shrinking opportunities to make a living.

That demographic reality coincided with profound changes in the world economy, particularly in Europe but reverberating globally. Each change left its mark on the Jewish people of Europe and the Muslim world. Together the changes marked all the people of these places, but affected Jews in particular ways.

The individual stories which seem so personally compelling and idiosyncratic took place in the context of these upheavals. The Jewish man who left the Lithuanian town of Acmene and peddled in Limerick, the man who went from Alsace to do the same in Donaldsonville, Louisiana, or the Romanian who trod the roads of the rural areas of Quebec—all told their stories in personal terms, emphasizing the names of towns left, family members and friends whom they joined in the new world. But all of them depended on massive global changes.

While economic historians have pondered at length the issue of when economic modernization took place, and even questioned the meaning of the term, all agree that something happened beginning in the late eighteenth century and continuing into the nineteenth. The first stirrings, the blossoming, and then maturation of the industrial revolution—technological strides in transportation involving canal building, railroad construction, and road improvements—challenged the Jewish economic way of life. The poor rural folk who had been tied to the land and to landowners began to flock to the big cities, where factory work took them out of the peasantry, destroying the Jews' rural customer base, and leading to dissolution of long-standing countryside arrangements.

Politically and culturally, Europe and the Ottoman Empire and North Africa also changed in relationship to emerging ideas of nationalisms, movements that sought to liberate people from the domination of imperial powers, defined as foreign and extraneous to the linguistic, ethnic, and religious essence of the local people. Nationalist movements and their leaders proclaimed the ideal and fictive homogeneity of groups of people, defined as nations, who they claimed had the right to sovereignty. That vision limited membership in the nation to a core group. According to the vision of the world construed by Romanticism, a cultural and intellectual current entwined with the growth of nationalism, nations had souls and national purity was a supreme ideal. For the Jews in all these places, regardless of how long their families had lived in these countries, nationalism and Romanticism converged into racism. Jews simply stood apart from the "imagined community," as eternal outsiders.[23]

This efflorescence of nationalism, among other changes, fostered intensified hostilities between one country or empire and another which in turn spurred profound changes in how societies operated. Russia, the Ottomans, the Austro-Hungarians saw the need for standing armies, and defined military service as obligatory for young men and as a way to transform the unruly multiethnic, multireligious people who lived under the empire's rule into a coherent whole.

Those forces, Jewish population growth, urbanization and industrialization, and the pernicious spell of racially inflected nationalism, might have sufficed as forces to propel outward the migration of millions of Jews who in the great century transplanted themselves to new lands. But positive forces pulled them to places where they thrived, and the aspirations of their migrations became fulfilled.

WORLDWIDE MAGNETS

Jews, like everyone else, had to have someplace to go and some way to get there. The discovery of the new world provided both. The European conquests of the Americas and the antipodes, simply put, opened up colossal expanses of land for the exploitation of resources. That development required the settlement of these lands by people, both the excess populations of the British Isles, France, and Iberia and people from other countries willing to come and do the work necessary to help wring a profit from land, be it in agriculture, mining, or logging. The development of the African slave trade and the subjugation of the indigenous peoples of these new-world regions cannot be disentangled from the histories of colonization and white settlement, and in all the places to which the Jews went they interacted with the slaves and their descendants, and with the native peoples as well. But the Jews' whiteness protected them and helped define these places, home to millions of African slaves and dispossessed original peoples, as good and fitting settings for Jewish settlement.

The development of new-world lands, under the aegis of colonization and then with the emergence of national independence in the United States, the republics of Latin America, and Canada, as well as the continued but benign (for white people) dominion of the British Empire over South Africa, New Zealand, and Australia, transformed economic relationships back home. It allowed for the importation of iron ore, lumber, fur, spices, and all the addictive foods that Europeans came to love, such as coffee, tea, and chocolate, while also providing an outlet for European manufactured goods. Those yoked developments upped the pace of industrialization and further transformed social relationships.

The transportation revolution in Europe and in the colonies and successor new nations facilitated the exchange of raw materials from the new world to the old and the finished goods in the other direction. That revolution also made possible mass migrations, starting in the late eighteenth and early nineteenth centuries. The opening of the Erie Canal in 1825 provided a safe and efficient means to get lumber, iron ore, and agricultural goods from the Great Lakes to the port of New York. This engineering feat made possible the migration of Americans from the East Coast to the Middle West, the development of the farms and mines there, the possibility of shipping those goods to Europe through the port of New York. Millions of Europeans migrated to the United States, filling ships that less and less carried manufactured products to an America now making its own.

Booms in canal building, the plotting and laying of roads, and the mammoth construction of railroads took place all over the world, both old and new. Developers and surveyors, armies and civil authorities came into regions defined as wilderness and made these lands habitable and profitable for commerce. Whether for extractive work like mining or for farming, be it as extensive plantations or more modest family holdings, the opening up of places once inaccessible to all but their native inhabitants stimulated the migration of people from near and far.

By the 1870s, yet another technological breakthrough spurred even greater emigration from Europe. The refinement of steamship technology allowed massive vessels to traverse the world's oceans. Even greater numbers of people from Europe could go to the Americas and from Europe, via Britain, to the antipodes. Steam travel, fueled first by coal and then by oil, shortened the travel time to a fraction of what it had been when sail power moved the ships. Vastly larger numbers of people could be transported at once, many crammed in steerage and second-class accommodations. Large international concerns made fortunes in the immigrant transport business, which begat more migrations. Those steamships docked in a number of new-world port cities, with New York the busiest and the one through which the largest number of immigrants passed. Around the world in the immigrant receiving countries, railroads, again an innovation of the nineteenth century, hooked up with the arriving ships so that immigrants could get out to their destinations. The development of steamship technology also cut to a fraction the amount of time required for mail to flow from immigrants to their families back home and the reverse, enhancing communication and enabling those in the destination setting to report quickly on possibilities for those who had not yet joined the emigrant flood.

Other innovations made the nineteenth the century of European immigration, including for the Jews. The first telegraph communication between North America and Europe took place in 1858, and although it took years to perfect the technology, the ability to send news from one spot to another facilitated mass human movements. By the end of the nineteenth century telegraph lines connected all of Europe with North America and beyond. The ability to communicate from faraway places with the folks back at home, and from back home to the new world, revolutionized the processes of immigration. The ability of women and men already in the United States or South Africa to inform their families that they should join them on the other side depended on swift and efficient communication. The ability of immigrants to transmit money to pay for steamship tickets via the telegraph created a new dynamic in the history of migration.[24]

The Jewish migration started and gained steam, turning into a flood, as a result of all these forces, which had nothing to do with them or with their anomalous outsider status in Europe, the Ottoman Empire, and North Africa. Their migrations would never have taken place without this transformation of the world. Jews in the Russian Empire, for example, began to emigrate in massive numbers only in the 1880s, a movement eventually culminating in the loss of about one-third of Russia's Jewish population. The 1880s, it happens, brought the first Russian government investment in railroad transportation, as it took over private railroad lines sporadically built since the 1830s. The movement coincided with the emergence of steamship travel and the improvement of the speed and reliability of the Atlantic cable in the late 1870s. Jews as well as their Christian neighbors left Lithuania and the Ukraine for places like Chicago, Buffalo, and Pittsburgh in the United States, and the industrial cities of England as well.

Certainly some specifically group matters shaped the Jewish emigration. The pogroms of Russia, which hardly began in 1881, the conventional date given for their inception; the "Hep-Hep" riots, which raged in Bavaria in 1819; and the popular violence directed at the Jews in Alsace in 1848 all convinced some Jews that a safer existence awaited them elsewhere. Measures undertaken by various states to limit Jewish economic and family options created the centrifugal force that stimulated migrations. In the early nineteenth century in parts of central Europe, Jews labored under the burden of the *matrikel*, state policies which limited the number of Jews who could marry. Other places limited marriages to the better-off Jews, those the government considered valuable and self-supporting. For many Jews poverty disqualified them for matrimony. Young Jewish men and women, in love already or eager to find mates, had a real incentive to leave for places like the United States, where they could get on with life with no such laws to burden them.[25] Mounting bureaucratic restrictions on peddlers hampered their already limited options in multiple places in Europe.[26] The Pale of Settlement in the Czarist Empire hemmed in the Jews geographically, preventing them from taking advantage of new economic possibilities.

Jewish organizational networks also played a role in shaping the Jewish migrations. In the Ottoman world and North Africa, for example, the students in the Alliance Israélite Universelle schools learned about opportunities available in the countries outside of their declining homelands. Their teachers and the school administrators encouraged them to take advantage of migration options in South America, for example, as a solution to the lack of opportunities at home.[27]

The Jewishness of the great nineteenth-century migration can also be illustrated by the preponderance of Lithuanians among the Jewish migrants. While Lithuanian non-Jews, primarily Catholic but some Lutherans as well, also migrated, going in large number to Chicago, Buffalo, Cleveland, Detroit, and Pittsburgh, they did so in numbers and proportions that hardly dominated the European or even the eastern European emigrant flood. Poles migrated in much larger number than Lithuanians among non-Jews. But among Jews the "Litvaks" made up the largest proportion of eastern Europeans until the second decade of the twentieth century. For places like South Africa, the British Isles, and much of Latin America they constituted either *the* largest number of immigrants or the largest number among the Ashkenazi immigrant population. Even in the United States, all regions included, with its complex mélange of Jewish newcomers, the Lithuanians, for decades, outnumbered Jewish immigrants from other places. And Lithuanians, with their long history of peddling and other river-based trade occupations, their familiarity with small-town life, their extensive dealings with farmers, and their comfort with linguistically mixed populations, provided the single largest cadre of new-world Jewish peddlers.

Jewish emigration from the Ashkenazic and Sephardic worlds moved along particular geographic and chronological arcs. The modernization of the European economies, with the massive changes attendant upon it, began in western Europe in the late eighteenth century and slowly spread to the east and to the Muslim lands. Therefore the first Jews who emigrated to new lands, and as peddlers, went from northern German-speaking areas around the Baltic and from that area which had been part of independent Poland, but at that very time had become incorporated into Prussia. By the 1820s, with both the development of the Erie Canal and the cessation of the Napoleonic Wars, "America" fever swept the southern German principalities, particularly Bavaria and the Rhine region, as well as Bohemia to the east and Alsace to the west. With the intense penetration of the railroad into central Europe and more remote European borderland regions, the migration scooped up Jews from northwestern Russia, Suwałki, and Lithuania, as well as Hungary and Galicia. By the 1870s, as steam travel became the dominant mode of transportation, the sources of Jewish emigration shifted decidedly to the east and the south. While until the 1910s the majority of Jews who left the Czarist Empire left from Lithuania, gradually increasing numbers of Jews from the Ukraine, Moldavia, and White Russia made their way outward.

So, too, in the early twentieth century, as the Ottoman Empire began to embark on internal economic development, the Jews' long-standing economic niche in petty trade, with peddling crucial, crumbled, and Jews from through-out the empire cast their lot with new lands. The opening of the Suez Canal in 1869 diverted trade from southeastern Turkey as well as from Damascus and Aleppo, places with robust Jewish populations of traders and the peddlers who moved their goods from place to place. After the 1908 Young Turk revolution, the government instituted mandatory military service for all men, Christians and Jews included, groups previously exempted. In an increasingly national-istic Turkey, one which came to define cultural citizenship as inherently tied to "Turkishness," Jews began to see themselves as not fitting in, as marginal people, in contrast to the relative normality they had sensed previously in the multiethnic, multireligious Ottoman Empire. The convergence of these forces encouraged emigration.[28]

The Jewish migration, like all transoceanic migrations, came to a virtual standstill with the outbreak of World War I but picked up again in its immedi-ate aftermath. For Jews the war brought tremendous dislocations, as the various warring nations surrounded the Jews, while the Russian Revolution, the subsequent civil war, and the emergence of central European nations as independent countries further complicated Jewish life. The closing of the doors to the United States upon the passage and implementation of the 1924 National Origins Act did not end Jewish emigration but redirected it. Jews turned their attention, as they had not before, to South Africa, Australia, and New Zealand, and to the various lands of South and Central America and the Caribbean. By this moment, international Jewish aid organizations based in the United States sought to facilitate the movement of Jews to new promising lands, and by the 1930s, with the rise of Nazism in Germany and the increas-ing difficulties of Jewish economic and political life in Poland, their migra-tions experienced another spurt.

Jews moved around this world, leaving the homes of their birth and child-hoods, for places abroad. They left places that held little for them in the quest for economic sustenance. The proportions of those coming from particular places such Alsace, Bohemia, Lithuania, Syria, and Morocco to those leaving other places varied over time, but everywhere emigration transformed the lives of those who stayed behind. According to one study of Jewish life in the dying rural Jewish communities of Germany—dying because of both the urban migration of the better-educated and more financially endowed and the movement to America of the others—"There was no village in Southern Germany which was not a frequent scene of leave-taking; a young man with his wooden trunks mounted on a shaky vehicle which took him to the nearest railway station, his ultimate destination being America."[29] Throughout southern Germany in these years Jews fretted that so few of their young would be left to support communal institutions.

Although those leave-takings no doubt provided occasions for tears over the possibility of lifetime separations, parents' fears for the safety of their children, and the sapping of communal fullness, leave-takings also brought with them the anticipation of remittances. A letter writer for the "Our Town" column in the Kovno, Lithuania, *Folkblat* of the mid-1930s described the town of Palanga, stripped of its Jewish population. "Many," the correspondent noted, "had emigrated. . . . The only 'bright spot' is that 70 percent of the Jewish population receives help from friends in Africa, America, and more recently a small number is aided from Palestine."[30] While these sources did not say so, the young man who left his southern German town and the one who escaped from Palanga to South Africa and the United States probably took their first steps in those lands as peddlers.

BEYOND TIME AND PLACE

How they launched their migrations also revealed global Jewish commonalities, defying the particularities of time and place. Single young Jewish men strategized with parents and siblings about going off to new worlds, returning only after some years of peddling, not to live but to find a bride and then go back to their new homes. The single men may have been the first of their cohort to have gone, or older brothers, friends, or cousins may have preceded them, paid their fares, and then set them up with peddling routes when they reunited on the other side.

The prospect of peddling in some new-world place changed family decision-making practices. The idea took such a powerful hold that, for example, in late-nineteenth- and early-twentieth-century Lithuania, "it became," according to one observer at the time, "fashionable to offer to a learned bridegroom a passage to South Africa as a dowry." While not all Jewish men who came to South Africa peddled, so many did that Lithuanian Jews assumed that going to southern Africa meant peddling.[31]

Married men thinking about emigrating to peddle had to decide what to do with wives and children in those initial years on the road. Some—and the number cannot be quantified—said their good-byes and left their dependents back home. The migrant husband, the new-world peddler called for his family only when he had saved enough to support a family and settle down in a store or some other stable enterprise. Other married men made somewhat different decisions. They emigrated with children and wives in tow, but left their dependents in some larger Jewish enclave where they had other family members to provide a base as the husband sought his livelihood on some far-off road, returning only during the major Jewish holidays. The wives left behind, be it back home or in the new destination place, often operated small shops as they waited to be reunited with their peddling husbands. For some the distances may not have been so great as to force upon the family extended separations. Rather, the immigrant wife held down the home as the peddling husband made his weekly circuit around the region, coming home on Friday and going off again on Sunday.

Many of these migrations went along steps. Memoirs and family histories reveal the life histories of Jews who migrated first to England, other parts of the British Isles, and Sweden, peddled, and then moved on to the United States, South Africa, or Australia, opening a shop, settling down into some more substantial and sedentary business. "The life of my great-grandfather," Edgar Samuel detailed in a conference presentation, "is a relevant case" of this kind of multistep, peddler-facilitated migration. Phillip Blaski, born in a town near Kalisch, in Poland, lived with a stepmother he disliked. To escape from her, he went first to Manchester, England. Here he anglicized his given name from Uri Feibush to Phillip. He married in England, and he and his wife attempted to make a living in the jewelry business. Although he intended to move on to America, he sailed instead for Australia, and at age twenty-two he settled in Melbourne, at the height of the gold rush. Phillip combined his jewelry business with peddling, going out weekly to the miners, selling jewelry while he bought gold dust from them.[32]

According to family lore, Australia had not been his actual choice. He had hoped to go to America, missed the boat, and used his ticket to go to the antipodes. Sidney Matz, on the other hand, eventually did get to America. He went first from Russia (probably Lithuania) to South Africa, where a brother awaited him, and from there to Canada, then across the border to Idaho, then to Wyoming and eventually Utah, peddling as he went.[33]

The multistep nature of the peddlers' progress also took place within any one country. The newcomers started out in one place, peddled, and then tested out new territories and regions where they had heard opportunities could be found. Young men landing in some East Coast port in the United States and planning to try their hand (and feet) at peddling more often than not made their way to the Middle West or New England or the South, brought there by word of mouth and the presence of relatives, friends, or townspeople from back home. The father of Arlen Specter, who would become a United States senator from Pennsylvania, came from the Ukraine sometime in the early twentieth century and "moved his family back and forth between the East Coast and the Midwest seeking work before settling in Kansas"—birthplace in 1930 of the future senator—"as a peddler." In and of themselves the individual stories have no great significance, but as an aggregate they narrate the lives of migrating Jewish men and their families, who blazed paths to new homes, with peddling the engine that fueled their movements.[34]

LANDS OF PROMISE

In the emigrants' imagination no place equaled the United States, unless the man or woman on the move had family members who already lived in, say, Cuba or Northern Rhodesia, in New Zealand or Chile. Absent the direct draw of family, the United States proved most attractive to the largest number. Peddling in England had declined precipitously since the early decades of the nineteenth century, when Jewish immigrants, primarily from Posen and other parts of northern German-speaking regions, had left those previously Polish lands to hawk in the countryside and in the small provincial towns. Most of these men did well enough and settled down as proprietors of comfortable English stores, although even some of them moved on to America. England's intensive railroad development in the middle decades of the century sapped opportunities for peddlers. Only garment making could accommodate large numbers of Jewish immigrants after the 1870s, and it hardly competed with America, with its booming economy and its constantly expanding geographic space open for settlement, realities that made it possible for on-the-road peddling to continue to serve as a route to eventual self-employment and comfort. In the British Isles such opportunities beckoned, but only in the economically sluggish regions of Ireland, Scotland, and Wales, places with nothing like the dynamism of the United States economy.

That much of the migration went from Europe and the Arabic-speaking world through England or some other English-speaking country indicated the magnetic pull of the United States, the prize par excellence of global Jewish migrations. After all, more than 80 percent of emigrating Jews went to the United States. Of those who did not, America seems to have been the place they wanted to go but for circumstances of one kind or another that diverted them. A stop in England, or in Sidney Matz's case South Africa and Canada, meant a chance to learn the language while on the road, engaging with it house by house, farmstead by farmstead, and opening up a larger store only after having mastered the local words and culture. English, Scottish, Welsh, Irish, and South African roads offered the Jewish emigrants moving educational venues upon which they familiarized themselves with the language they needed for that most desirable place of all, the United States. When they arrived in America, often defined by others as English or Irish Jews, they graduated from peddling and opened businesses, got married or reunited with wives and children, and planted themselves in settled communities.[35]

The United States offered Jews the grand prize in the age of migration. But a few other places functioned as miniature Americas. For Lithuanian Jews, South Africa represented a destination of choice, both for the rich economic opportunities available to white European immigrants and for the growing concentration of their kin, friends, townspeople, and other Lithuanian Jews. It became a Litvak outpost. The form of Yiddish that developed in the lands beyond the Cape of Good Hope, the communal and religious patterns, the cooking style all bore the marks of Lithuania. The route to this land came via England, and some stayed only long enough to get themselves on oceangoing ships, while others spent some time there, embarking there on their first newworld peddling ventures. Cape Town and Johannesburg emerged as major centers of Jewish life, places where the former immigrant *smous* assumed positions of leadership in the Jewish community and achieved civic respectability.[36] Sephardim from the Ottoman Empire and North Africa opted in large number for South and Central America, although most of the Polish Jews who also went to Argentina, Mexico, Cuba, Brazil, and the like saw these places merely as way stations to the United States.[37] In any case, these countries came to house substantial Jewish populations for whom peddling had provided the men's first work experiences. Some Latin American cities, like Mexico City, Buenos Aires, and Havana, over time developed robust Jewish communities, with multiple synagogues, mutual aid societies, newspapers, political clubs, and informal social networks, making these places attractive enough to stay in rather than going north to the United States.[38]

Jewish peddler immigrants engaged in "gravitational migrations," seeking out particular places where family, friends, and well-defined economic possibilities existed for them. They left homes bound specifically for Tupper Lake, New York; Chico, California; Cork, Ireland; Bulawayo, Rhodesia; Shamokin, Pennsylvania; or Otago, New Zealand. Here brothers, uncles, cousins waited for them, ready to get them launched. While over time most Jewish immigrants and certainly their children abandoned these small-town destinations for larger cities, these places had been the initial magnets which drew them across the oceans, as had the opportunities of peddling.[39]

Even a cursory survey of the gravitational dynamic that pulled Jews from specific places to specific places—with peddling the rope that pulled them to their new worlds—demonstrates the patterns of the Jewish migrations on a global scale. Sephardic Jews from the Ottoman Empire and various places in North Africa, such as Morocco, streamed to nearly all of Latin America and the Caribbean, drawn particularly to Argentina and Mexico, Chile and Uruguay, Colombia and Peru. While Jews from that mammoth swath of land also went to England, South Africa, and parts of the United States, the Spanish- and Portuguese-speaking new world attracted them in particular.

The geographic scope of the Sephardic migration reads like guidebook to the new world. A handful of Jews from Syria, with its strong French influence and presence, found their way to Haiti, with its French-based language, where they labored as peddlers. Many Sephardim who knew Ladino, a Jewish language built on a bedrock of Spanish, opted for various places in South America, including Portuguese-speaking Brazil.[40] More specifically, Jews from Montastir, also known as Bitola, in what would decades later become Yugoslavia, did not just go to South America but headed for Chile, where, like nearly all the Sephardim, they labored as peddlers, or semananiks. That level of geographic specificity shaped the life of Jews in the Amazon basin, most of whom came from Tangier, Tetuan, Rabat, and Casablanca. A field worker for the French-based Alliance Israélite Universelle in 1906 visited Iquitos, the largest city in the Peruvian rain forest. There he met "more than two hundred of our former students from Morocco." Back in Tangier, Isaac Pisa wrote, "They speak of Iquitos as . . . a fabulous city. . . . It is typical of [a] Tangerian to make his fortune in Iquitos." And what did the Tangerian and Moroccan Jews do in the rain forest?[41] "They travel up river by canoe or steamship," sell- ing by the waterway to the people who worked on the rubber plantations, stopping at each dock up and down the river.[42]

But the predominance of Romance languages, French, Spanish, and Portuguese, does not contain the full range of places where these Jews went and where they peddled. Jews from the Balkans peddled in and around Manchester, England, and throughout the sugar-plantation regions of Jamaica. They showed up in South Africa, the Lithuanian stronghold, and made their way to the United States, where, between 1899 and 1924, some twenty thousand from Thrace and the Aegean regions arrived. As did their Ashkenazi brethren, whom they saw as quite different, and vice versa, more than 80 percent stayed in New York, planting small satellite communities in Seattle and Atlanta. And in all those places, they started out by peddling.

Elsewhere in South America, which also experienced a Christian migration from Arabic-speaking lands, a kind of gathering of non-Ashkenazi Jews took place. Jews from Syria, the Balkans, Anatolia, Egypt, and Morocco coalesced into multinational Sephardic communities in Panama, Colombia, Mexico, Cuba, Venezuela, Chile, Uruguay, and elsewhere. Jews from the Syrian city of Aleppo, for example, joined in this migration, and by the first decade of the twentieth century, thousands of them honeycombed the agricultural districts of Argentina, selling trinkets, Catholic religious objects, and household goods. While they may have started the flow to Argentina, Jewish immigrants from throughout the east opted for these places. They, along with Jews from other parts of North Africa, the Middle East, and the Near East, carried in their packs soaps and notions, suspenders and neckties, watches and jewelry, and laid the basis for a new kind of Jewish community, a trans-Sephardic one, a community in which their religious rite, *minhag Sepharad*, defined the basis of Jewishness, rather than their languages or their particular national political status. (Only in Argentina did Ashkenazi Jews come to outnumber the Sephardim.)[43]

South Africa and Ireland, as well as towns in Northern and Southern Rhodesia, could rightly be seen as outposts of Lithuania, with each of those places connected to particular towns and provinces of this sending society. The South African connection, for example, linked the tip of Africa to the province of Kovno.[44] Among those who showed up in southern Africa, sizable groups came from Schloss, Samsten, Grubin, Zagger, Coldingen, and Talen, small places in the province of Courland. From Kovno, knots of friends and relatives hailed from the specific towns of Taurage, Wilkomire, Roisani, Plungya, as well as villages from around Vilna, such as Ershinsky and Supran—all tiny Lithuanian towns suffering from economic stagnation and Jewish overpopulation.[45] The Zionist leader Nahum Sokolow at the turn of the twentieth century referred to South Africa, vis-à-vis the Jews, as a "colony of Lithuania."[46]

Jews from the towns of Akmene and Shavli ended up being the Jews of Dublin, Limerick, and Cork, and a few even smaller communities in the Irish countryside, making up what one Irish Jewish writer referred to as the "Gaelic Gollus," or the Gaelic dispersion of the Jews. While many had spent some time in England first, most only stopped over there briefly, since transportation routes did not link Ireland and northwestern Russia directly. Their intimate connections with each other from their premigration homes facilitated providing shelter to newcomers, assisting the immigrants in getting together a pack of goods to peddle in the countryside.[47]

Like Ireland, Sweden attracted a relatively small Jewish immigrant population at the same time that so many of its own women and men emigrated abroad. But like it and other small destination points, it attracted a relatively homogeneous group of Jews from just a few small sending places. Indeed, the smaller the destination place, the more finely tuned the gravitation from specific originating sources. No more than a few thousand Jews, mostly house-to-house peddlers, went to Sweden from the late 1860s through the 1920s, and almost all came from the town of Posiat in the province of Suwałki, a region falling between northeastern Poland and southern Lithuania. As in the Irish case, relationships from back home facilitated the orientation process and the launching of each new Jewish immigrant peddler.[48]

Mid- to late nineteenth-century Australia received an influx of both Polish and Lithuanian Jews, many of whom had spent some time in England. Australian Jewish immigration history offers one narrative not replicated elsewhere, but despite its uniqueness, it still demonstrates global Jewish patterns. Among the convicts transported to the antipodes from England, Jews born mostly in Poland, as well as the English-born children of Polish immigrants, laid the foundation of Jewish communal life. Some of these, like Henry Abrams or Jacob Cohen, had peddled in England, and the crimes for which the authorities deported them stemmed from the peddling careers. They had been convicted of peddling stolen goods, of being fences. Other Jewish immigrants to Australia took to peddling only when arriving there, seeing in the occupation a reasonable path to economic stability.[49]

AMERICAN EXCEPTIONALISM

All of these places stand in bold contrast to the United States, which attracted immigrants not from any one place disproportionately but—for Jewish immigrants as for immigrants as a whole—from the broad spatial diversity of the migrant population. No one place of origin dominated. While some eras brought more immigrants from one region, followed by subsequent streams from elsewhere, immigration to America took its shape from the sheer diversity of its immigrants and the fact that that no one immigrant group defined the totality of the immigrant experience.[50]

Ashkenazim far outnumbered Sephardim, but the latter settled in many of the same places where the former lived. So, too, Jews from eastern Europe, who came latest during the age of the great migration, arrived in numbers far greater than those who had come earlier from central Europe. Jews from central Europe arrived first, primarily from the German-speaking states that became Germany in 1871. They hailed from Bavaria, Baden, the Rhineland, Hesse, and in the tens of thousands from Posen. The mid-nineteenth century brought Jews from Alsace, but Lithuanians, Hungarians, Bohemians, and Galicians arrived then as well. By the late 1860s Suwałki, the source of the Swedish Jewish immigration, began to send particularly large numbers to the United States, and then the Lithuanian migration took off in earnest, to be followed by the end of the century by the Romanians and then in the 1910s by the Ukrainian and White Russian Jews. Jews from the Ottoman Empire had come to the United States by the 1890s. All of these Jews interacted with one another, creating institutions together and eventually marrying across group lines, and yet simultaneously they maintained separate communal structures. And all of them peddled.

Their peddling resembled the patterns of Jewish settlement of the United States. Edward Cohen, self-described "peddler's grandson," quoted the account in a family memoir of his grandfather—a Romanian Jew who peddled in Louisiana—spending his weekends off the road in New Orleans. When liberated, momentarily, from his route, he would "rest, drink whiskey with the Alsation peddlers and play poker all night." For a new arrival in the United States, this weekly respite in the Crescent City from peddling gave him a chance to broaden his contacts and meet other Jewish immigrants, including these from Alsace, whom he might never have met had he not migrated and not peddled.[51]

Jewish men from all these places peddled, and peddled all over the United States. But some groups at some times headed for very particular destinations, based on the languages and origins of potential customers. Alsatian Jews, like Eddie Cohen's grandfather's poker-playing and whiskey-drinking pals, with their knowledge of French clustered in Louisiana, a state that supported a French-inflected culture and a French-speaking population. Jews from eastern Europe, familiar with Polish, Lithuanian, and Ukrainian, easily made their way as peddlers and then became shopkeepers in the steel-mill and coal-mining regions of Pennsylvania, Ohio, and West Virginia, where they reunited, figuratively, with their old customers. In the middle decades of the nineteenth century, as waves of non-Jewish German speakers came to the United States and settled in cities, small towns, and rural areas in the Middle West, Jewish peddlers followed them. Able to speak their language, and also familiar with the intricacies of their tastes, the young Jewish men from Bavaria, Westphalia, the Rhine region, and even Posen and Lithuania found a good first customer base.

But choice of location in the United States transcended linguistic preferences. In hundreds of small towns in the Middle West, New England, upstate New York, and the Deep South, Lithuanian Jews, familiar with small-town Jewish life, moved in and took to the roads to peddle. So, too, Jewish peddlers from places like Bohemia and Alsace, but also those from Rhodes and Morocco, knew what it meant to live and sell in a borderland. They had left many regions made up of linguistically, religiously, and ethnically mixed populations. Jews knew how to negotiate commercially in such settings, and adjusted easily to, say, upstate New York with its American (for lack of a better term here), Irish, and French-Canadian population base. Likewise selling in California to Spanish and English speakers, as well as to Native Americans with their many languages, and in the South to African Americans and whites made such places and their heterogeneity not shockingly new but just an American iteration of the old-world jumble of peoples, all customers or potential customers.[52]

Family and friends in one place, already ensconced in some business, welcomed the new immigrants who could peddle their wares to remote customers. Max Vanger, for a time a peddler in the Canadian Maritimes, mostly operating outside of Halifax and Saint. John's in the second decade of the twentieth century, recalled that family relationships rather than the particularities of the place drew the immigrants in, and that peddling provided the mechanism. A sixteen-year-old leather worker by trade in White Russia, Vanger grew to despise the smell of leather. Although his parents objected to his emigration, he wrote to an uncle in Canada asking for help. When the uncle agreed to assist him, he, as he wrote, "stopped taking orders [and] told everybody that I was going to America. I did not know that Canada was a separate country, but it did not make any difference to me." Vanger did not much like the work in which his uncle set him up, peddling, but "I did not give up." Indeed he triumphed, even expanding the scope of his customer base farther out of town: "We got to Fredericton . . . and started to peddle from house to house . . . and we did quite well although I hated it and when roads dried up we started to go to the country." It really did not matter what kinds of customers he sold to, or from whom he acquired his goods. His mobile trading provided him with the bedrock upon which to get started in his new world.[53]

What kinds of places did the Jewish emigrants go to in order to peddle and start their new world lives? Certainly some places proved to be more amenable to peddling than others. Topography, weather, and the nature of settlement patterns in some areas made peddling difficult. Much of the American Southwest, characterized by homesteads and *haciendas* miles apart from one another, beaten down by the brutality of the sun, led most of the Jews who went to New Mexico and Arizona to opt for shops in places like Santa Fe, although Mike Goldwater, best known as the grandfather of Senator Barry Goldwater, peddled for a time around Gila County, Arizona.[54] Jewish peddlers, traversing the road, particularly by foot, faced excruciating winter conditions, cold and massive snow drifts, in Manitoba, on the Iron Range of Minnesota, and in the Dakotas, as well as in Vermont and Maine, and some of them engaged in seasonal peddling, limiting their on-the-road selling to the clement weather. This made these less than desirable destinations, although some Jews in the upper Midwest, the New England frost belt, and the Canadian prairies peddled year-round, despite the snow drifts and the subzero temperatures that extended for months.

New-world Jewish peddling took place in a Christian world. With the exception of unconverted native peoples in Australia, southern Africa, and the Americas, Christians made up the customer base. But unlike the Christians back home, most new-world Christians had had no contact with Jews before opening their doors to the Jewish peddler.[55] True for the British Isles, South and Central America, southern Africa, Sweden, Australia, and New Zealand, this absence of previous exposure to Jews helped shape the peddler-customer interchange. All of the peoples, regardless of race or class, to whom the Jewish peddlers sold can be considered as blank slates upon which the peddlers, their first Jews, could leave their mark, teaching them what and who a Jew might be.

In some cases, in various microregions, Jewish peddlers in North America sold to people they had actually known back home—indeed, people to whom they had once before sold, as peddlers. Jewish peddlers entered the homes in the United States and Canada of German, Ukrainian, Polish, Hungarian, Czech, and Lithuanian women, themselves recent immigrants. This reunion on new-world grounds offered the Jewish peddlers a chance to sell to people whose languages they already knew, whose customs they comprehended, and whose tastes they understood. They did not have to struggle with new and unfamiliar languages. Hostility may have lingered from back home, but in the new world, the Jewish peddler did not serve as the middleman between Christian peasants and the marketplace as he had before migration. Most of these central and eastern European immigrants, in fact, rather than making a living in agriculture as they once had, had come to America to work in coal mines, steel mills, and other industrial enterprises, ones with which the Jews had no connection. Jewish peddlers and their shopkeeper coreligionists provided this immigrant industrial proletariat opportunities to evade the clutches of the notorious company stores, where employers who paid paltry wages further enriched themselves by selling goods at exorbitant prices. The Jewish peddler, the American replica of his old-world progenitor, rather than serving the employer or landowner, served the customer directly.[56]

Jews from the Ottoman Empire and the Arabic-speaking world also found a religious landscape different from that back home. Instead of selling to Muslim customers and some few Christians, mostly Eastern Orthodox, they came into societies populated by Protestants and Roman Catholics. They had not only to learn new languages but to accommodate the religious sensibilities and calendars of these customers. In Central and Latin America, Moroccan Jewish peddlers became the purveyors of rosaries, Catholic holy pictures, and statues of the Virgin Mary and other saints beloved to the Catholic masses.

Whether selling to Catholics or Protestants, the peddlers opted for places where certain conditions prevailed. Enough people had to live there who wanted to have, and could afford, new material goods. But they had to be poor enough or far enough removed from the marketplace that they had little choice where to get their desired objects. The places had to support few nearby stores, and potential customers had to be restrained by poor roads, which made travel difficult for anyone other than the peddler, who did not worry about ease. Rather, he benefited from the difficulties faced by the women and men of the area.

Peddlers had to arrive at just the right moment, when low-level material conditions stood face-to-face with new economic and social realities. They did best when regions experienced revolutions in taste, which created appetites for previously unattainable or even unknown goods. Relatively poor people had to find their pockets jingling with cash, deposited, as it were, by massive changes in the social and economic order. Jewish peddlers arrived in the late eighteenth century in the northeastern English city of Sunderland. Dutch and Bohemian immigrants, as well as some Lithuanians from the town of Krottingen, took to peddling in a place described at the time as one where "there seemed to be no middle-class people, thousands excessively poor with but a few wealthy. You might have walked down High Street and have seen scarcely a woman with a gown on except on Sundays, the habiliments being a calamankey [a nearby area] petticoat, a cotton jacket, and linen blue-and-white checked apron with a bib." The town had "no market place" to speak of. The Jewish immigrants who streamed across the Channel and continued north came as the town experienced an upward tick when it became a stop on the coal-transporting network south from Scotland. Women could now afford some lace, ribbons, buckles, a necklace or brooch, a second apron, or even an additional dress. These women embraced the Jewish peddlers and the handful of Jewish town merchants, among them a jeweler and silversmith, who outfitted the peddlers.[57]

Ireland in the late nineteenth century, likewise, welcomed Jewish peddlers as the survivors of the potato famine of the 1840s began to want tea, watches, pictures with gilded frames, tobacco, pots and pans, sugar, clothing, and household goods. Before the Great Hunger, Irish peasants had lived with scant material possessions. Few owned tables, cutlery, or plates. Despite the damp weather, few had shoes. Men and women rarely possessed more than one change of clothing. As a result of famine's devastation and the massive emigration, rural Ireland changed. The population thinned out, remittances from relatives working abroad flowed in, and farmworkers earned higher wages than before. These economic factors stoked material desires. Poor tenants became somewhat less poor farmers, and dwellers of thatched cottages with earthen floors, devoid of windows, moved into small cabins, places that cried out for curtains, carpeting, pictures and picture frames to hang on the walls. So Conrad Arensberg in 1937, when the last of the Jewish weekly vendors still wended their way through the Irish countryside, commented in his ethnographic study on the cooking pots that hung from the fireplaces, and the furnishings of the ubiquitous special west room, "all 'fine' pieces of furniture, symbolic brass objects brought in by the bride at marriage . . . blessed objects, crucifixes," a far cry from the typical homes of the prefamine years.[58]

Even in the United States the passage of time from the late eighteenth century into the middle of the nineteenth coincided with a spike in material consumption, as Americans increasingly adorned their bodies with a better grade of clothing and stocked their homes with a higher standard of furnishing. Increased consumption began with the better-off classes and spread to the middle classes, who with the aid of peddlers, not just Jews, satisfied the desire of the nonelites to indulge in emulative spending, hoping to adorn themselves and make their homes resemble those of their economic betters.[59]

The Jewish immigrant peddlers headed for places experiencing "revolutions of rising expectations," which opened up fertile fields for entrepreneurs willing and able to bring goods to people relatively disconnected from cities and towns. These not very well-off customers could buy only on credit, but they had some pounds, dollars, or pesos to purchase what they wanted. Innovations in transportation and the creation of popular print media stimulated further aspirations for goods, some that earlier generations could not have imagined or even known.

In other places, North America, South Africa, and Australia, all places launched and developed as land frontiers, immigration from abroad brought settlers to essentially unsettled lands. Migration begot further migration, and expansion proceeded inexorably. More people meant more demand for consumer goods. The more remote the settlement—the American Far West, the Australian outback, the South African Transvaal—the more crucial the niche filled by the peddlers. Probably no one would have moved to Oregon or Nebraska, British Columbia or Manitoba, in their frontier days had they not believed that they would shortly have pots and pans, dishes and silverware, tablecloths and eyeglasses, and the other accoutrements of the settled lives they had left. People moved to those places to take advantage of inexpensive land for farming, and peddlers followed just a few footsteps behind.[60]

Jewish immigrants continued to come to places as peddlers so long as the places needed their services. When regions outgrew this kind of primitive marketing, the immigrant peddlers went elsewhere, or headed for the cities to set up shop. Jewish immigrants went to these places to peddle as long as no one else did the same. Jewish peddlers in the middle of the nineteenth century flocked to the KwaZulu-Natal region of South Africa, but by the end of the century, as immigrants from India developed competing economic activities, the Litvaks turned their attention to the Transvaal.[61]

DIVIDED LANDS

Nearly every place the immigrant Jewish peddlers went, with the exception of the British Isles and Scandinavia, they stumbled into societies in which color mattered. In some places—Canada, South Africa, Australia, and New Zealand—the color divide followed a native-versus-European colonist divide. Where one stood across the native-European chasm shaped life choices, economic opportunities, and political participation. The United States, the countries of the Caribbean, and much of Latin America fissured along a tripartite color spectrum. Those of European lineage held all or nearly all political and economic power, while African slaves and their descendants, as well as the native peoples and other nonwhites, contended with powerlessness, economic deprivation, and lack of meaningful (or any) citizenship. Immigrant Jewish peddlers came to places where their whiteness, as defined by custom and law, facilitated their migrations and made their peddling fundamentally successful.

While the Jewish peddlers, including those who emigrated from the Muslim lands, benefited from being white, they sold to everyone and anyone. White, black, or tawny, it made no difference: customers were customers, business was business. The color of the customer's skin mattered not at all to the peddler who exchanged goods for cash. Sales to Native Americans and African Americans did not cause white customers to refuse to do business with Jewish peddlers, nor did it stymie the peddlers' trajectory from the road to sedentary and respectable commerce.

In some places Jewish peddlers sold to independent farmers and their families. Outfitted with backpacks, peddlers made their way throughout the United States, Canada, Australia, and southern Africa, going to farmsteads widely separated by space. The farmers relied on the peddlers, as primitive roads and vast distances kept them from markets. The peddlers offered household goods, clothing, and other items that enhanced life in isolated settings. In other places, immigrant Jewish peddlers sold to people who lived and worked in servile or semiservile work situations. They made their way onto cotton plantations in the American South worked by slaves. This literally captive clientele, many of whom had no clothes or household goods of their own choosing, could enhance either what they wore or how they furnished their meager quarters by buying what the peddler carried.[62]

Even larger numbers of Jewish peddlers came to the southern United States after slavery, when emancipation created great opportunities for them to sell to both whites and African Americans, the families of the tenant farmers and the hired hands who worked the plantations. The South provided masses of customers to Jewish peddlers among the women and men who worked in the textile mills and furniture factories of Georgia and South and North Carolina, poorly educated and desperately poor laborers. The peddlers provided them with an alternative to the stores owned by landowners and factory owners.

Jewish immigrant peddlers opted to go to places where men and women made their living, however minimal: in logging and mining camps, and on plantations, such as those in South and Central America that produced rubber, coffee, and sugar. When the United Fruit Company, owned by a former Jewish peddler to the American South, Sam Zemmuray, opened its massive banana plantations on the north coast of Honduras, Jews from eastern Europe flocked there to sell as itinerants to the workers.[63] During the rubber boom in the Amazon of the late nineteenth century, one commentator noted that the region had been "overrun by Hebrew peddlers."[64]

Each of these enterprises concentrated workers who labored in gangs, under highly supervised conditions. Employers provided housing for the workers, made up of indigenous people recruited to labor after their own economies had been destroyed, former slaves and their progeny, and immigrants from abroad attracted by work and wages. To these workers, native and foreign born, Jewish peddlers provided the clothing and household goods that spelled the difference between a miserable existence and a slight step above that. The workers, laboring on a coffee plantation in Jamaica, harvesting sugar in Cuba or rubber in Colombia, experienced their first contact with a cash economy, learning how to use currency to pay for goods. Newly ushered into the capitalist way of life, these women and men who had previously functioned in barter economies learned about this new way of life from Jewish peddlers who taught them the meaning of money.

These places had much in common with the coal mines and steel mills of western Pennsylvania and West Virginia and the cotton textile mills that dotted the small towns of the Carolinas and of New Hampshire and Maine. They resembled, as far as the Jewish peddlers saw it, the dozens of Welsh iron and steel towns of the Merthyr-Dowlais region, and the mining towns that dotted the Rhondda and Cynon Valleys of Wales in the 1870s. Situated in nonurban regions, these areas depended upon the mines and mills, where masses of workers spent their days churning out coal and steel, tables and textiles. The laborers in turn bought the goods that the peddlers carried.

Nearly all of these areas grew out of "rushes" and "booms," the gold and diamond rushes of South Africa, New Zealand, and Australia, the rubber rush of the Amazon, the coal rush of mid-nineteenth-century Pennsylvania and West Virginia, the California Gold Rush of the 1840s, as well as the rubber boom of the Amazon. Just as Jewish peddlers followed the shifting frontier in the United States, moving from western New York and the Middle West to New England, the Deep South, and the prairie states to the Pacific Northwest and the Southwest, they learned about the discovery of gems and minerals unearthed in faraway places. The Jews did not flock to these places to descend into the mines or to pick up axes and hew the trees in the logging camps. For the most part they did not plan to grub a stake and pan for gold. Rather, they saw golden opportunities in hefting packs on their backs, filling them with sundry goods, and going from camp to camp, mine to mine, mill to mill, selling to those who did the actual labor.

Hearing the news of one rush or boom or another, potential Jewish immigrants activated their communal networks and headed out to new regions of the world, whose people constituted their greatest resource. The men and women who wanted low-cost goods and could pay for what they bought drew the peddlers across oceans and landmasses. It mattered little what kind of place they went to. They did not care particularly if they took their first new-world steps on the roads of more or less advanced countries, or if they opted for tropical, subtropical, or temperate climates. They functioned pretty much the same whether they went to places like the United States, which drew in millions of other immigrants, or Ireland, Wales, Jamaica, or Chile. Wherever they went, they perforce relied upon other Jews to get them started.

JEWISH NETWORKS AND THE PEDDLERS

The entire new-world peddling experience depended upon the existence of webs of relationships that reflected the Jews' age-old connection to trade. Young Jews showing up in one place or another, no matter the country or continent, sought out other Jews, often, though not always, individuals with whom they shared ties back home. Those Jews already present in a place had likely spent time themselves on the road as peddlers and provided the newest arrival, the would-be peddler, with such basics as a place to stay, food, and, most crucially for the peddling experience, contacts to wholesalers, who then offered the goods to be sold.

The wholesaler, at times just a shopkeeper, extended credit for a line of merchandise and a route, basically a map of where the new peddler should go. He offered guidance on how to get to his *medinah*, or kingdom, and the nuts-and-bolts as to language, habits, and tastes of the customers. The shopkeeper or wholesaler gave the neophyte peddler a list of words in the local language, but written in Yiddish for the Ashkenazim, with such key phrases as "Hello, ma'am" and "Would you like to look in my bag," or the Spanish, French, Portuguese, Swedish, Afrikaans, Cherokee, or Mayan equivalents.

In so many cases, in numbers that cannot be counted for even any one place, let alone for the entirety of the new world, the businessman who provided the peddler with his start-up happened to be a brother, brother-in-law, cousin, or uncle. Moyses Benguigui left the Moroccan city of Salé in 1909, bound for Brazil, where his uncle Azulay Pazuello already kept shop in the state of Pará. Armed with a loan from his uncle, Moyses went off to the Amazon basin, peddling fabrics, tools, and medicines. Julius Weis's cousin David put him up in Natchez for a week after a forty-two-day voyage across the Atlantic and offered him two options: either work as a clerk in the Mississippi store or take to the road and be his own boss. Julius opted for the latter, as "my disposition had always been to work for myself." His cousin offered to "give me a few words as would be most necessary in selling goods . . . and as soon as these were somewhat mastered I was ready for business. We selected a small assortment of goods. . . . He bought me a horse, saddle and bridle . . . and I was fully equipped." These two stories differed not at all from those of young Alsatian Jewish men from Metz who went to Louisiana, or those from Raishishok in the Lithuanian province of Kovno who went to the Cape Colony. This pattern repeated itself in the millions around the Jewish world.[65]

The Jewish network involved more than Uncle Azulay Pazuello's sense of family obligation or that of cousin David. Jewish businessmen, at every level, helped launch the new peddlers. Jews around the world sold goods imported from abroad, through Jewish economic chains. The farther removed the place was from the major centers of production, the more the goods came from far away. Jewish peddlers in Jamaica and Cuba sold goods that came via Jewish economic networks from Britain and the United States. The Jewish *smous* of South Africa carried goods made in England and shipped halfway around the world. Jewish manufacturers produced many of the goods. Jewish exporters facilitated their movement across oceans and entrusted them to Jewish importers, who through a chain of lesser merchants, including wholesalers, warehouse owners, and shopkeepers, placed the goods into the hands of the Jewish peddlers, who then dispersed the items into the countryside and into the hands of the customers whose homes they entered.

This kind of transnational Jewish business flowed between Jews in the major centers of developed countries to the less-advanced places where so many immigrant Jews took to the road. A former peddler who had operated around Mexico City recalled that American Jews, also once but no longer peddlers, made a living as "jobbers," who supplied the "stockings, ties, socks, little knives, razor blades" that the peddlers stuffed into their packs and which "we carried on our shoulders."[66]

In some places the boundary between the metropolis where the goods came from and the hinterland where the peddlers sold the goods blurred. American, German, and British Jewish businessmen, at the high end, lived in or spent extended periods of time in Mexico, Cuba, South Africa, and Jamaica, supervising the peddlers' operations. These same affluent Jewish businessmen living in the less-developed places also assisted the small struggling Jewish communities founded by the peddlers and the shopkeepers, binding tighter the connection between business and community.[67]

The United States, with its massive size and the large number of Jewish newcomers, operated as a domestic version of this same global phenomenon. Jewish immigrant peddlers existed at the bottom of a linked chain headed by manufacturers in New York, Chicago, Baltimore, Cincinnati, and other large cities, who worked directly with Jewish warehouse owners who facilitated goods and credit for the peddlers. Jacob Epstein, a Jewish immigrant from Russia, an erstwhile peddler, established himself as a peddler warehouse owner in Baltimore, the Baltimore Bargain House, in the late nineteenth century. He made a point of meeting new Jewish immigrants disembarking at the port, greeting them, and got them started as peddlers who operated in western Maryland and Maryland's eastern shore, as well as West Virginia, Kentucky, and indeed all through the South.[68]

Epstein and his Baltimore Bargain House facilitated the immigrants' entry into peddling, something of financial benefit to Epstein. Simeon Hecht also operated a peddler warehouse in Baltimore, and he too made it his business to help numerous new Jewish immigrants to get out on their roads. Epstein and Hecht competed for the peddlers' trade, thus enhancing the new immigrants' agency, allowing them to pick and choose between these two and indeed other suppliers.[69] A description from South Africa could just as easily be applied to South Carolina. An 1891 article from the Russian Jewish newspaper *Hatzfirah* described the first moments of the peddler's life after landing at the Cape:

> After the newcomer has rested from his long and arduous journey and regained his strength, his benefactor, for a few pounds sterling buys some inexpensive wares, teaches him the Hollands names of the merchandise, and the prices, puts his wares in a basket which he loads on the newcomer's back and sends him away from his house like Noah sending the dove from the Ark . . . thus to make the rounds of the farms and sell his wares.[70]

Often the formal apparatus of the Jewish community, founded and staffed by successful merchants, directly assisted newcomer peddlers. Fusing business and community interests, organizations like the United Hebrew Relief Association of Chicago provided interest-free loans to peddlers. It helped the would-be peddlers secure their required peddler licenses, taught them how to negotiate the city, county, and state bureaucracies, and signed for and bonded them, so that the newly arrived could quickly set out on the road and start selling.[71]

Around the world, whether Dublin or Rio de Janeiro, local Jewish businesses depended upon the newcomer to peddle their goods to the customers in the hinterlands. In Ireland many former peddlers became picture frame makers, and Jewish weekly men carried these quasi-luxury objects around the countryside. In Brazil, as in so many other places, Jewish textile manufacturers outfitted peddlers, who in turn loaded their bags with cloth, clothing, and sewing implements. Suppliers, wholesalers, and shopkeepers participated with the peddlers in a single integrated economy. Each on his own rung, they operated together.

Opportunities proliferated in the place where the Jews went as peddlers, and each place had its own history, its own chronology. Opportunities for Jewish peddlers followed major ecological, demographic, and economic transformations. As to the United States and the other frontier societies, European outposts shaped by colonialism, no Jews, peddlers or not, would have shown up but for the white penetration of native lands. The decision of colonial rulers and their successors in South America and the Caribbean to recruit Indians, enslave Africans, and then bring the descendants of slaves to work on vast plantations to produce sugar, bananas, rubber, and coffee enabled Jewish immigrants from Syria, Morocco, and the Balkans, collectively called *turcos*, and others from eastern Europe, referred to as *polacos*, to sell to the workers and their wives. While not frontier societies, England in the late eighteenth century, Sweden in the middle of the nineteenth, and Ireland at the century's end experienced commercial revolutions which allowed growing numbers of women and men to want to buy more.

Each place had its own history, and its history marked the Jewish peddlers. British authorities, for example, sent dozens of Jewish hawkers, recent immigrants from Poland and Germany or their sons, convicted of crimes, to the antipodes. Many resumed peddling in their new home "down under," selling to aborigines and the British settlers. By the mid-nineteenth century waves of Irish immigrants came to Australia, and Jewish peddlers followed them. With the gold rush of the 1850s more Jews arrived along with miners, and with agricultural development, the numbers of Jewish peddlers increased; as they did elsewhere, they serviced diverse populations, all eager for the peddlers' goods.[72]

So, too, New England's transformation from a region of small independent farmers to a region of textile mills, with looms operated by local women along with immigrants from Ireland and Quebec providing eastern European Jewish immigrants with customers to whom they could ply their wares. South and North Carolina in the late nineteenth century evolved from a zone of tobacco and cotton growing into one where people made a living spinning cotton in factories, and the women and men who labored in these mills, labeled derogatorily as "lint heads," received the Jewish peddlers, newly arrived from Lithuania. Jewish immigrant peddlers headed for lumber camps in Georgia, in upstate New York, on Michigan's Upper Peninsula, and in Oregon. Just to round out this travelogue, documenting the spread of Jewish peddling and the development of new labor systems based on the exploitation of natural resources, new Jewish immigrants set out to peddle in the Mesabi Iron Range of northern Minnesota and among the thousands of workers in the steel mills of Pennsylvania and the copper mines of Montana, as well as to the men who constituted the labor force of the large-scale commercial fishing industry in Nova Scotia, and their wives. In all of these places workers earned just enough beyond bare subsistence so that they and their wives could avail themselves of the goods carried in the peddlers' packs.

The nexus between peddling, the Jews' familiar way of making a living, and the great migration stretched across national borders, oceans, and continents. It drove their movements outward from their multiple old worlds, places which held out little for them. It propelled them simultaneously to a number of new lands, which they believed did offer prospects for success, for carving out a comfortable and more secure place in the world. The migration depended upon the technology of transportation and the changes in the places to which they went. It depended upon Jewish economic chains of relationship, which coincided with chains of community. But when peddling they very much had to rely upon themselves, as one by one, on their own, they made their way to their customers' homes.

2

Road Runners

Jewish Peddlers in Their New Worlds

Just as peddling helped launch the modern Jewish exodus out of old homes, so too, it drew the Jews into a wide new world. Peddling's fundamental characteristics enabled them to achieve their migrations' goals. While not all Jews peddled upon arrival in new lands, such a large number did that it constituted a mass experience which served the economic and political needs of nearly all, including those who did not pick up a pack and take to the road. It literally opened doors for them, although not all succeeded at it. Some failed miserably, and a scant few experienced meteoric economic mobility. But most who peddled managed to accomplish that which they had set out to do, to live more securely and freely than they had before they commenced their journeys.

New-world Jewish peddling differed little around the world. In all these places, the Jewish peddlers came as unknowns, arriving in countries and regions devoid of a Jewish past or presence. The expulsion of the Jews from England in 1290, for example, lay so shrouded in the distant past that no Englishwoman or -man who greeted a Polish Jewish peddler in the late eighteenth century would have had an inkling that Jews had once lived in their county, had conducted their business, had been slaughtered and the survivors cast out. In Sweden, Canada, Mexico, Jamaica, Cuba, and elsewhere in the Caribbean, in each of the Latin American republics, in southern Africa, Australia, New Zealand, Ireland, Scotland, and Wales, no Jews had ever lived, save some lone stray individuals, before the great Jewish migration and the peddlers' arrival.

A QUESTION OF NUMBERS

We can never know how many Jews peddled in the new world because it constituted a passing stage in the lives of the immigrants. For one, many immigrant Jews started out in some other line of work but switched to peddling for some amount of time, and nearly all immigrant peddlers moved on to other occupations. Census takers would have had a hard time finding and enumerating them. In the United States, with its ten-year census cycle, an immigrant Jewish man who arrived in, say, 1871 and peddled until 1876 would never show up on an official form as a peddler. Similarly, peddlers were likely to be on the road when census takers came to town, so many itinerants slipped through the cracks. As peddlers they rarely had fixed abodes, so few city directories carried their names and described how they made their livings. Rather, they came in and out of particular towns or cities, where they rested on the weekends, paid off their creditors, replenished their stocks, and went back to the roads, rendering them invisible to official scrutiny.

Histories of specific Jewish communities spanning the globe contain random, usually unreliable tallies of the numbers of Jews who, at various times, peddled. Each numerical portrait constitutes a guess or snapshot of a specific moment. Peddlers' licenses, required everywhere, might provide hints, but not every jurisdiction asked peddlers to supply their religious affiliation on license forms. In Sweden peddlers did have to list religion, but in the United States they did not. Last names on license applications might provide a clue to Jewishness, but only a clue.[1] And uncountable numbers of peddlers did not register because they did not want to pay the license fee. Sometimes, however, historians do not need to guess. In Ireland, for example, schools listed pupils' religion and fathers' occupations, and according to such documents for Cork in the decades of the late nineteenth and early twentieth centuries, a majority of the Jewish youngsters in Cork listed their fathers as "travelers." In individual life histories, gathered from around the Jewish new world, people refer to themselves, their fathers, other male family members as having endured a stint in peddling. But these scattered sources do not constitute accurate quantitative data.

Internal Jewish communal narratives, works of history, or celebration volumes merely say, for any given period of time, that just about everyone peddled. The author of a history of the Jewish communities in the south of Wales felt no need to be more exact. In telling the story of the Jews in the town of Port Talbot, for example, he noted that the first Jew there, Raphael Levi, "started in the usual line of business and with his pack, travelled in the vicinity of Swansea." The historian's choice of "usual" says it all.

Change the proper noun and this statement could be repurposed for the experiences of Jewish immigrants in all destination settings, for some period of time. The indeterminate formulation—the "usual" occupation for the Jewish immigrants—or the comment that "most Jews" or "a majority of the Jews" made a living as peddlers when they first arrived in Indiana, Cape Town, New South Wales, Cork, Manitoba, Newfoundland, Chile, Jamaica, and beyond will have to do.[2]

Commentary during the migration years likewise perforce fell back on "many," "most," "a lot," and often just "all," highlighting the importance of peddling to Jewish immigration and in the life of the communities they founded. Havana's Yiddish-Spanish newspaper of the 1930s, *Oyfgang*, surveyed the situation of Jews in Peru and declared that "most" of the seven hundred Jews in Lima made a living as peddlers, and because so many labored in that capacity, "the most important Jewish organization in the land is the credit association of Hebrew peddlers which provided small loans to the men who went out into the countryside as well as in the city streets."[3] *Havaner Lebn*, a Yiddish magazine of the same decade, reported on Jewish life in nearby Honduras, noting of young Jewish men, "all of them are peddlers; mostly clothes, but whatever they find."[4]

SMALL TOWNS, BIG CITIES, AND THE PEDDLERS

Peddling spread Jewish populations out from the ports of disembarkation. While Jews in the modern era became an urban people, many also fanned out to smaller towns and deeper into the hinterlands. While most stayed in the big cities, vast numbers moved via peddling into the countryside. Peddlers returned to the metropolis on the weekends. If married, they typically left their wives and children in these communities. A number of peddlers went farther out into the hinterlands to seek opportunities in less-settled regions that housed small Jewish enclaves. The peddlers operated out of the tiny nodes of Jewish life, small-town replicas of the big cities. To these small towns they returned on the weekend, resting, settling up with their creditors, acquiring new stock, and then heading to the road. As the number of new Jewish peddlers increased, the towns began to support increasingly robust and active Jewish communities. When the peddlers gave up their mobile lives, they tended to set themselves down in those small communities, opening stores and adding to the number of small-town Jews.

In some cases a small town that served as a peddlers' hub grew over time into a large and then larger city, with a robust Jewish population. Cincinnati served as a frontier outpost when the first Jewish peddlers arrived and flow-ered in the Queen City. St. Louis attracted Jewish peddlers before it became a large city, as did Detroit, Milwaukee, and Minneapolis. Chicago formed as a village on the edge of the prairie wilderness but mushroomed in size and im-portance into something inestimably larger. Even in its earliest days, the 1840s, it operated as the nerve center for midwestern Jewish peddlers. Even as the city and its Jewish population grew exponentially, Jewish immigrant ped-dlers relied on it. They got their goods directly or indirectly from Jewish wholesalers and warehouse owners in Chicago. In this nearly universal pattern of Jewish geography, peddling drove the population outward, providing the economic reason for the creation of the hubs of Jewish life.[5]

Peddling in each country and each region and subregion had its own chro-nology. Since only immigrants peddled, each history pivoted on each nation's history and politics of immigration. Jewish peddling in Ireland, Scotland, and Wales began to ebb after the first decade of the twentieth century with the 1905 Aliens Act. Jewish peddling dried up in the United States after the 1920s, when congressional legislation ended numerically unrestricted immigration of Europeans. Each country in Latin America for a time encouraged and then restricted immigration, as did Australia and South Africa. Although men of the immigrant generation may still have been on the road after the restrictions went into effect, few new recruits took the peddlers' places, and as they one by one saved enough to get off the road, no new Jewish immigrants filled their shoes or their packs. The 1930s brought something of a minor renaissance for Jewish peddling when German and Polish Jewish refugees came to Australia, Cuba, and South and Central America.[6]

The many individual histories of peddling, by country and region, con-formed to changes in the basic economic and physical development of the place. As each place developed and became denser in settlement, people had fewer needs for the country peddlers. As cultural norms for women changed and they felt comfortable going to markets by themselves, they did not have to wait at home for the peddler, affectionately referred to as the "department store on wheels." As governments invested resources in road building and as mail service improved, customers could satisfy their material wants by thumbing through the enticing pictures of the Montgomery Ward catalogue, published in 1872, the Spiegel catalogue of 1888, and the Sears catalogue of the 1890s, the latter two founded by the sons of immigrant peddlers. Not that Jews stopped peddling in the United States, but they went to more remote regions and sold goods to customers in places beyond the reach of the catalogues.

WORLDWIDE PATTERNS

But that lay in the future, and during the age of the great Jewish migration, peddling pulled millions of Jewish men to the world beyond Europe, the Ottoman Empire, and North Africa. The life histories of new-world Jewish peddlers, regardless of time and place, abound with the personal details of chain migrations, of brothers bringing over brothers, and uncles bringing over nephews, who in turn brought over other relatives. The stories reveal how husbands migrated, saved their money, and then sent for wives and children. Added together, these literally millions of stories about migration, family reconstitution, and peddling amounted to a crucial chapter in Jewish history. Centrifugal forces launched the Jewish migration, like all others, while centripetal ones drew them to particular places.

The particular places they went to offered nothing specifically attractive *except* the presence of family members who could provide the newly arrived immigrants with their first access to economic opportunities. Nothing particularly notable characterized Mauch Chunk, Pennsylvania, in the 1830s except the coal mining companies that had operated there since the 1790s, and the miners and their families in and around Carbon County. Joseph Seligman, who in the middle of the nineteenth century founded J. & W. Seligman, a powerful investment bank, showed up there as a young immigrant from Bavaria because a cousin, Lewis Seligman, already lived there, having become an established merchant. Joseph opted for peddling. According to a brother who joined him in the anthracite coal town shortly thereafter, Joseph "expended $300 for jewelry—rings, bracelets, and watches—some gold plated, others German silver. With these goods as a loan and the $40 given by mother," he "went to work peddling, and on the first day sold more than $100 worth of goods. . . . [He] kept at the occupation and went through Pennsylvania . . . with good success." Joseph called for his brothers, one by one, to join him. From there the band of Seligman brothers, reunited in America, settled down in Lancaster with a store and ultimately stood at the helm of a major firm with worldwide reach.[7]

Brothers particularly set migrations in motion. They came from large families, and one brother would follow another across the ocean. Philip Schochet, who went from Russia to Minnesota in the 1880s, reminisced, "Brother Herman," already in the United States for a few years, "arrived from the Country" to greet his newly immigrated sibling. Herman "fixed me up a pack [of] dry goods and a suitcase [of] notions and sent me out on the train 50 miles west from Minneapolis with Myer Moses." Moses, an uncle, then took over the tutelage of the neophyte peddler, giving him "the lesson how to peddle;

took me along for a whole day. The following morning we parted and he gave me a road," directing him to go "from town to town, and the country was all covered with snow and places 2 feet high." Schochet, who eventually settled in Faribault, Minnesota, would never have chosen the upper Midwest without the brother and the uncle paving the peddling way for him, and without their lessons, he might not have ended up a comfortable wholesaler, dealing in iron and other metal.[8] Charles Wessolowsky's brother Asa had come to Georgia from Posen. He had gotten started on the road, carved out a peddling route, and written to his brother to join him. He expected Charles, in fact, on a precise date in 1858; when Charles, who would later edit the *Jewish South*, arrived later than planned, Asa chided him for having squandered a full week when they could have been "on the road."[9]

Uncle Meyer tutored Philip Schochet in the rules of the road. Uncle Ruben Leib Levine did the same in Hagerstown, Maryland, for the newly arrived Louis Singer, who told his story in nearly similar terms. Uncle Ruben "made me up a pack of dry goods and notions. The pack weighed about 25 pounds more than I weighed. He took me out to the country. He told me when you come to a house to knock on the door, and if the people ask you, . . . open your pack and say, 'Madam buy.'"[10]

It would be impossible to mention even a fraction of the examples of brothers and uncles bringing over their male kin as part of the Jewish peddler migrations. Relatively poor families who wanted to migrate, or who realized that some of their children had to, could rarely afford for all go at once. Someone, typically a young man, served as a kind of scout, the first link in a long migratory chain. He would learn the ropes, establish a relationship with a supplier, develop a customer base, and save money to pay the fares of one, then another, and then another male family member. Each of these in turn went out on the road.

The segmented, male-based migration made sense. If all family members had arrived together, dependent family—small children, women, and older parents—would have impeded the peddling venture. Dependents drained rather than created resources. Children in particular consumed, and their migrations had to follow the carefully planned steps of the pioneers. Wives, too, constituted economic liabilities in the early migration stages. After all, in an age before effective contraception, a wife meant babies and more babies. Those babies no doubt would have been welcomed and embraced, but they had to wait until they could be fed and raised.

New-world Jewish migrants who had no desire to go back to the places from which they had come engaged in a careful calculus of deciding who should go when and where. The need to send men, bachelors on their own or with male relatives and friends, or married men whose wives remained back home, pre-dominated. Because they hoped that their children would acquire some educa-tion and become part of the middle class of their new lands, these men also deliberated about when and how to create or reunite their families. The first family member to go, whether a single or a married man, entered into a mercan-tile relationship with one or more Jews already present in the destination set-ting. Usually a former peddler someplace, but now a shopkeeper, he provided the immigrant with his first bundle of goods, fixed him up with a route, offered some pointers on the customers' ways of life, a few basics of the language of the land. Often that included a slip of paper with phrases in the local language written out in Hebrew characters. The peddler, obviously, had to pay the shop-keeper back, with some profit, for the goods he had taken out on the road.

Often family members provided the credit. Indeed, the very individual whose remittances and encouragement drew the immigrant to a particular new-world place served as the launcher of the peddler's career. If not a relative, then a townsperson from back home who had made the transition from peddling to shopkeeping. And if the merchant-supplier and the neophyte peddler shared neither kinship nor hometown relationships, Jewishness was a sufficient link. Jewish merchants extended trust and credit to the newly arrived. Jacob Lehmann came to the United States and began his career before the Civil War peddling goods to the planters of sugarcane in southern Louisiana. Within a few years he opened a country store in Donaldsonville. He dealt intensively with the newly arriving Jewish peddlers, mostly from Posen and Alsace, who, one by one, went out to those same plantations and to other farmers in the re-gion. Lehmann, or Lemann, as he spelled his name in America, operated at the nexus between peddling and fixed-place merchandising.[11] Likewise, in much of Latin America, particularly in the Amazon basin, Jewish merchants of Sephardic background supplied the later-arriving immigrant Jews from Poland, as well as others from the Levant, with their stock, and in the process helped flatten this presumably powerful divide in the Jewish world.[12]

A mutually beneficial relationship—the provision of goods to peddlers and the peddlers' marketing of those goods house to house to customers who could not easily get to the store—worked in everyone's interest. Each side needed the other, and this erased or at least eased class inequities within Jewish communities, small ones in particular. This mutuality blunted compe-tition among the peddlers and between the settled Jewish shopkeepers and the peddlers. The success of the shopkeeper meant the success of the peddler, and the good fortunes of the peddlers enhanced those of the shopkeeper. All the parties in this intra-Jewish transaction had to be in sync with one another.[13]

Because Jewish migrations hinged globally on peddling and only men peddled, wives and children stayed back until the peddler father could become a
stay-at-home, in-the-shop father. The stories numbered in the millions and
took place all over the world, but maybe the experience of Esther Surasky
Pinck can illustrate the trend. She arrived as a small child with her mother in
Aiken, South Carolina, in 1896 from Knyshin, near Bialystok. Her father, a
peddler, preceded them by six years. Upon coming to the United States, he
stayed briefly in New York City, then moved south, joining an uncle in Aiken.
Peddling in the countryside, equipped with a Russian-English dictionary, he
launched himself in Aiken and in six years squirreled away enough money to
open a store and pay the fare for his children and his wife to join him.[14]
Similarly, Shimsel Cohen, an immigrant from Lithuania, joined his brother in
Bangor, Maine, in 1906, "secured a horse and team and operated as a peddler
for a few years." Then, almost as if conforming to a script, he laid away his
money and called for his wife to join him. Together they set up a confectionary
store in the Maine city. Over the years their family grew as they brought over
other kin from Lithuania and produced a crop of American-born children.[15]

Bonds of responsibility connected Jews to one another even when kinship
did not. Those links tied them together through networks of business and community. Since established Jewish merchants had much to gain by facilitating
the influx of more and more peddlers into their region, to disperse their goods
and enhance their operations, the peddlers, rather than being annoyances, interlopers, or embarrassing new immigrants, instead served a crucial purpose.

Jewish communal assistance for new peddlers transcended kinship. Jewish
peddling functioned as the bottom level of a vertical Jewish economic chain.
Non–family members offered start-up support for the newcomers. On one
level they did this because it constituted a fundamental Jewish communal obligation, the provision of *gemilat khesed*, acts of kindness such as interest-free
loans. Communal leaders understood that they owed other Jews practical aid.
When Rabbi David Wasserzug of Johannesburg died in 1918, his obituary in
the *Jewish Chronicle* sang his praises, reporting that he had "obtained licenses
and permits" for many of the "poor Russian Jews in the Transvaal, . . . to
travel as hawkers."[16] He and many other Jews around the world no doubt believed in the Talmudic principle "All of Israel are responsible for each other."

Lazarus Straus had a similar story. Straus, whose sons would eventually
include Nathan and Isidor, who became coowners of Macy's department store,
and Oscar, who served as the United States ambassador to Turkey and secretary of commerce, came to the United States from Otterberg in the Rhenish
Palatinate before the Civil War. Lazarus arrived in Talbotton, Georgia, armed

with a letter of introduction from several Otterberg Jews in Philadelphia, who vouched to the Kaufman brothers (Oglethorpe, Georgia, wholesalers) for his reliability and credit-worthiness.

Straus, far from a poor peddler, still turned to Jewish sources to begin his American peddling career. He peddled only briefly, but he peddled nonetheless. Although the story of the Straus family became the stuff of American Jewish legend, the letter of introduction, the connection with local Jewish merchants in a small town, the reliance on Jewish sources for credit, the move from peddler to shopkeeper within the context of a vertically articulated Jewish economy—all conformed to the experiences of most.[17]

The Straus story contains one more small detail that makes it typical rather than extraordinary, although the long-term outcome made it unique. The family first came to Philadelphia and only subsequently headed for the hinterlands to peddle. Untold numbers of Jews emigrated from some back-home place, landed and spent some time in the big city, be it New York or Dublin, Baltimore or Havana, and later, having made some useful contacts, moved on to more remote, less-settled areas to do their peddling. One family among many who did this eventually set itself up in 1889 in Michigan's Upper Peninsula. The wife in the couple, who eventually ran a clothing store in the town of Newberry, called for her siblings, all living in New York City. She did that, no doubt, because she missed them and believed life might be somewhat more salubrious in this remote area of forests and mines. But she did it also because, as she saw it, they "needed help in the store, and besides, there was money to be made peddling among the farms and lumber camp." That is, beyond family bonds, the peddler relatives could expand the catchment area of her Newberry store.[18]

Responsibility made good business sense as Jewish manufacturers, wholesalers, owners of warehouses, shopkeepers, even junkyard owners depended on the peddlers. Without peddlers, the owners of the stores could deal in only a limited stock of goods, circumscribed by the number of women and men who could physically make it to their shops. This then handicapped the wholesalers and the peddler-supply company owners, who had fewer opportunities to expand their operations. Without the peddlers, the junkyard dealers would have had to go out on their own to get their tin, bones, paper, rags, and other discarded objects, which the peddlers collected, cutting then the amount of salvage material they could sell to manufacturers and jobbers. Every one of these people, all Jews, depended on the peddlers, and they all shared an economic stake in one another's activities, all bound together by shared Jewishness.

Those with means, the settled shopkeepers or the wholesalers, helped the newcomers in multiple ways. They assisted the tyros to navigate the licensing system, something requiring knowledge of the local language, law, and bureaucracy. They provided the goods, advising the immigrant where to go in this strange new country, how to get there, and what sold best to what kinds of customers. The patron had much to gain from this assistance. After all, the peddler would be selling *his* wares, extending *his* commercial reach.

PATHS TO PEDDLING

Most immigrant peddlers started out that way. They arrived in their new land. Another Jew outfitted them and they headed for the road. They had migrated knowing that they would get started this way. Others entered peddling as a second-stage occupation, having tried something else that had not worked out. Or they realized that peddling offered benefits that other modes of making a living did not. In various parts of the United States, Canada, and Latin America, Jewish aid organizations like the Baron de Hirsch Fund tried to place new Jewish immigrants in agriculture and set up Jewish agricultural communities. Not all of these colonies failed, but most did, and the erstwhile Jewish farmers turned to peddling instead. Some Jews in Manitoba, for example, began as farmers but opted for peddling as something with a better future. So, too, Jews in the U.S. Industrial Removal Office, founded in 1905, recognized that the men whom they placed in jobs outside of New York quickly left those positions and opted for peddling instead. According to the 1914 report of the National Conference of Jewish Charities, based in New York, "a comparatively large number of those [immigrant Jewish men] who were sent to cities such as Gary [Indiana] soon gave up the relatively well-paid situations to which they had been sent and took up other work such as peddling." The author of this report on "Levantine" Jewish immigrants to the United States, David Da Sola Pool, explained to the charity group that it should not view as a failure the move by the beneficiaries of their assistance into peddling. Rather, he suggested, "it betokens an initiative, a desire to be one's own master, an ambition to take up work where the prospects of advancement and development are brighter than they are for an employee in a factory or steel works and perhaps a desire to be free to observe the Sabbath and religious holy days."[19]

Peddling beckoned Jewish immigrants because it fit into their communal and kinship system. Many peddlers, who with time settled down in a store, continued peddling as an outreach operation of their fixed businesses. This small detail demonstrated peddling's attractiveness and its centrality as a strategy. Typically the Jewish shopkeeper maintained some kind of peddling operation, allowing him to get his goods out to a broader clientele than those who could reach the store. Although he himself might no longer go out on the road, he recognized the business value of maintaining contact with his old customers, the men and women in the hinterlands. Who better to bring his town goods to the clients he had cultivated while on the road than a male family member or a friend just arrived from back home? Where no such newcomers showed up, then any new Jewish male immigrant would do, and that young man essentially recapitulated the life history of the one who came before him.

Shopkeepers who decided to keep peddling themselves needed someone to stand behind the counter, keep the shelves stocked, engage with customers, and maintain the books. Who better to do that than a wife? Indeed, once they married or reunited with their wives, the former peddlers, now shopkeepers, often turned some of the day-to-day operations of the business in town to the women, as they, the men, spent part of their time going out to the customers in remote regions. This mode of operation worked well, particularly in the early days of the sedentary merchant's career. As the in-town store prospered, however, and as the family grew with the birth of children, the men did less peddling and left it to the newer arrivals from abroad.

The tight bond between Jewish peddling and shopkeeping reflected the reality that, beginning in the middle of the nineteenth century, across the United States and throughout much of the new world, Jews played a conspicuous role in retail business in communities of all sizes. In 1872 in Columbus, Ohio, for example, not only did every Jewish family but one go into the clothing business, but Jews owned every retail clothing store in the state capital. A Johnstown, Pennsylvania, newspaper claimed in the 1870s that no non-Jews sold clothing. Seventy percent of Indianapolis's clothing establishments had Jewish owners. In one town after another Jews owned all or most of the jewelry stores, optical shops, and dry goods stores, some of which transformed over time into department stores.[20]

The connections between the peddlers and the shopkeepers, the bonds forged between Jewish business and Jewish community, went deeper. The shopkeeper's sedentary operation functioned as the hub of peddler activity on the weekends. To their stores and communities the peddlers came after the week on the road. There they paid their debts to the shopkeepers who had outfitted them, then picked up the goods for the upcoming week. All over the world, in small dispersed towns and in larger cities, the regional hubs, Jewish stores, mostly dry goods, operated by former peddlers and their wives, sustained those who went out on the road. These Jewish-owned stores provided peddlers with the stuff they needed to sell and provided them with the cash they might lend to customers, cash-poor women and men.

Sedentary Jewish merchants, the sources of goods and credit, supported a number of newcomer peddlers who relied upon them. The merchants gave each peddler a route and instructed him where to go, as well as how to get there. The merchant-creditor did not want more than one peddler going to the same houses, covering the same territory. They strove to prevent peddler competition. Conversely, the peddlers did not want to encroach on someone else's territory, knowing that suppliers would not appreciate such poaching, and it also went against their own business interests. The peddler wanted to have his customers, loyal women who knew and trusted him, and whom he could trust as well. He had to grant that exclusive right to his brother peddlers as well. Each had his own base and each prospered, however slowly.

COLLECTING JUNK

Wherever peddling took place it followed a universal tempo that took the peddler from walking the roads to having an animal-driven wagon, which they first rented and then owned. As peddlers made that transition away from foot-work to the luxury of a horse-, ox-, or donkey-pulled wagon, they twisted even more tightly the bond between themselves and the better-off, settled merchants. With the acquisition of a wagon many began to collect scrap, which they either gathered themselves or paid others to gather for them. As they emptied their wagons of the jewelry and picture frames, eyeglasses and watches, fabric, clothing, hardware, needles, and the like, the peddlers filled the empty spaces with old bones, discarded bits of tin and iron, rags—pretty much anything that someone would eventually buy for reuse.

Whether the customers collected the junk for the peddlers—the word had no pejorative connotation in the Jewish economic lexicon—or the peddlers scoured the landscape for the scraps themselves, the peddlers helped give birth to a thriving sector of the new-world Jewish economy. Everyplace Jews went in this age of migration, some gravitated to the salvage business, and Jewish scrap yards spanned the globe. An early form of recycling, the Jewish scrap business became a cornerstone of local Jewish economies. On his return trip to town, after the week on the road, a wagon peddler might sell the detritus to the Jewish shopkeeper, who in turn worked out arrangements with jobbers, and scrap yard owners—other Jewish immigrants and former peddlers—paid for what others considered worthless. Often the peddlers themselves sold directly to junkyards or to manufacturers who knew the value of this seemingly worthless material. However they collected, hauled, and sold off the junk, they did so for a profit, however marginal. And they did so in the context of a fully articulated Jewish economy, with Jews buying from and selling to one another, thus solidifying the personal, communal, and economic connections between Jews in their destination settings.[21]

One story will illustrate the global dynamic. Nathan Alpert made his way to the United States in 1903 from the Belarusian town Soly. He peddled in and around Scranton, Pennsylvania, and then ended up in Detroit before his final destination, Traverse City, Michigan. He brought his wife, Fruma Zlata, and his son Abe over in 1904. Nathan peddled religious objects and pictures to the local farm families. On his trips to the countryside he learned about the value of a ginseng, a root that grew widely throughout the region. Nathan collected the ginseng, which he dried out in his house, hanging it from the ceiling so that his small children could not get it. He then started taking the dried ginseng to Chicago's Chinatown, a lively market for the herb.[22]

This took place around cities and towns around the world. The Jewish stores from which the peddlers operated and which former peddlers owned drew together the multiple strands of their new world experiences. It did not matter how large or small the community, it took place wherever Jews lived. Jewish peddlers selling in Westchester County, New York, used New York City as their base, while Jewish peddlers who operated in and around Michigan's Upper Peninsula orbited around Bay City, a tiny Jewish enclave. On-the-road peddlers functioned in a world that linked the hinterlands and the metropolis, the rural areas with town life through goods and credit.[23]

One description of this from Winnipeg could easily have come from New South Wales, Limerick, or Chile. The daughter of such a shopkeeper, looking back to the 1880s, recalled that "at his [Finkelstein's] store, those of the group who became peddlers were given their first start, and later their stocks were replenished. They went off to trade with the Indians . . . and English in the surrounding territory." While the shopkeeper clearly occupied a superior position to the peddlers, Bella Weretnikow Rosenbaum nonetheless remembered, "Business was nearly always good—they had customers waiting for them. Thus they prospered and, in due time, most of the peddlers opened stores of their own."[24]

Newly arrived immigrants took up peddling by acquiring their goods from these stores, shopping around and picking up items from some or all of them, based on what local Jewish merchants believed customers wanted. The longer any individual peddled in a region, the better he got to know his customers. The larger his reputation grew, the more clout he carried within the Jewish economic network, and the more and better goods and lower prices he could command and then pass on to the people on his route. All of this depended on intracommunal trust. The peddler had to trust the merchant to provide reliable stock, and the merchant had to trust the peddler to come back and pay for that stock, so that the merchant in turn could pay his creditors. Peddler and shop-keeper expected to profit on the sale of the items since without the profit there could be no justification for the whole enterprise, the migration included.

In communities around the world Jewish men, usually established mer-chants, gave interest-free loans to those wanting to start peddling. Hebrew loan associations popped up wherever Jews settled in large enough number to be able to amass some funds. In 1895 in Detroit such an association came into being, charging members five cents a week. A 1903 article in the *Detroit Free Press* reported that the organization typically lent new immigrants five dollars to acquire a stock or fifteen dollars to upgrade to horse and wagon.[25] Established Jews in Montreal created the Baron de Hirsch Institute in the 1880s. Named for a French Jewish philanthropist, the Quebec organization lent money to those eager to go into business, including peddling.[26] Indeed, throughout Canada, the Jewish Colonization Association, founded by Hirsch in 1891, set up a special committee, "Loans for Peddlers License and General Help to Establish Themselves."[27] In Brazil in the 1920s, Polish Jewish immigrants turned to the local *laisparkasse*, a savings and loan society which extended start-up capital to newcomer peddlers, while in Mexico in that decade B'nai B'rith, a worldwide Jewish fraternal organization, directly helped new immi-grants, also primarily from Poland, to purchase hammers, saws, sickles, whet-stones, inexpensive clothing, mirrors, plaster saints, and crucifixes to take into the countryside. B'nai B'rith's Mexico City lodge tried to negotiate with Jewish importers, there and in the United States, to increase the amount of credit they would extend to the newly arrived immigrant peddlers.[28]

Peddlers did not just depend on aid from other Jews. They also organized themselves to negotiate collectively with the settled merchants who provided their goods and credit. In Uruguay, for example, from the 1910s through the 1930s, Jewish peddlers, *cuéntaniks*, formed a number of societies, such as La Sociedad Commercial Israelita, La Corporación Commercial, and La Cooperativa Comercial Israelita del Uruguay, to negotiate with suppliers, hoping to secure reduced rates for goods, better financing, and more ample credit. In parts of Canada, Chile, and Cuba, peddlers worked together to en-hance their bargaining power with their Jewish creditors. Peddler collective action depended upon the constant town-based weekend clustering where peddlers met, shared stories of misery on the road, and as a group complained about their suppliers, coming up with strategies as to the best ways to improve their lot.[29]

The tempo of peddling reflected local levels of the development of transportation systems. Where and when only primitive roads linked customers and suppliers, peddlers undertook circuits of more than a week in length, staying out on the road for longer periods of time. Regions blessed with canals and railroads allowed peddlers to ship their goods from their town base to one or more depots along the way, timing their arrivals with the arrival of their goods. Peddlers with wagons particularly benefited from advances in transportation, and they could cover a much wider territory than those who trudged by foot. Jewish merchants owned the depots to which they sent their goods, and these coreligionists thrived on the peddler business. Some peddlers serviced families that lived on the outskirts of cities, and the itinerant merchants went to their customers either by foot or by streetcar. No matter how he got out of town and onto the road for his weekly path, his mind, no doubt, remained fixed on Friday, when he would come back to what constituted, for him, civilization.

Jewish suppliers advertised in newspapers around the world. Paid notices in Jewish newspapers touting the availability of peddler wares, in places as far apart as Winnipeg, New York, Chicago, Cincinnati, London, and Brazil, reflected the centrality of peddling for the Jewish economy and the pivotal role of peddling in the global migration. The peddlers' suppliers, most of them former peddlers, offered more than just goods at low prices to the peddlers. They also provided the information the peddlers needed on how to apply for a license. They directed the peddlers to specific routes, making sure that no peddler veered onto someone else's terrain. Beyond the information, the owners of the supply houses stood as guarantors for the peddlers when they took out their papers, vouching for the new immigrants ready to go out on the road, armed with their state-issued licenses.

All over the world some former peddlers set themselves up as peddler suppliers, and as such they became agents in the immigration business. In the early nineteenth century Henry Moses, who took the name Zender Falmouth, set himself up in Falmouth, England, as a supplier of peddlers. One young arrival to England, Israel Solomon, recalled, in his autobiography, that "Zender kept a stock of buckles, small cutlery, jewelry, and matches to supply the hawkers, and gave credit to young men on certain conditions and, where it was necessary, advanced money to obtain the hawker's license. The conditions were to return every Friday early enough to participate in the minyan [the Jewish prayer quorum of ten men], and on Sunday morning to square up their accounts by paying the money owed for last week's sales, and to receive fresh goods on credit." Zender Falmouth's supply of goods and credit served as a lodestone for new Jewish men who made the journey across the English Channel from Poland and the northern Germanic states.[30]

His story repeated itself an ocean away. Sixteen-year-old Jacob Epstein, an immigrant from Russia, saved up $600 by 1881 from his two-year stint as a peddler in the hinterlands of Maryland. He gave up his itinerant existence and rented a small store in Baltimore, which he stocked with jewelry, oilcloth, fabric for dresses, and patterns, pins, needles, thimbles, and kitchenware. From one tiny space he created the Baltimore Bargain House, which grew over the course of the early twentieth century. He changed the goods he carried to satisfy what he believed the customers wanted. Epstein sold his "bargains" to the peddlers, the thousands of new Jewish immigrants, whom he hoped would buy from him rather than from some other Jewish-owned peddler supply company in Baltimore or elsewhere. Certainly the most successful of the peddler suppliers in the cities on the Chesapeake, Epstein cleverly figured out how to corner the peddler business, coming up with the scheme of standing at the docks, meeting the incoming ships at the port, and identifying the immigrant Jewish men disembarking. He offered to set up these men, individuals obviously eager for work, with peddling supplies and direct them to routes throughout the American South, the Chesapeake region, and West Virginia. As these newcomers then brought over their relatives to peddle, they, too, got their stock from the Baltimore Bargain House.[31] "Falmouth" and Epstein operated nearly a century apart and on opposite sides of the Atlantic, but operated basically the same way.

The new immigrant who got off at an English or American port must have truly appreciated meeting Zender Falmouth or his equivalent in Dublin, Montreal, Toronto, Winnipeg, Cape Town, Buenos Aires, or Havana, waiting at the docks, providing the immigrant with a ready-made opportunity to get started on the roads of his new home. For the new immigrants the existence of Jewish trade networks and communal resources served as a sign or omen that they had made the right decision when they had chosen to migrate.

New-world peddling spawned subsequent peddling. Lithuanian Jews came to Scotland in the early twentieth century. They hawked their goods to the miners who lived south of Glasgow. As they accumulated some savings, they communicated with family and friends back home, singing the praises of the Scottish mining region as a place to make a living. That news drew the newcomers to the region who showed up and went to work for their friends who had provided the information and the means to start. Known in Scotland as "trebbelers," a corruption of "travelers," the peddlers sold the goods acquired from the shopkeepers and wholesalers. This same kind of subdivision or subcontracting took place in Ireland with the weekly men, also referred to as travelers, as it did among the Jewish immigrants who came from Syria to Mexico or Poland to Cuba.

THE ADVANTAGES OF PEDDLING

Peddling played a not inconsiderable role in stacking the odds in favor of the decisions of millions of Jews to migrate. It offered a degree of flexibility, allowing its practitioners to diversify their operation and economic scope, even while being forced to be on the road. Once in the new world, immigrant peddlers extended their economic activities with moneylending, performing both economic acts simultaneously, selling goods to customers while lending money. As they sold on the installment plan everywhere, they seamlessly segued into lending money to customers, poor people with limited resources. The money itself came from settled Jewish merchants who profited from these transactions, as did the borrowers who needed cash. The customers used the money to pay for the goods purchased from the peddler and for other purposes as well. In Ireland and Wales this constituted a nearly universal experience. Elaine Crowley's recollections of being *A Dublin Girl* in the 1930s referred to her poor family's heightened material aspirations and the "weekly," "the Jewman," who took low interest on the money he lent. Although this took place in Dublin, the urban Jewish peddlers, like their rural counterparts, went house to house, apartment to apartment, crossing into their customers' living space on a weekly basis, and selling goods on the installment plan and offering ready cash.[32]

The first novel written by an Irish Jew, Joseph Edelstein's *The Money Lender* (1931), depicted, much to the chagrin of the Dublin Jewish community, the life history of peddler Moses Leventhal and his journey from poverty in Lithuania to his death in Ireland as a wealthy man, his wealth derived from his nefarious and heartless money lending. The novel traced the misery of his boyhood in Lithuania, where he read in *Hatzfirah* many an article extolling the benefits of migration, the lure of peddling, and Jewish success in the new world. *The Money Lender*'s protagonist came to Ireland through friends and fellow Jews from "Wexney," who equipped him with a kit of goods and put him on the road peddling in the countryside. His creditor, a fellow Wexney native, encouraged him to lend money in order to enlarge his earnings and hasten the day when he could stop peddling. The novel depicts the tragic implications of Leventhal's money lending, which ruins an innocent young woman who borrows more than she can pay back. Peddling led to money lending, which in turn destroyed the life of the borrower and soul of the lender.

Peddling also existed in the context of pawning, yet another occupation that Jews pursued in Ireland, Wales, much of the American South, South Africa, and elsewhere. Irish memoirs abound with the details of the pawn, and Jews comprised many, although not all, of the local pawnbrokers. The poor relied upon pawning for their survival, and both urban and rural Jewish peddlers, the men who had sold the goods in the first place, frequently bought the items back in the course of return visits. In cities like Dublin, former Jewish peddlers opened pawn shops, probably dealing with the same customers whose apartments they had once entered.[33]

Peddlers sold their goods on the installment plan, adding small amounts of interest on the cost of the goods. The customer chose the item and put down a negotiated amount. The peddler then came back, week after week, to get the money owed from that purchase. He also showed new wares. The peddler hoped that the customer who owed him money for something bought on a previous visit would buy something else each time.

These itinerant merchants could carry new goods as customers requested them and as they, the peddlers, learned about them. They could respond to novelty by stocking and displaying it. As sewing machines became available at an affordable price, peddlers started offering them. With the development of phonographs and records, these wares began to be offered. Peddlers with wagons sometimes carried photographic equipment and took their customers' portraits. Peddlers showed customers catalogues with pictures and descriptions of consumer goods, and when a customer expressed an interest in a particular item, the peddler ordered it and brought it into the customer's home.

Peddlers responded to customer demand and complaint. Meyer Guggenheim came to Philadelphia in 1847 from Switzerland, choosing a route in Pennsylvania's anthracite coal region. When the women to whom he had sold bottles of stove polish complained that the product left their hands dirty, he asked a friend in Philadelphia to analyze the substance to figure out what caused the discoloration. Guggenheim's friend helped him concoct a new batch of cleaning fluid devoid of the offending substance. The peddler, soon to become millionaire, went back to his customers with a better stove polish, one that left their hands clean.[34]

Peddlers, particularly the unmarried, could earn weekly, in small sums, money that went beyond what they owed their creditors. They had no overhead and few expenses. These savings provided the basis for a slow but appreciable accumulation of capital, which enabled a transition from foot peddler to wagon peddler to storekeeper or owner of some other business. Some Jewish immigrants working in other kinds of enterprises, dissatisfied with their sluggish mobility, decided to peddle in order to accumulate savings more quickly. Mary Cohen, an immigrant from the Netherlands, living in Oakland, California, in the 1870s concluded that her husband Isaac would do better economically as a peddler than as a carver and gilder of picture frames. She persuaded him to go out and peddle. Isaac and Mary Cohen changed their surname to Magnin, and out of Isaac's peddler earnings they accumulated enough to open a store, I. Magnin, eventually one of the country's most high-end department stores. Joe Goodman's success was much more modest than I. Magnin's, but like Isaac Cohen, this Jewish immigrant, who ended up a solid grocer in El Paso, Texas, left one field of work, in Goodman's case garment making, for peddling. Caught in the grips of the depression of 1893, Goodman, an immigrant from Lithuania, decided to leave his sewing machine and take up a 160-pound peddler's pack, with which he made his way through northern New York. He eventually moved to El Paso, opened a grocery store, and emerged as a leader in the local Jewish community. Had he stayed a sweatshop worker in New York, he probably would not have achieved the self-employment or the leadership status he desired.[35]

In fact, rather than being a last resort for unskilled Jewish immigrant men, a dumping ground for those who could do no better, peddling represented a first step on an ascent that not just anyone could achieve. Some tried peddling and failed. "My father," recalled Bella Rosenbaum of her immigrant life in Winnipeg, "a small scholarly man with a carefully trimmed, pointed red beard . . . tried his luck at peddling, but unfortunately it seems he did not have any luck."[36] Abe Gellman from Kamenetz, Poland, also tried peddling. His friends who tried to set him up "did everything possible to have made me satisfied but unfortunately the business they were in wasn't to my liking. . . . It was peddling merchandise with a horse and wagon outfitted like a small store on wheels with shelves, show cases and selling in the suburbs of Chicago. It was honest, fair work but I couldn't get accustomed to it."[37] Friends of Adolf Kraus, a Bohemian immigrant who came to the United States at the end of the Civil War, persuaded him to peddle "in some district where I would be forced to learn to speak English." Kraus, using the last of the money he brought with him from Blowitz, "invested in Yankee notions and started on a peddling tour in Connecticut." He hated it, and "I was . . . a . . . dismal failure as a peddler . . . because it was very distasteful to me and my heart was not in it." Kraus, who later became a lawyer and Jewish communal activist, saw one silver lining in this failed experiment. He recalled that "the farmers I came in contact with on this trip were very hospitable. I stayed at some of the farms for days at a time, helped to do the chores . . . played with the boys, and in that manner soon picked up considerable English."[38]

Stories of failed peddlers abound. A contributor to a Yiddish-language immigrant memoir project recalled that "after one day peddling it did not take me long to realize that peddling is not for me." He opted instead to labor in a sweater factory.[39] Ben-Moyshe Laikin, another contributor to the memoir project, came to Philadelphia to join a cousin who owned a wholesale warehouse. His cousin outfitted him as a peddler, but he could not do it. He found it impossible to knock on someone's doors, engage in some small talk before trying to make the sale. Unable to peddle, he had to go to work in the cousin's warehouse. As he saw it, working inside stymied his progress in learning English, and throughout his life he regretted his inability to peddle.[40]

Ben-Moyshe Laikin knew something. He figured out that as a way to get started in his new land, peddling had a greatest potential for opening the doors to success. It provided those who could do it with the most efficient way to learn the lay of the land and its people. He and nearly all those whose impressions have survived understood that new-world Jewish peddling constituted a temporary stage in the lives of the men who could do it. For nearly all, peddling consumed just a few years, from their arrival until they accumulated enough to move into a sedentary mercantile occupation, in which they no longer had to endure days and weeks on the road away from family and community. Owning a store meant no more dependence on customers for places to lodge, no more nights sleeping in barns or fields if no customer offered a bed. It meant a wife, children, a reconstituted family and life in a Jewish community, something that most wanted. Migration based on peddling enabled immigrant Jews to integrate into their new country. It offered them the swiftest path toward learning the language of the land, a not inconsiderable asset for a group of people who had no intention of returning to the places they had left.

Peddling not only made possible the transfer of Jews as individuals via family networks from Lithuania or the Ottoman Empire to Ireland or South Africa, Mexico or Chile, but it served as the soil from which Jewish communities took root around the world. The history of Jewish peddling involved community as much as business. Conversely, even the time off the road, intended to satisfy communal needs, had an economic side to it as well. After all, if Friday night and Saturday day constituted Jewish holy time, spent in rest, religious worship, food, and pleasures of various kinds, Saturday night brought the peddlers and the merchants back to the reality of the mundane world of business. At that time, once the Sabbath had come to an end, the peddlers made their way to the stores or warehouses of their creditors, paid them for last week's jumble of goods, and then started loading up their packs and wagons with the stuff they would hawk during the next week. Sunday sent them back onto the road.

Time on the road and time off the road made peddling an enterprise that connected the "holy" and the "mundane." Peddling drew Jews, individual by individual and family by family, to specific places that had previously had no Jews or so few as to make community impossible. But with each additional Jew and Jewish family, these places became increasingly attractive as destinations for yet others.

THE WEEKLY CYCLE

The peddlers sold on a weekly circuit, heading out on Sundays or Mondays, depending on the distance they had to travel to begin their routes. They trod the roads, or rode on the wagon, and visited the customers' homes one by one. Fridays all the peddlers made their way back to the town, reuniting with one another and with the shopkeepers, and with their wives and children, living briefly as members of a Jewish community. Here they spent the Sabbath, as well as the Jewish holidays. In smaller places some peddlers lodged in the homes of the shopkeepers, further cementing the bonds between them, and tightening the connections between commerce and community. Here peddlers experienced a different life from their lives on the road. Simon Wolf, who in the middle of the nineteenth century would emerge as a political leader of American Jewry, grew up in Uhrichsville, Ohio, living with his extended family, the operators of a general store. Out of that store, he recalled in his *Reminiscences*, "twenty to thirty Jewish peddlers . . . with their packs, weighing from one hundred to one hundred and fifty pounds, would start out into their rural districts of the state." At a moment in time when the town had no synagogue, no rabbi, no formally structured community, the peddlers, who "managed always to return on a Friday, so as to be with us on Saturday," participated in the religious services which one of Wolf's uncles held in his home.[41]

Wherever the peddlers went, whatever country or continent, they lived their lives according to a set pattern of weekdays on the road and weekends at rest. For all their suffering on the road, for all their exertions carrying heavy backpacks, they may have been among the few people anyplace who enjoyed a five-day work week. Almost all Americans until the 1930s worked six days a week. Jewish store owners had a difficult time closing their stores on Saturdays, the most popular shopping day, and Jewish factory workers had to clock in on the Sabbath regardless of their sensibilities. But peddlers could treat Saturday as a day of rest. Rabbi Emil Hirsch of Chicago's Sinai Temple, an advocate for Sundays as Sabbath, noted with humor or irony, "Only millionaires and peddlers can observe the Jewish Sabbath."[42]

Like the peddlers who spent a few days every week at the Wolf family store in Uhrichsville, their peers around the world experienced these moments as times when they interacted with other Jews. In these two days of respite they reverted to their familiar language, Yiddish for the Ashkenazim, Ladino or Arabic for the Jewish immigrant peddlers from the Muslim world. In time off the road and in the shelter of the Jewish enclave they partook of Sabbath religious services, conducted informally at first, but over time, as congregations developed, in more formal settings. During their forty-eight hours without a pack on their backs they could eat familiar and kosher food, prepared in the styles of Lithuania, Romania, Alsace, Bavaria, Morocco, or whatever the places of origin of the Jewish families with whom they stayed. In larger places, Jewish women opened and operated boardinghouses for peddlers, part of the formalization of communal life. These boardinghouses provided women, many of them widows, with a chance to make a living and provided the peddlers with camaraderie in a Jewish setting, so different from the five nights spent on the road.

During these weekends the bachelor Jewish peddlers could meet single Jewish women, the daughters, sisters, and other female relatives of the shopkeepers. Those meetings took place around the world, and they evolved from chance meetings to formal courtships, marriages, leading to the formation of new Jewish families, swelling the size of the town's Jewish population, and enabling the creation of new and more formal Jewish institutions.

Part of that increasing institutional elaborateness can be traced back to the peddlers' presence. One peddler, M. S. Polack, who sold seasonally in a territory that went from southern Pennsylvania through South Carolina, combined his peddling with providing ritual circumcision for Jewish male infants. An immigrant from Germany in the 1830s, a time when few Jewish functionaries existed in the back country of the fledgling nation, Polack helped create American Judaism as he sold his wares. He kept a circumcision logbook in which he noted both the date of the child's birth and the date of the circumcision, and we can see that he could not always arrive on the obligatory eighth day after the birth of the baby. Frontier life and the demands of peddling trumped the demands of the Jewish law. Yet Polack's peripatetic life as a peddler allowed him to range widely over the countryside and fulfill this deeply felt and almost universally assumed communal obligation.[43]

The fact that Jews in these scattered communities started to need the services of a *mohel*, a ritual circumciser, meant that some Jewish women had arrived and that their presence had shaped the new-world Jewish culture built on the peddling economy. Jewish women in even modest-sized Jewish communities set up networks of support for Jewish peddlers. Only the rare Jewish woman peddled in the new world. Irving Katz's mother stood out as an exception. In recalling the immigrant experience of his parents, Max and Rebecca, writes that his family's "mainstay was our horse and wagon. Sometimes father, at other times mother, went through the countryside villages peddling notions and any other goods available. . . . Mother went more often because father was still engaged in studies which Mom always encouraged."[44]

WOMEN AND PEDDLING

The scarcity of women peddlers in the new world reflects the fact that many male peddlers arrived as bachelors or, having left wives back home, effectively lived as bachelors. The arrival of women spelled the family's transition to sedentary life. Women may not have peddled in new-world settings because of the absence of extended family to watch children and perform domestic functions while the women went out on their routes. Katz did not share with his readers whether his father, while studying, also cooked, cleaned, did the laundry, and minded the children.

The absence of women from the road allowed them to take on other activities and roles, economic and communal. Women in the towns and cities more often than not sustained the family store, that commercial and communal hub that supplied the peddlers. They operated stores so that their husbands could peddle, collect scrap, and go to larger cities to inspect and buy goods. Women all over the Jews' new world also ran boardinghouses for peddlers, either during the week, as they made their way through their territories, or over the Sabbath, when the men returned to the hubs of Jewish life. And some women who did not operate actual boardinghouses still opened their homes to the peddlers on the weekend, providing them with food, clean linens, and the other accoutrements of restful time off the road.[45]

The women took upon themselves, whether formally or informally, the obligation of *hakhnassat orkhim*, or hospitality for strangers. Simon Wolf, in his recollections of life in the small Ohio town, extolled the "hostess," his aunt, who offered "loving care and attention" to the men who gathered in her home and her store. Jewish peddlers who arrived, in Uhrichsville or its global equivalents, turned to the wives of peddlers and storekeepers for food and shelter.

In numerous small communities such women's activities laid the basis for formal organizing, constituting the first Jewish communal venture, sometimes predating the first cemetery. But even if the cemetery came first, the women's group organized to provide for the wayfarers, the peddlers in the new world. This act led to the growth of the Jewish voluntary organizational infrastructure. In towns around the world Jewish women's organizations, like the Female Hebrew Benevolent Associations in the United States, provided short-term interest–free loans to men trying to get started in peddling without family to help them or local businessman to launch their careers. Jewish histories of places such as Knoxville, Tennessee, rural and small-town North Dakota, and upstate New York, among many others, told this story of organized Jewish female benevolence, directed toward assisting the peddlers who floated in and out of their communities.[46]

Jewish women in the towns and cities from which their peddler husbands ventured out played a more decisive and shaping role in the formation of Jewish communities than they had in Europe before migration. Their ability to create the Jewish communal organizations which fit their needs and did not parallel those founded by the men reflected that empowerment. In many moderate-sized communities, for example, Jewish men tended to organize multiple congregations organized according to the places in Europe that they had come from. Polish, German, Bohemian, and Russian congregations sprouted up. Men, who spent much time on the road, opted for ethnically homogeneous religious institutions when they came back to town. The women, however, in one town after another created a single unified women's benevolent society, one that transcended places of origin. All the Jewish women in Albany, Georgia, or Akron, Ohio, banded together, attended meetings, and performed their self-assigned functions despite their varied geographic backgrounds. To what degree did this reflect the reality that these women lived five days out of seven with each other, without men? Did their intense dependence on one another, given their husbands' absence, erase boundaries that divided the men, who spent their days solo on the roads? As their husbands left for their road trips, the women, it seems, sought each other out. Being a Jewish woman who found herself without extended family no doubt proved to be lonely, and encouraged one to value the companionship of, and solidarity with, other Jewish women, regardless of whether some had come from Lithuania and others from Alsace. As these women perceived it, they had so much in common with one another that place of origin mattered little.

Perhaps because of their husbands' absences, they met, socialized, and learned from the non-Jewish women around them as well. Almost all of the

Jewish children went to public school, engaging with peers of other religious and ethnic backgrounds. This brought the women also into contact with the larger Christian world, and as the only parent present a mother often participated in activities associated with the education of her youngsters. As shopkeepers, the Jewish women struck up acquaintances with other women, from whom they learned the details of new-world cultures; thus they formed bonds with their female neighbors over domestic and personal matters. Sarah Thal, a Lithuanian Jewish immigrant, wife of a peddler, lived in the upper Midwest and met "Mrs. Stratton. She wove rag carpets." Thal considered the carpets beautiful and wanted to learn how to make them herself. From that same woman, "I learned to make citron and green tomato pickles and cakes and pies." Some learning went the other way as well, "and I taught my neighbors how to make coffee cake, potato salad, cottage cheese, noodles, etc." From Mrs. Stratton and her counterparts around the Protestant, English-speaking world, Jewish women learned how to raise funds for their Jewish activities through strawberry socials, bazaars, and white elephant sales, and to apply such words as "benevolence" and "ladies" to the *hevrat nashim*, or the women's societies, they founded, and whose activities in part helped the peddlers.[47]

The way Jewish women forged reciprocal relationships with non-Jewish women depended to a degree on their husbands' peddling. With husbands gone, Jewish immigrant women could socialize with whom they wanted and how. That weekly absence allowed them to develop economic activities and shape the communities in which they lived. After all, five days out of seven women outnumbered men, and Jewish women used their weekly numerical preponderance to develop their own new-world lives.

Peddling shaped Jewish marriage patterns around the new world. In Argentina, for example, in the early twentieth century, groups of Jewish men, all bachelors from Damascus, peddled along the Riachuelo River, spending their weekends in the Boca and Barracas neighborhoods of Buenos Aires. When they could get married, they wrote to the young women from back home, who arrived accompanied by their brothers, who then themselves took up the peddling life in the new world.[48] In other cases—and numbers and rates cannot be computed—peddlers met young Jewish women in the towns from which they peddled. The daughters, sisters, female cousins of the shopkeepers became the partners for the young men ready to get off the road. Other peddlers found that their sisters back home served as informal matchmakers when they were ready to settle down. Because marriage facilitated shopkeeping, getting married meant more than just love and family, although those values mattered greatly.

In other cases, known to us only serendipitously because someone saved a cache of letters or produced a family memoir, Jewish men met, fell in love with, and decided to marry non-Jewish women. At times those women agreed to convert to Judaism, and the peddler-husband brought his fiancée or new wife to some hub of Jewish life for a conversion and a Jewish wedding. Marcus Spiegel, an immigrant from Bavaria, peddled in the 1850s in Ohio, leaving an extended family in Chicago. On his journeys in and around Union County he came frequently to the home of Stephen Hamlin, a Quaker farmer. Hamlin's daughter Caroline and the Jewish peddler fell in love. Spiegel's family tried to dissuade them from marrying. Caroline Hamlin, according to her daughter's memoir, rather than being offended by the aggressiveness of Henry Greenbaum, the family member who hastened to Ohio to put a stop to the marriage, found herself charmed by him. Caroline and Marcus got married in August 1853 by a justice of the peace in Stark County, Ohio. They then went to Chicago, where Caroline commenced her studies for conversion to Judaism. She converted, learned German, picked up German Jewish cooking tips, and over the course of her lifetime became an active and energetic member of the Chicago Jewish community, continuing this beyond Marcus's death in the Civil War during the Red River campaign.[49]

The story of Marcus Spiegel and Caroline Hamlin illustrates several other aspects of Jewish peddling in the new world. Caroline Hamlin, the daughter of a substantial white Protestant farmer, represented the nation's dominant American population. On her father's side the family had migrated from England to Virginia in 1637, and her mother's forbears also had deep roots in colonial Virginia. The Hamlins settled in Ohio at the turn of the nineteenth century, counting themselves among the first wave of pioneers to the territory. Marcus Spiegel, the German Jewish immigrant, a lifelong observant Jew, had no trouble coming into the Hamlin home as a peddler with his sack of wares, mixing with them, and wooing their daughter. After all, the objection to the marriage came from his family, not hers.

Peddling gave Jews a chance to shed some of their outward difference, as perceived by others. Wherever they peddled, local commentators noted their elegant dress, with tie and waistcoat, a bowler or top hat upon their heads. Even for peddlers still bearded and marked as Jewish, their sartorial choices emphasized their dignity, not the occupation's dinginess. They understood that customers might be less likely to open the door to a bedraggled man wearing tattered clothing.

The positive valence that accompanied Jewish peddling took a notable twist in the United States. No doubt by an accident of timing, when Jews entered American peddling, they did so by supplanting the Yankee peddlers, a group with unimpeachable American bona fides. Although Americans lampooned the Yankee peddler for his alleged sharp dealing and shrewd business sense, Yankees still represented the oldest of white Americans, the descendants of New England and the nation's founding fathers. For the Jews to step into the Yankee's shoes, and to do so via peddling, gave them an economic and cultural history profoundly different from those of their non-Jewish coimmigrants from Ireland, Italy, Poland, and elsewhere, who entered America as laborers on railroad crews, on canal-digging gangs, or in mines and steel mills. In popular discourse Irish immigrants tended to be depicted as akin to African-Americans, slaves or not. The Jewish peddlers, on the other hand, entered into the popular consciousness as akin to their Yankee predecessors.

While Jewish peddlers also sold to nonelite customers, people unlike the Hamlins of Union County, Ohio, they always identified with their social betters. They did not seek to integrate into the less well-off, nondominant classes in their destination societies. In South Africa, for example, the Jewish *smous*, or peddlers, dealt most intensely and most often with Boers, the Afrikaans-speaking whites of Dutch origin. But Jews gravitated towards the English-speaking, British-oriented elites. The smous sent their children to school to learn English, to model themselves along English lines of bourgeois behavior and success. Jewish peddlers who came to Quebec, divided between French and English speakers—a chasm that corresponded to the poorer and better off in provincial society—sold heavily to the French denizen of the small rural towns. But they sent their children to English schools and sought integration into the Anglophone world. In regions of the United States divided by race, class, language, and religion, Jews expected to integrate into the white, middle-class, English-speaking, and Protestant populations. So, too, in Ireland: though the Jewish weekly men conducted business transactions with Irish Catholics, they took their cultural cues from the English-leaning middle class.

In the Caribbean and Central America, where Jewish peddlers plied their trade in the small towns among the plantation workers, they aspired culturally to become part of the cosmopolitan culture of the cities, and wanted to be associated with the white Europeans. Despite the overwhelmingly Catholic nature of those societies, Jews, though they had few illusions of real integration, held up those elites as the people whose other institutions they sought to enter.

In short, by marrying Caroline Hamlin and becoming the son-in-law of a substantial Quaker family, among the oldest in the nation, Marcus Spiegel, who never wavered in his commitment to Judaism and Jewish communal life, used his peddling experience to become American in more than the sense of acquiring citizenship. Marcus and Caroline's story says much about Jewish peddling in the new world and the matter of language. When Marcus entered the Hamlins' parlor to spread out his goods, he did so as a speaker of English. Although he may have had an accent, he commanded the language of the land. Marcus and his family had come to America in 1846, and his marriage to Caroline, who knew no German, took place in 1853. Less than ten years after his arrival in America, Marcus could speak English well enough not only to sell dry goods but to court a well-off, probably reasonably well-educated young woman.

All over the world where peddlers went, whether they spoke English, Spanish, French, Afrikaans, Portuguese, or Swedish, they had no choice but acquire the dominant language. But peddlers sold not only to the speakers of the dominant languages. They also developed routes which had them selling to speakers of Mayan, Sioux, Cherokee, Gaelic, and many others. One description of Jewish life in Bolivia as late as the 1940s noted that since the Jewish peddlers there spoke only to the Indians, "they speak the dialect of the Indios. They appear in the most outlying villages, where hardly any Europeans have ever been."[50]

They had no choice but to learn languages. Their occupation demanded it. They could, in the initial stages, get along with a few stumbling words, armed with a sheet of paper provided by a friend or their shopkeeper creditor, with such phrases as "Would you like to look in my bag?" in one language or another, written in Yiddish or Ladino or Arabic. But the more a peddler could say in the customers' own language, the more eloquently he could tout the quality of his goods. The more he could engage in the small talk that humanized the relationship, the more he could sell.

Typically the peddlers slept in the home of their last customer of the day. A warm bed in a customer's home far surpassed sleeping in a field, in the back of their wagon, or in a barn. When a peddler lodged with the customer, being able to speak, maintain a conversation, and get to know his hosts improved his chances of making a sale. Learning Spanish or French, or whatever other language predominated, made good business sense. Peddlers wanted to learn the dominant language because they had no intention to return to their places of origin. They had moved for good, and that reality demanded of them an instant engagement with the local culture. The alacrity with which former peddlers became part of local civic life testified further to the fact that peddling equipped them linguistically to experience integration into new societies.

PEDDLER WOES

For all the recollections of communal help, family reunification, and ultimate success, the actual pursuit of the occupation often proved excruciating, lonely, and difficult. In memoirs and autobiographies, children's recollections of their fathers' tales throb with laments about heavy packs, cold weather and hot, loneliness and isolation. From around the world peddlers' own accounts resound with the details of struggling under heavy loads, trudging through muddy roads or dusty ones, going out in rain and snow, of misery and often shame, at having to knock on doors and obsequiously appeal to the women whose languages they barely understood. Their complaints differed little from one place to the other. Those who bemoaned their circumstances in South Africa, Cuba, or Mexico fixated on the heat, the beating of the sun on their bodies. Those who sold in Vermont or Minnesota or Michigan recalled shivering in the cold and the blizzards. The basic act of peddling called for tremendous physical exertion. Henry Lazarus, who peddled in north Florida and southern Georgia, told his children, "There was only one way to tell the summer from the winter out there. In the summer, the trips were hot, monotonous, dusty, and slow; in the winter, they were cold, monotonous, dusty, and slow."[51]

One of the most often cited American peddler narratives, a diary that covers two years in the life of Abraham Kohn, a Bavarian immigrant who began his American life peddling in New England in the 1840s, described with bitterness a farm woman's refusal to let him sleep in her house: as "she was afraid of strangers, she might not sleep well." She had no mercy for him, sending him out into "the worst blizzard I have ever seen. O God, I thought, is this the land of liberty and hospitality and tolerance? Why have I been led here?" Although Mrs. Spaulding eventually relented and let him stay the night in her home, Kohn felt nothing but unhappiness with peddling. "O God," he invoked again, "our Father, consider Thy little band of the house of Israel. Behold how they are compelled to profane Thy holy Torah in pursuit of their daily bread." He continued in a similarly silvery but miserable vein. "O misguided fools, led astray by avarice and cupidity! You have left your friends and acquaintances, your relatives and your parents, your home and . . . your language and your customs . . . only to sell your wares in the wild places of America, in isolated farmhouses and tiny hamlets." Employing again the apostrophe, he added, "O that I had never seen this land, but remained in Germany, appreciated to a humble country craftsman! Though oppressed by taxes and discriminated against as a Jew, I should still be happier than in . . . America, free from royal taxes and every man's religious equal though I am!" Despite invoking the appeal of Germany and his wish that he had stayed there, Kohn made no effort to go home. He, like nearly all his cohort, soldiered on.[52]

Many young Jewish immigrant men considered peddling physically draining and shameful. Bernard Horwich, who came to Chicago from Lithuania in 1860, described the occupation as humiliating and balked at the idea proposed by his friend Mr. Goldstein, a peddler himself, "that I buy some goods and take up peddling. I disliked the idea very much. It seemed so humiliating."[53] Abe Gellman also went to Chicago, and the friends who greeted him tried to help him get started. They "did everything possible to have made me satisfied," he remembered. But "unfortunately the business they were in wasn't to my liking though they gave me a job. It was peddling merchandise with a horse and wagon . . . in the suburbs of Chicago." He admitted, "It was honest, fair work, but I couldn't get accustomed to it." Nathan Sokol came to Birmingham, Alabama, in 1909. He recognized that as he had "no trade on hand to earn my first meal from, so I had to take to peddling which I despised more than anything in the world. It took many moons to break myself in to the idea of knocking door to door begging people to buy something from me."[54] The father of art critic Bernard Berenson and Senda Berenson, the founder of women's basketball, also peddled on a route on the outskirts of Boston after emigrating from Lithuania. On one occasion he knocked on a door of a home in Concord and the woman who bought from him invited him into the house. By chance his son, then a student at Harvard, happened to be in her home. Not knowing that the peddler was father to the college boy, she exclaimed: "Guess who is in the drawing-room! A young man named Bernard Berenson." The father hastily collected his goods and left, not wanting his son to see him in such a servile position. Both the son, who sought entry into the American educated elite, and the father, burdened by his box of goods, would have cringed at the idea of meeting under such circumstances. Another time, as the elder Berenson clattered down the aisle of a train, loaded down with his wares, he spied his daughter with a group of her school friends. Again, terrified of embarrassing her, of having her chums find out that he made a living as a peddler, he got off the train and waited for the next one.[55]

The overall misery of the peddlers, their weekly encounters with loneliness and isolation, emerged as a theme around the world. Isaac Mayer Wise, the founder of Reform Judaism in America, as a recent arrival from Bohemia considered the condition of the Jews he met in America miserable. He met an old friend from back home who laid out for him the details of new-world peddling, "Our people in this country . . . may be divided into the following classes: the basket peddler—he is as yet altogether dumb and homeless;

(2) the trunk-carrier, who stammers some little English and hopes for better times; (3) the pack carrier, who carries from one hundred to one-hundred and fifty pounds upon his back, and indulges the thought that he will become a business man someday." Wise's informant, a Mr. Stein, added that some peddlers move up the ranks of a "wagon-baron, who peddles through the country with a one or two horse team. . . . At first one is the slave of the basket or the pack; then the lackey of the horse."[56]

Newspapers, Jewish and others, reported on peddler suicides. London's *Jewish Chronicle*, for example, provided terse notices from around the world of Jewish peddlers who for reasons unspecified took their own lives. The local press in various places also let readers know that here or there someone found the body of Jewish peddler, dead at his own hand. The *Atlanta Constitution* on July 29, 1882, informed readers of "A Jew Peddler's Suicide," as the headline read: outside of St. Louis, in the town of Lindley, Illinois, "Moses Kuntz, a Jew peddler from St. Louis committed suicide by shooting himself with a revolver. Depression and ill-health were the cause." Did the particularities of peddling, the long days on the road, the need to assume a cheerful mien with his customers who may have viewed his knock on the door as an annoying intrusion, the need to flatter them to make a sale, and the daily absence of family and friends push Moses Kuntz over the edge? Did peddling ruin his physical and mental well-being?[57]

That obviously cannot be answered. But ample evidence exists that many peddlers suffered as a result of the onerous burden that they literally carried. A man in Philadelphia placed a letter in the *Yudishe Gezetten*, a Yiddish newspaper, in 1876 begging for help. His twenty-five-year old son, a man with a wife and two small children, "went out to peddle in the country with a stock worth $140 and I have not heard from him again."[58] Had the man gotten injured? Had he died as a result of foul play or illness? Or, had he used his opportunity out in the country to abandon his wife, his children, his elderly father and try to assume a new identity, start a new life? Maybe he met a woman, fell in love, and decided to jettison his wife and previous life?

The issue of Jewish male marital desertion extended beyond the realm of new-world peddling, but peddling and migration offered men a chance to liberate themselves from familial bonds and obligations. It provided a perfect vehicle to leave home, go out on the road, and then just not come back. A Wilmington, Delaware, newspaper ran an article in 1883 entitled "How a Jewess Overhauled her Runaway Husband." It reported on one Fanny Saponitz from Philadelphia, who traveled to Delaware in search of her husband, Lewis, "a peddling Jew." She found him living with his father in Dover and indignantly filed a complaint with the local authorities, who arrested the errant Lewis, sent him to jail, and fined him. While the story ended with Lewis admitting his error and returning to Fanny, other such desertions did not culminate in reconciliation and reunion. Peddling actually offered Jewish immigrant men a superb cover for desertion.[59]

The shame and the misery, the cold weather and heat, the loneliness—all shadowed new-world Jewish peddling. In no way could it be seen as anything other than hard, particularly in the pack-peddling stage. Surely many who found themselves out on the road in a blizzard or a heat wave questioned their own judgment, asking themselves, as Jacob Kohn had, why they had bothered to migrate if in the new world they performed the same odious occupation that Jews did back home.

But however miserable they felt about peddling, it came as no surprise to new Jewish immigrant men that on their arrival in whatever new land, someone handed them a backpack, outfitted them with a mess of goods, and sent them out onto the road. They also knew that they would not spend a lifetime doing so and that sometime in the future they would step off the road. And they recognized, through information gleaned from those who had been out on the roads before them, that in their new homes they would in the main encounter customers who would nearly welcome them and would make the years on the road something other than hell on earth. Most peddlers and their customers depicted a relatively harmonious symbiotic relationship between Jewish immigrant sellers and the non-Jews who bought from them. They expressed warm feelings, one for the other. Jacob Kohn, who complained so bitterly about the snow, who warned the youth of Bavaria to stay home and not expose themselves to the hardships of peddling, who questioned his decision to have left home, and who excoriated Mrs. Spalding for her reluctance to let him sleep in her home, went on to note that once she relented, she welcomed him in for the night, and they spent a fine evening, even singing together as they sat protected in her farmstead while the blizzard raged outside.

I. J. Schwartz devoted his book-length poem *Kentucky* to "Josh," an immigrant Jewish peddler who traversed the eponymous southern state where he eventually settled down as a shopkeeper among the local farmers, black and white. In Schwartz's poem, until Josh found the place to lay his pack down his life consisted of

Tramp, tramp, tramp, tramp, in the soft red sand
Baked in flour-white dust
The tall bony figure bent

From head to foot—from the old bowler hat
To the hard, dried-up boots.

Josh, a former sweatshop worker, had left his children back in New York, children "Whom he had not seen for years / While wandering in search of bread. / So, with a pack, he set out on the road." He dreamed of quickly earning enough money to reunite with his children and give up this life, "feet sore, his heart heavy, / A pack on his back, a stick in his hand." Josh, in this extended lyrical depiction of a peddler's life, intuited that by traversing the roads as he did, he trod on a long path of the Jewish past, that as he "passed with his heavy pack / It seemed strangely familiar to him, / Known from old times." But Josh also knew that his fate lay in the hands of his customers, the women and men who lived in "the new, the free and enormous land."[60]

3

Along the Road

Jewish Peddlers and Their New-World Customers

When J. Ida Jiggetts wrote *Religion, Diet, and Health of Jews* in 1949, she felt the need to explain why "I, a Negro, am sufficiently interested in the Jewish people to study and write about them." She invoked her experiences growing up in the American South, citing her memories of "the visits of a Jewish peddler who sold beautiful linens, shawls, china, and other goods." The weekly visit of the peddler sparked her interest "in the labels I read on the merchandise," and she found fascinating "his explanations of the folkways of those countries from which the goods had been brought." He opened her eyes to "how Jews lived," and described "the country from which [he] came." He detailed his history and told her that "the men in his family, since the 18th century, had been forced by law to be peddlars, money lenders, second-hand dealers, or physicians." These visits sparked a lifelong interest in Jews and Jewish culture, and she recalled with particular fascination the "Hebrew words he sometimes spoke to my father."[1]

Jiggetts's words offer a portal into the world forged by immigrant Jewish peddlers and their customers, not just in one home in the southern United States but worldwide. Peddlers, Jewish immigrants to strange new places, could not have functioned as well as they did on their own. Even the sources of their Jewish enclaves would not have sufficed to make possible their ultimate successes.

Their fate lay just as much in the hands of their customers, non-Jewish women and men who opened their doors in response to the peddlers' knocks. Customers welcomed them and bought from them, and the women in particular became more than just supporting actors in this drama that transformed the Jewish world. These women, as they dealt with the peddlers, altered consumption patterns in their societies. They forged a symbiotic relationship with the Jewish peddlers.

Perhaps this is an obvious point in thinking about all migrations, particularly those based on commerce: successful outcomes depended upon a synergistic relationship between newcomers and those whom they encountered. The history of new-world Jewish peddling reveals that despite differences in class, race, ethnicity, religion, and language, Jews and their customers changed each other's lives. Jews had left places that marginalized them, defined them as the quintessential outsiders. They migrated to places where they experienced the positive fulfillment of their dreams, and achieving that fulfillment depended on the goodwill of the non-Jews who readily purchased from them.

Commerce shaped this phenomenon, which relied upon the development of trust between buyer and seller. However much the two differed from each other, their interactions hinged on the reality that one had something to offer the other, and the other wanted it badly enough to expend resources on it. Each had an equal stake in the transaction. Neither held more power than the other. The seller had the goods and set the price. But if the customer considered the item not worth the price, she just declined the deal, leaving the seller with a pile of unsold cloth, clothes, glasses, picture frames, needles, or thread. She could not be compelled to buy, particularly if the transaction did not involve necessities, such as bread or fuel. In the buying and selling of tablecloths, suspenders, picture frames, and jewelry, items easily done without, the customer in fact held the advantage.

But she, the potential customer, might very much want the cloth to brighten her dinner table or the picture frame to adorn her walls. Towels, bed linens, and jewelry, she might reckon, could improve the quality of her life. She might have little chance to get those items elsewhere, and at so low a price. So the seller gained a bit in the politics of the transaction. Customer and merchant engaged in a dance, choreographed by desire and availability and the common interest of both to exchange items for cash, at a price acceptable to both.

Peddling as a variant of selling added an element of intimacy not replicated in shops and other emporia. It took place in the customers' homes. The peddlers saw how their customers lived, met their children, got to know their neighbors, and if they slept over and ate at their tables, as so many did, they came to be temporary members of the household. This profoundly shaped new-world Jewish experiences. They developed ideas about their customers that transcended traditional ideas of non-Jews as "just *goyim*," as an undifferentiated Gentile mass, not to be trusted and sharing little in common with Jews.

The peddler's visits changed his customers as well. They had to struggle to understand the peddler's halting English, Spanish, Swedish, Cherokee, French, Afrikaans, or whatever language of the land. When customers invited the peddlers across their thresholds, to eat at their tables and sleep in their homes, they overcame their own parochialism, forcing themselves to think about the world in more complicated and bigger terms than before. That happened to J. Ida Jiggetts as a child and probably to her parents as well. The Jewish peddlers never denied their Jewishness, and the customers always knew that a Jew, not a Christian, had entered their domestic spaces. The act of peddling erased linguistic, national, and religious differences as barriers to human interaction. Over time the peddlers ceased to be alien, as customers noticed what they and the peddlers had in common. Regardless of the real differences, both customer and peddler yearned for the same outcome of their encounter, and the experience put them on the course toward common citizenship.

When Jews sold, as they did around the world, to women and men of subordinated or subjugated status, they performed on a weekly basis a kind of subversion of regnant social norms. Peddlers came into the homes of African Americans, onto Native American reservations, and into the dwelling places of indigenous Africans in South Africa, Maori in New Zealand, Aborigine in Australia. Here these otherwise subservient and conquered peoples had the upper hand over a white European. The Jew may have been the only white person whom the customer could have treated rudely, in whose face she could slam the door or refuse entry. The Jew had no power in her home. He could not coerce her. The peddler wanted something from her, hoping that something inside his pack would appeal to her. He had to engage her with respect and charm, in her language, on her terms. Without those, he would have no sale.

Jewish peddlers had to conduct themselves respectfully no matter to whom they sold. Whether selling to white women or black, Protestant or Catholic, native born or immigrant, poor or more economically comfortable, individuals from the dominant group or the inferior one. To succeed the immigrant peddler had to be personable and nonthreatening. Despite his newness to the land, he had to talk to the women who opened the doors and find ways to engage with them, one by one.

Everywhere they went they developed the skills needed to win over their customers. They fulfilled the goals of their migrations and did so because their customers welcomed them, liked them, and bought from them. Evidence came from around the world of the peddlers' success, of their ability to overcome hardship, develop those personal relationships with customers, win their trust, and get their sales.

Boer customers in South Africa, for example, made possible the realization of the aspirations of tens of thousands of Lithuanian Jews. A Jewish writer sitting in Russia in 1891 commented on the fate of so many young Jewish men who at that moment streamed to the Cape of Good Hope. He depicted the difficulties of their lives as smous but he acknowledged the payoffs they had achieved after years trudging on roads continents and oceans away from Lithuania. The writer of this piece for *Hatzfirah*, N. D. Hoffman, lamented how "bitter indeed is the fate of this pedlar, or *tocher* or *smous*, as the Afrikaners call him." He wrote:

> For days and weeks he trudges the countryside visiting the farmers, his heavy basket upon his shoulders and burning rays of the African sun beating down upon him. He will climb high mountains, descend into valleys and knock upon the doors of the Afrikaner to sell his wares.

But the readers of *Hatzfirah*, many of whom, as they read this piece, might have been contemplating their own migrations, also, as they read on, learned about the other side of the immigrant-smous experience. "In these months . . . he will acquaint himself with the character of the Boers, learn a little Hollands, and become familiar with the customers of the land. He will then begin to feel at ease. . . . The Afrikaners, who are by nature humanitarian, will pity the poor unfortunate pedlar and will buy some of his goods. . . . Slowly the sun of success will begin to shine upon him."

In contrast to the privations of the "poor unfortunate pedlar," Hoffman chronicled his upward mobility from pitiable smous to someone who had graduated to donkey and cart, to ownership of some horses and mules, until he could become a storekeeper. The author personally knew "some exceedingly wealthy men . . . now regarded as honoured merchants, who arrived here penniless and destitute and became poor struggling pedlars. . . . Thanks to their industry and business acumen they have met with great success and are now at the peak of their good fortune."[2]

Hoffman valorized the acumen and hard work of the Jews. He also acknowledged the goodness of the customers. He considered them "humanitarian," noting that they facilitated the peddlers' success. Clearly Hoffman did not probe the racial dimensions of life in South Africa, the condition of the native Africans, or the split between the British and the Afrikaner. Those matters lay beyond his concern. He just wanted to show that the customers to whom the *tochers* peddled their wares deserved some credit too.

A world away, in Maine in the middle of the nineteenth century, observers took note of the similarly positive relationships that flourished between Jewish peddlers and customers. Here, too, in this radically different climate, this same kind of mutuality took root. The Maine assessment came from an unlikely and as such possibly objective source, the reports of R. G. Dunn, a credit rating agency, which canvassed people as to the trustworthiness of local businessmen throughout the United States and Canada. Dunn reporters went around and asked about this merchant and that, noting in their ledger books what had been said about each one.

In their voluminous commentary on local businesses, agents for R. G. Dunn never hesitated to remark when the subject of their inquiry happened to be Jewish. Most of those remarks emphasized the negative when it came to Jews. They repeatedly used pejorative language about Jews, pointing out their flaws, and attributing those flaws to their Jewishness. Dunn did not like Jews partly because Jews avoided local banks and other formal credit sources when they needed capital. Since Jewish merchants operated within the closed realm of the Jewish economy, reporters for R. G. Dunn could ascertain little about their business transactions, and castigated Jews for moving about too much and for not owning local real estate.

Yet even with R. G. Dunn's tendency to deprecate Jews as shady and sneaky, its agents commented regularly in their distinctive and terse notations, full of idiosyncratic abbreviations, that local people, in this case in Maine, had little negative to say about the Jews. Indeed, most people who transacted business with Jewish merchants respected them, the peddlers in particular. While local people knew that Mayer Waterman, a peddler in Kittery as of October of 1847, "has no visible property in this town except a horse and wagon and a load of DG [dry goods]," they "never heard a word angst [against] his char[acter], is unmarred, said by some to be rich. Strictly temperate," not a minor comment in the state which passed the nation's most stringent antialcohol law, just a few years later in 1851. A year later, the reporter found Waterman "still peddling—respected by many. Has no R.E. [real estate], no other visppy [visible property] except horse, wagon and stock. Yet is said to be rich. A very quiet gentlemanly man." As to Solomon Silverman of Blue Hill, Hancock County, the Dunn investigator noted that he "is an honest man . . . is attentive to his bus [business] and always on the move. . . . Gets his in NY. . . . has no attachable ppy beyond the contents of his cart. . . . Diligent in his peddling." Finally, locals considered Lewis Bloomberg of Waterville in 1883 to be "a man of gdhbts [good habits]. Indu [industrious]. Hon [hon-est], for the past 2 ye[a]rs has driven a peddlers cart." The operative words here, "good character," "gentlemanly," "good habits," "respected by many," and "never heard a word against," counted for much with the credit bureau. Drawn from local gossip and acquired by asking around, these words reflected popular views about some specific men who plied the roads of Maine, selling from house to house. At least as far as the people of these towns in rural Maine saw it, the Jewish peddlers attracted only positive attention.[3]

The author of *Kentucky*, I. J. Schwartz, also tapped into this sentiment, as he depicted his peddler character, Josh. Schwartz's book-length poem, like N. D. Hoffman's description of the young Lithuanian Jewish men in South Africa, juxtaposed the misery of life on the road with the local residents' warm embrace of the peddlers. Schwartz presented Josh, of the "red pointed beard . . . / The eyes strained and bloodshot," as a suffering man, miserable while on the road. Exhausted, Josh knocks on a cabin door, looking to make a sale and to find a place to rest for the night. A farmer with a loaded gun opens the door. In answer to the question, "Who are you?" Josh replies, "A Jew, who seeks a place to rest his head." Rather than pumping him full of buckshot or throwing him out into the night, the farmer puts down his gun, offering the peddler a meal, a bed, and human companionship. Over the course of the poem's next verses the farmer and his wife lay out a table of food, of which, Josh explains, he can eat only a little of because of his religious principles, but eat he does. His hosts observe him in prayers and then eagerly look through his merchandise, inviting their neighbors over also to delight in what Josh carries in his bag. After this one night the local folk encourage Josh to get off the road, stay in their town, open a store to sell the stuff he had been carrying on his back. They invite him to become part of their community.[4]

Kentucky, Maine, and South Africa, places so far removed from each other, so different in climate, topography, economic base, and demography, all welcomed Jewish peddlers. In these places and everywhere else in the new world, Jewish peddlers came every week to the same homes, stopping by to collect payment on goods previously purchased, hoping that customers would want some new item, previously unavailable. But if one week he had sold a customer shoddy goods, acted rudely, or behaved inappropriately, he ran the risk that the next time he showed up she would slam the door in his face and shoo him away. Not only would she not buy from him again, she might not pay him the full amount of money she owed. He would have to strike her from his list of steady customers and find someone else to take her place.

The customer had another tool in her kit to keep the peddler in line. The customer, an insider member of a local community, could tell her friends and neighbors, the women she went to church with, many of whom she may have grown up with, to shun this particular peddler. The customer poorly treated by the immigrant Jewish peddler had the power to besmirch his reputation, and without that reputation he failed. The people of Maine who spoke with the R. G. Dunn reporter told of the Jewish peddlers' gentlemanly behavior, sobriety, and honesty. They could just as easily, if the situation necessitated it, describe the men as sharp, lascivious, and dishonest.

SLEEPING OVER

But they did not. Peddlers understood that to accomplish their goals, to earn money and settle down, they needed to behave on the road and in their customers' homes in exemplary ways. They not only wanted to make a sale but hoped to sleep in their customers' homes. Because peddlers operated on a weekly cycle and sold on the installment plan, they came to the same houses on the same days every week, collecting payment for goods previously purchased and exhibiting new goods they knew the customers did not yet have.

After all, they had been inside their homes, had seen whether, for example, they hung pictures on their walls or whether the husband wore a watch. Knowing that a particular woman had purchased a tablecloth, a peddler speculated that sometime thereafter he could entice her to consider cloth napkins. Peddlers also knew who would be each day's last customer, and they planned accordingly. To the friendliest people, perhaps the biggest spenders, the nicest ones who let them sleep in the house by the fire and not in the barn with the animals, they showed up with the setting of the sun, while visiting the less friendly and stingiest earlier in the day, long before having to think about sleep.

A bed in a house had much to recommend it as opposed to sleeping in a field, a ditch, a forest, or even in the back of the wagon. How much better the bed or pallet inside compared with stretching out under the open sky, exposed to the elements, on the hard ground, worried about wild animals and bandits attracted to unarmed men with goods and cash. Sleeping in a customer's house also deepened the connection between peddlers and customers. It meant spending more time together independent of the commercial exchange, conversing, engaging in a cultural exchange. As that relationship deepened, the peddler developed increasing fluency in the vernacular, and the customers came to see the peddlers as human beings with whom they had spent some time, talked, shared details of their personal lives. This enhanced the opportunities for future sales. For the peddler this strengthened relationship offered greater comfort but also constituted one more step on the road toward fulfilling the goals of the immigration, toward getting off the road altogether.

The simple act of sleeping in customers' homes meant much for Jewish immigrant peddlers and made the experiences of Jewish immigrants markedly different from those of other newcomers to these same places. No other immigrant job offered this kind of prospect for intimacy and mutual understanding. The majority of Irishwomen who migrated to the United States spent time in domestic service, living in their employers' homes. But they hardly sat around, talking, swapping stories, and since they served the meals, they did not eat at their employers' tables.

This mutuality predominated. Regardless of who the Jewish peddler's customers were, nights spent in their dwelling places provided global lessons in specific local cultures. Dave Pearlman, like so many late-nineteenth-century Jewish immigrants, left Lithuania in 1884 for the United States, peddling in and around Americus, Georgia. Being new to local mores, Pearlman, defined by law and custom as white, lodged regularly with one African-American farm family. He recounted to Jewish friends who had preceded him to America that the farmer and his children took it upon themselves, around the dinner table, to teach Dave "the words for the items on the table . . . [and to] help him form simple sentences, using the words he had memorized." Other peddlers, in their memoirs, told of customers who, in the evening, helped the peddler learn the dominant language. An act of human kindness—teaching the foreigner, handicapped by his ignorance, the language and customs of the land—probably allowed poor customers to feel superior to someone.[5]

Peddlers sold not only to people who spoke the dominant language. In Ireland they had to learn English and Irish, in South Africa, English and Afrikaans, in Quebec, English and French. In the United States peddlers went into the homes of speakers of various Native American languages, as well as those of Spanish speakers of the Southwest, French speakers in New England, and an array of immigrants from around the world. In these homes they picked up enough French, Norwegian, Italian, Slovenian, Finnish, Portuguese to make their desired sales and establish personal connections with all customers. In northern New England, French speakers from Quebec bought from Jewish peddlers, and as one community history stated quite simply, "Pripstein . . . in time learned French well enough to travel around the villages and farms of the Lower Laurentians selling . . . to farms and villages."[6]

As a result of lodging in customers' homes, peddlers picked up bits and pieces of the local culture. Their experiences in peddling provided lessons in the history, customs, and mores of the place. Jewish peddlers slept in the homes of southern planters, and did so often enough that some plantation houses maintained special rooms for the peddlers. During those nights in the "big house," in the parlors and kitchens of the slaveowning classes, the peddlers learned firsthand the meaning of whiteness. Oscar Straus's father came to America from Bavaria and peddled in rural Georgia and "was treated," according to his son, "by the owners of the plantations with a spirit of equality that is hard to appreciate today." Straus the younger, whom Theodore Roosevelt would name secretary of commerce, recalled that "the existence of slavery drew a distinct line of demarcation between the white and black races. This gave to the white a status of equality that probably otherwise he would not have enjoyed to such a degree." Straus's father learned that law and convention deemed him white and that slavery helped shore up his status.[7]

The learning went the other way as well. The Jiggetts family learned much about Jewish life in Europe and acquired some Hebrew words. The peddlers taught other customers as well. Customers asked the peddlers about their lives back home, in places they may never have heard of like Lithuania or Alsace, Bohemia or Rhodes. One peddler memoir from Georgia related that an American farmer, Mr. Bedford, plied the peddler, named Yampolsky, with questions in the evening after dinner and before sleep. Besides asking his guest to write out his name, since Bedford had never heard anything like it, he asked, "Where did I come from? . . . what kind of country? . . . what kind of city?" Yampolsky gave the Georgia farmer and his family, as best he could, a lesson in geography, an excursion to a place that they would likely never go to.[8]

FOOD AND INTERFAITH ENCOUNTERS

Mr. Bedford posed another question to Yampolsky, one that non-Jewish customers asked around the peddler's globe. He wanted to know, "What was my religion? . . . Why didn't Jews believe in Jesus Christ?" Queries about the Jews' Jewishness grew out of a sense of curiosity and amazement. It became a matter of discussion, particularly over the matter of food. The wife, whose decision it was, according to most accounts, to allow the peddler to sleep over or not, invariably asked him whether he would care to eat with the family.

For Jewish peddlers this proved to be no simple matter. Some peddlers admitted in their narratives that after a day on the road, after lugging a huge backpack, they ate anything offered to them, even if they preferred to observe the Jewish dietary laws, or *kashrut*, which strictly delineated what could and could not be eaten. A peddler who adhered to dietary law should have said no to anything his customers offered. He should not have eaten off their plates, used their utensils, or consumed anything cooked or baked in their ovens. But life on the road made such punctiliousness difficult, if not impossible. Some peddlers in their narratives stated categorically that they did not care about kashrut and did not feel the need to justify their food choices. They just ate whatever appeared on the table and enjoyed a home-cooked meal. Often self-described as religious back home, when on their journeys to the new world and away from families, they shed restrictions to which they had previously adhered. Others recognized that peddling undermined strict adherence to the dietary rules; when on the road, they must eat what they could. The consumption of kosher food would have to wait for the weekends, when they went back to the nearest Jewish enclave, or even until they stopped peddling and created their own homes and communities.

But most peddlers among the few whose thoughts have survived expressed uneasiness about eating the food served. They felt compelled to announce to their generous hosts that they could not eat this item or that, that while grateful for the offer, they would have to say no to some or all of the food on the table. Men steeped in a system that divided the world's food into the edible and the inedible found that most of their customers' fare fell squarely in the latter. The peddlers usually refused anything other than fruit, vegetables, bread, or eggs.

Such refusals must have amazed the customers, inevitably leading to yet another question, namely, why the peddler could not eat food that everyone in the family consumed. Why would anyone turn down bacon or ham or squirrel or bear? After all, who would the customers ever have known who as a matter of religion eschewed pork chops? They knew religious difference, understanding the divide between Catholics and Protestants, the latter subdivided into multiple denominations. They understood differences in nationality and race, but where would they have encountered men who claimed that their religion forbade them from eating bacon or ham?

Around the globe the peddlers answered the women's questions directly and straightforwardly. As a Jew, the guest might say, he could not partake of this food, and many housewives, who liked accommodating the peddlers, went out of their way to meet these dietary needs. Rather than be offended by the peddlers' unwillingness to eat the family's food or appalled that someone said no to their home cooking, the women worked out ways to feed the peddlers, respectful of Jewish law. Numerous women, as described in memoirs, kept aside a separate pot for the peddler to use when he came by. He could fix his own food. These Christian women learned about kashrut and had the right items available when the peddler showed up. Cherokee Indians referred to the Jewish peddlers as "egg eaters," knowing the Jews would eat only eggs cooked in their shells.[9] In the South African Transvaal and in the Irish Midlands, farm women also set aside eggs for peddlers, and let the men prepare their meals in their own pots.

Customers around the world asked about Jewish dietary practices, and peddlers' answers provided them with lessons in comparative religion. The father of Leon Schwarz peddled in Alabama after the Civil War period. Once, according to family lore, he "sat down to eat in a farm house and was served pot-liquor, fried bacon and some greens served with side meat." The elder Schwarz, either because he did not care or just felt hungry, "pitched in and ate heartily." Surprised at his willingness to consume the food, his hostess interrogated him. "Mr. Schwarz, I am surprised to see you eat pork. I thought Moses ordered the Jews not to eat any hog meat." As the story went, the peddler surveying the table and seeing nothing but pork, replied, "Ah, madam, if Moses had travelled through Perry County, Alabama, he would never have issued such an order."[10]

For their part, peddlers often worried that refusing to eat the food could offend their hosts, whom they hoped to cultivate as potential buyers of additional goods. How, the peddlers asked themselves in word and deed, could they stay true to Judaism's strictures and not engender ill will among the women and men at whose tables they sat? How could they avoid snubbing their customers' hospitality? A memoir of Jewish peddling in New Zealand told of a peddler who in 1863 came to a hotel in a small town "where they put on ham and eggs for breakfast." The peddler, eager for a sale, tried to do nothing that could be defined as impolite. When the proprietress left the room, "he threw [the unkosher food] into the fire. In an instant it blazed and set fire to the chimney and there was a great consternation."[11]

BIBLE STORIES

By virtue of their inability to eat the food, the peddlers, then, no matter how low their level of Jewish learning, became translators or interpreters of Judaism to women and men of the new world, people who probably had not met a Jew before. The peddlers' role in exposing their customers to Judaism transcended food, although food loomed large. In many places, particularly in the American South and southern Africa, the Jewish peddlers and the Christian family, after dinner, sat down to read the Hebrew Bible, the Old Testament, together. More than in any Catholic setting, in solidly Protestant societies the Old Testament offered a common text, a meeting ground for immigrant Jews and Christian customers. One South African memoir, that of Casper (Kasriel) Sober, a Lithuanian peddler, who eventually carried photographic equipment along with his goods for sale, offered the following about his customers:

> The Boer farmers were very ardent readers of the Old Testament and Bible. Every day after the evening meal and before bedtime, the family including all the colored help, had to sit around the table. The wife or the oldest son brought out the Bible. . . . The farmer would read a chapter or town and explain it. . . . If there was ever a stranger, he was invited to read the Bible.

The readers included the smous, the Jew from Lithuania, who in Sober's case came with considerable religious learning from back home. Because he had told them that he would not eat the food, they assumed that he had to be extraordinarily religious and must be a clergyman. "Being a 'preacher,' " as the Afrikaner family saw it, "I often had the job of reading and explaining chapters of the Bible. It gave me lots of prestige with the farmers who advertised me to other farmers."[12] Yet another peddler told of the "traditional Afrikaner hospitality" he experienced in Namaqualand, in the Cape Province. "I clearly recall . . . Oom Theunis Van Niekerek, of the farm Aronegas. A massive, but gentle man." The peddler remembered that "evening discussions . . . generally centered around biblical matters," conversations in which the Lithuanian-born smous could participate.[13]

The customers' lessons in Judaism took place as they observed peddlers in prayer. They saw, no doubt for the first time, Jewish ritual paraphernalia, the prayer shawl, the leather strips of the tefillin, which the peddler wound around his head and his arm in his morning rites as he stood facing east. The sister of a Newfoundland Jewish peddler recalled that "her older brother, a very religious man, was accidentally interrupted one morning when he was saying his morning prayers" in a customer's home. "The man of the house, seeing the tfillen . . . the peddler had put on . . . mistakenly thought he was putting a rope on his head and ran to his wife to report that 'there is something wrong with Mr. Wilansky. I think he wants to take his life.' "[14] A Mr. Schachat, a Litvak who peddled in Robertson, in South Africa's Western Cape Province, lodged routinely with J. F. D. Kriel, an Afrikaner farmer. Kriel paid homage to Schachat in his memoir, remembering from his boyhood that the peddler, who came to sell stuff out of his "Magic Box," as the children called it, sometimes "spent his weekend with us in fast and prayer. From sundown his candle would burn and we would watch, fascinated at the old man's strange prayer ritual." On a regular, non-Sabbath day, the smous began his "morning . . . by reading a verse from the Bible. He would then don his long striped jerkin or Toga. . . . Prayers were recited standing up but in a rocking position."[15]

Max Bloom's customers who lived in and around Ironton, Ohio, also acquired details of Jewish religious practice via their peddler-teacher. Every Passover as he came around to them he distributed pieces of matzoh, an act, according to his son, that provided one of his "father's greatest joys." He liked teaching his customers about Judaism and Jewish customs. The customers may or may not have actually liked the matzoh, the crackerlike substance consumed during Passover, but Bloom's matzoh distribution revealed the comfort he felt in sharing his Jewishness with his Christian customers.[16]

Such stories came from around the new world, Protestant places particularly. A Jewish peddler in the area of Northfield, Minnesota, who covered a forty-mile territory often could not get home on Friday and spent his holy time with one particular family. In the narrative passed down in the peddler's family, he, Moses Menahem Zieve, known locally as "Holy Moses," typically arrived Friday afternoon. He slaughtered a chicken for himself according to Jewish law and prepared for the Sabbath. No doubt he prayed by himself Friday night and Saturday morning, and as the story handed down went, "a child in the customer's family, would go out Saturday night to check the skies." If he saw the requisite three stars which spelled the Sabbath's end, he would run into the house with excitement, yelling, "You can smoke now, Moses."

These new-world ecumenical experiences transpired everywhere the peddlers went. Christians and Jews learned from each other. In small towns in the American South, peddlers and former peddlers taught Bible in local Christian Sunday schools. The Christian ministers welcomed the peddlers into their churches to teach both children and adults about the Old Testament, a text the guests presumably knew well. "Holy Moses" and his customers, if the story can be believed, actually engaged in the most dramatic example of such interfaith contact. According to the granddaughter of this Lithuanian immigrant:

> The German immigrants who settled the area around Northfield, worshipped together in a community church. There was no regular preacher, for lack of funds. On Sunday mornings, then in this community church, my grandfather occupied the pulpit and preached to this

German-speaking congregation. His language? A carefully selected non-Hebraic Yiddish. His subject? The Torah portion of the week. And in serving this Christian community over many months, he won their gratitude—and an affectionate but reverent title. They called him "Holy Moses."[17]

He had no doubt also won their loyalty, which meant both goodwill and commercial success. When he or subsequent Jewish peddlers stopped at the homes of his former "parishioners," they could count on a warm receptions and robust sales.

If Zieve had not left Lithuania, he probably would never have entered a church, something forbidden by Jewish law. Had his German customers not emigrated, they would have never heard a Yiddish discourse on the *parsha*, or the Torah portion of the week, delivered by an Orthodox Jew. Without the peddlers' journeys into the new world, ordinary Christians would have never learned about the various element of the Jews' practice, his prayers, diet, and Sabbath observances. As it happened, though, these otherwise exotic details became a matter of explanation and interpretation in the course of the forging of positive relationships across religious lines.

Peddlers sleeping in the customers' homes further advanced intercultural exchanges, which then solidified the bond between buyer and seller. The peddler typically offered to pay his hosts for the bed and food, and the customer typically refused. The peddler then tried to leave behind some item as a gift: candy for the children, a decorative pin for the wife, some trinket. Yampolosky, after his night at the Bedfords' home, wanted to present his hostess with a tablecloth "that I noticed she had admired. They refused vehemently. Mr. Bedford said that if they accepted the tablecloth, it would be as though they had accepted money from a guest. They told me that they were very religious people and wanted to perform many charitable acts here on earth so that they would arrive in heaven with a bagful of good deeds."[18]

Christians and Jews learned from each other. The Jews learned to accommodate to the Christians' calendar. The Drain family lived in Oregon in the 1850s, still a frontier society, where settlers lacked many consumer goods. A Jewish peddler, according to the family story, made the difference between deprivation and access to some longed-for finer things. When sometime in the early winter "Grandmother Drain" told the peddler, Aaron Meier, that she desperately wanted a new darning needle, Meier replied, "My people do not celebrate Christmas . . . but I suppose you good people will soon be having a holiday with presents." She answered in the affirmative, and the peddler declared that he would "give the ladies of Pass Creek Canyon each a Christmas present," offering them darning needles to make their lives easier.

The narratives about peddler-customer relationships reverberated with the tones of religious harmony. Rather than being offended by the peddlers' un-willingness to eat the family's foods, most Christian hosts respected the Jews' religious integrity. Rather than finding the Jews' form of praying bizarre, cus-tomers described it with respect, and the Jews commented repeatedly on the customers' generosity and their sincere professions of Christian charity. Certainly in the United States, the most important peddler destination, this mutuality reflected the strong strain of religiosity that pervaded civic life. Since the 1830s, if not before, foreign observers noted that Americans viewed religion as a benign force for promoting virtue. As embodied in the memoirs of the peddlers and customers, Americans praised Jews' observance of the dictates of their religion. Rather that condemning Judaism as a perfidious re-ligion that rejected the divinity of Jesus, the peddlers' customers considered the practice of Judaism in their homes as a positive good.

In all of this religious exchange between customers and Jewish peddlers, accounts of customers attempting to convert the peddling Jews to Christianity are rare in the memoirs, autobiographies, and family and communal histories. The case of Charles Goldberg was an exception. Goldberg peddled in Missouri in the 1840s and fell deathly ill. He collapsed from his illness at the home of a minister, who nursed him back to health. This act of kindness caused the peddler to embrace the faith of the family that had healed him.[19] Other narra-tives have nothing to say about missionary efforts directed at the peddlers by the men and women whose homes they entered. At a time when evangelical activity consumed Christian leaders, customers rarely sought to bring the message of the gospel to the Jewish men who came into their homes to sell eyeglasses and tablecloths.

A CONVERGENCE OF SELF-INTEREST

Customers had much to gain from a good relationship with the peddlers, something that missionary activity might have severely jeopardized. They wanted what the peddlers had to sell, and at a reasonable price. They wanted to be treated honestly and fairly. They had little money, and every penny mat-tered. Cultivating the goodwill of the peddler, greeting him with a smile, let-ting him sleep in the house for the night— or so they must have hoped—would ensure quality goods at reasonable prices. This calculus involved women in particular. By using their hard-earned cash to buy goods from the peddlers, they enhanced their standard of living. Once, not so long before, these women had owned no towels, sheets, pillowcases, bedspreads, and tablecloths, or pictures with frames to put up on their walls. Now, with the peddlers' visits, these luxuries were within reach. With transformations of the local economy and the advent of the peddlers in their regions, these women could live at a higher level than their limited resources had previously made possible. They could have some of the accoutrements of bourgeois life, employing consumption as a way to erase the profound and obvious inequities they endured.

That the wives of plantation workers in Cuba, Jamaica, Brazil, Chile, Colombia—indeed throughout Central and Latin America—bought neckties, suspenders, belts, and watches for their husbands from the peddlers spoke volumes about the meaning of material goods. These same women, like their counterparts in Ireland and in the coal mining towns of Wales or the steel towns of Pennsylvania, lived with little, as they scrimped daily to make ends meet. That they chose to buy for themselves bits of ribbon and lace, that they considered themselves entitled to jewelry and hair combs, revealed their desire to announce to themselves and their neighbors their self-worth. They had the right to go to church on Sunday morning wearing a brooch or a necklace.

They met the peddlers at specific historic moments. The intrusion of capitalism and the expansion of large-scale business ventures changed societies around the world. Jewish peddlers came in and took advantage of new opportunities. When Shell Oil opened refineries in Curaçao in 1919, for example, it not only launched a decade of local prosperity but altered the lives of those who previously had not lived in a money economy, offering them cash wages. This made the Caribbean island an attractive destination for Polish Jewish peddlers, who offered newly monetized laborers the opportunity to buy novel goods on the installment plan. Using the Dutch word *kloppers*, knockers, they literally did that, going house to house, selling household goods, watches, clothing, inexpensive jewelry, and record players. A former rural peasant, now a worker for Shell Oil, no doubt paid poorly, could now nonetheless possess a record player, a watch, a bracelet, all of which meant much to himself and his family. They could think of themselves as not just dispossessed peasants or exploited workers but as owners of consumer goods.[20]

The arrival of peddlers into remote areas, particularly those inhabited by once self-sufficient people who had lived outside the sweep of European economic influence, transformed the material level of those who lived there. Jewish peddlers, immigrant men in search of new homes, stumbled into regions only recently "discovered" by European colonizers. An observer of what would in the distant future be called Zimbabwe pointed out that the

Jewish trader, "with his wagon full of cloth, ornaments and European food, barters his wares for the grain and meal of the natives; he encourages their vanity and their tastes for luxury, and the Mashona who a few years before thought it sufficient clothing to have two or three jackals' tails hung from his loins, today requires a tall hat or a second-hand frock coat. . . . Vanity and desire for luxury increase every year."[21] The British author Percy Hone, a believer in the civilizing impact of colonialism, saw the Jewish peddlers as valuable agents in the advance of the Empire.

That women all over the world purchased jewelry from the Jewish peddlers, as well as hairpins, lace, ribbons, cloth, and patterns to sew new dresses, reflected customers' sense of entitlement. A woman's husband might be a miner, cotton tenant farmer, or owner of a hardscrabble plot of land. But her purchases revealed her desire to proclaim her dignity. She had the right to dress with respectability and in a style that erased some distinctions that marked her as inferior to others around her. The goods women bought from peddlers, few of them necessities, represented an important moment in their lives and in that of their communities. Eyeglasses commonly came out of the peddlers' packs, and the need or desire to own a pair accompanied rising literacy rates, the emergence of mass-circulation magazines in distant places by improved postal systems, and the rise of popular entertainments. In South Africa, Ireland, and parts of the United States, peddlers with access to wagons began to carry photographic equipment. For poor families to want their portrait taken, with everyone decked out in their best clothes, transcended just a simple discretionary expenditure of cash. The portrait purchased from the peddler, to be displayed on a wall in the home, betokened a revolution in family life and a desire to assert visually that the people who lived here deserved to have their images preserved.

The goods carried by Jewish peddlers in early-nineteenth-century England, described by poet Robert Southey, could, with the right tweaking of language, have been carried by their descendants in early-twentieth-century Havana or Wales:

> There are Jew peddlers everywhere traveling with boxes of haberdashery on their backs, cuckoo clocks, sealing wax, quills, weather glasses, green spectacles, clumsy figures in plaster of paris, which you see over the chimney of an alehouse parlor in the country, or miserable prints of the King and Queen, the Four Seasons, the Cardinal Virtues, the last Naval Victory, the Prodigal Son, and such like subjects; even the Nativity and the Crucifixion.[22]

Each item had historically and culturally specific meaning. Some spoke to the aspirations of women to enhance their domestic aesthetics. At a time when women increasingly came to be associated with the home sphere, when the maintenance of a beautifully appointed living space expressed a woman's fulfillment of her duties, the "figures of plaster of paris" testified to her good taste, her refinement. The religious pictures need little explanation, exhibiting the family's piety, while the painting of the naval victory announced their patriotism, so robust after England's triumph over Napoleon and the end of the years of war. Writing implements allowed women to express themselves, an emerging trend in the nineteenth-century culture of domesticity. For men they helped them carry on their commercial functions. The clocks demonstrated the increased rule of time, befitting an increasingly urbanized and mechanized world in which individuals had to meet the demands of an efficient society. No one needed these goods, but they improved the lives of their purchasers, and the Jewish peddlers served as the agents of fulfilling desire.

Each item Southey described as being offered for sale by Jews in the English countryside had equivalents around the world, from practical haberdashery to Christian iconography to novelty items like spectacles and luxury goods produced for the relatively poor masses. Each item cemented the relationship between Jewish peddlers and new-world customers, embodying their common interests.

For new-world farmers in the United States, Australia, and South Africa, living spread out, far from one another and with little chance to go to town, the Jewish peddler also carried information about matters global, national, and even local. He didn't only bring goods customers wanted, he transported gossip from farm to farm. The farmers and their families mostly stayed put, but the peddler went to town every weekend and acquired firsthand news of all sorts. He interacted weekly with people like the Jewish shopkeepers and peddler warehouse owners, some of whom had been to Havana, New York, Dublin, and Cape Town, and the peddler shared tidbits that he had gleaned with the customers.

Peddler oral histories contain countless references to the goodwill engendered by bringing the news to isolated homesteads. One former peddler, Hyman Bernstein, shared his experiences with an interviewer for the 1930s Works Progress Administration. He did not stint on the difficulties he experienced, how excruciating were the miles of walking between the farms of rural Illinois, Iowa, and Indiana, some "fifteen, twenty, and thirty miles apart." But as he recalled, "there was no rural mail delivery in those days. Months would pass without a newspaper. The farmers were hungry for news." He began his peddling in 1871 and reported to all the farmers about the great Chicago fire, which he had witnessed. He remembered that "everybody wanted to know about the fire. I would sell my goods and bring news." Bernstein, the rural equivalent of a town crier and a newspaper, "always made a good day's profit at each farm house. The farmer's wife always gave me something to eat and a place to sleep." He kept kosher, but they gave him "fresh eggs, bread and butter and milk."[23]

ADVANTAGES OF BUYING FROM PEDDLERS

Some customers had specific reasons for patronizing peddlers, opting for them over town merchants. Law and social practice kept Native Americans on their reservations and out of white settlements in the American West. Jewish peddlers came to their communities, saving them from the scorn and violence they might have endured in town. Wolf Morris sold on the reservations to the Tolowas and Yuorks in Del Norte County, California, in the 1870s, inaugurating them into the cash economy. Morris's transactions assisted in diversifying his customers' economy, which had previously relied primarily on dentalia, or mollusk shells. Morris and hundreds of other Jewish peddlers in the United States provided Native Americans with an alternative means of obtaining goods.[24] Jewish peddlers like Julius Meyer, an immigrant from Germany known by the Pawnee as "Box-Ka-Re-Sha-Hash-Ta-Ka"—curly-headed white chief who speaks with one tongue—like other Jewish peddlers, bought up Indian artifacts on his various journeys, offering the impoverished people on whose lands he sold a chance to make money for objects previously without market value. Indeed, Jewish peddlers like Meyer helped stimulate a market for Indian arts and crafts in cities around the world, which in turn transformed the reservations' economies.[25]

When slavery still prevailed, peddlers who came onto plantations and sold to both planters and slaves played a small role in the development of an autonomous economy among the slaves. As owners allowed slaves to earn money by selling produce from their gardens, and from renting themselves out to other plantations, slaves took advantage of the peddlers' arrival to vary their clothing and buy items beyond what the planters gave them, to enhance their dwellings with furnishings of their own choosing.

Slaveowners actually feared the Jewish peddlers. They fretted that peddlers might help slaves run away, and that they disseminated abolitionist ideas and antislavery tracts. In fact, the southern white planter class had no reason to worry about the Jews as abolitionists in peddlers' clothing. The peddlers did not come in to change social or political relationships. What they thought about slavery they kept to themselves, unless they approved of it. In only one documented case did Jewish peddlers liberate a slave. As described in Kate E. R. Packard's *The Kidnapped and the Ransomed*, two peddlers, the Friedman brothers of Cincinnati and Tuscumbia, Alabama, conspired to purchase Peter Still and then free him.[26] Slaveowners perhaps should have been more concerned that the ability of slaves to earn money and use it to buy goods from the peddlers was a manifestation of individualism and personal agency that undermined the system. But if the planters worried about the subversive implications of the peddlers coming on to their lands, they did not stop them, and they, along with the slaves, looked forward to the arrival of the peddlers.

After slavery was abolished, African Americans in the South repeatedly experienced humiliation when going to stores in town. They had to enter through a separate entrance and could not handle the merchandise or try on clothes. The peddlers who came to their homes, despite the strictures of the regnant racial code, could allow the customers whatever they wanted, shielded by the privacy of closed doors. Peddlers purposely addressed their African-American customers as "Mr." and "Mrs." or "Ma'am," far cries from the "boy" or "girl" they heard from shopkeepers and other whites. In the prevailing racial system, which sought to preserve the hierarchy of slavery, the peddlers may have been the only white people who regularly came into the homes of African Americans without the power of the state behind them.[27]

Customers gained much from connecting with the peddlers, beyond the attractive wares and the news. Many clients had economic incentives to opt for peddlers over sedentary merchants: peddlers sold their goods at lower prices than did town merchants. Whether women bought from smous in South Africa, weekly men in Ireland, semananiks in Argentina, or kloppers in other parts of South America, they acquired goods for less money than if they shopped in a store. Peddlers who sold on the installment plan charged less interest than did fixed-place merchants, who had to factor in overhead that the peddler did not incur.

More specific reasons drew some to peddlers. In mining communities and on plantations around the world, the peddler provided an alternative to the company stores, the shops owned and operated by the employers, mine and mill owners, and the landlords of estates who used consumption as another way to profit from their workers. The company store or the plantation commissary abetted the powerful as they exploited their subordinates. The Jewish peddlers who made their way to, say, West Virginia or Jamaica or Alabama did not represent those who extracted excruciatingly difficult labor for low wages from the workers. Outsiders, they did not, according to the customers, participate in the exploitive system. The Shavsky brothers from Kishinev peddled among the logging camps of northern California. So enthusiastically did the loggers' families embrace these two Jewish peddlers and turn their backs on the company store that the owners declared the Shavskys personae non grata in the camps, denying them the privilege of going house to house. The Shavsky brothers improvised. They parked themselves and their wagon at the edge of the camps, just beyond the official boundaries, so that customers could easily get to them.[28]

The economic benefit of transacting business with the peddlers extended even farther. When selling to customers who lived near forests and wilderness regions, peddlers entered into arrangements with their customers to barter for furs, hides, herbs, and feathers, which the Jewish peddlers recognized as commodities sellable for a profit. The peddlers, in conjunction with Jewish scrapyard owners, saw money in items like these, stuff strewn through the countryside, lying there ready to be gathered and then sold. No one owned the herbs that grew in profusion, just waiting to be picked. The miners or steel-workers who spent leisure time hunting game for food found in the peddlers an eager market for pelts, hides, and bones. In South Africa, Jewish peddlers participated in the expansion of the ostrich feather trade, picking up plumes that would eventually end up on the hats of fashionable women in New York, London, and Paris.

Customers reveled in their ability to extend their meager earnings by gathering these items. Farmers, miners, textile workers, and their wives did not make a living by means of this stuff. They spent their days raising wheat or cotton, extracting coal, or tending looms, but what the peddlers wanted from them could be collected and transformed into either cash or goods from the peddlers' sacks. Old bones, for example, had great value, as did scraps of paper discarded as trash. It cost nothing for the miner and his family, the tenant farmer on a cotton plantation, the logger and his wife, or the factory worker to devote some time to collecting ginseng or saving up the bones from last's week's soup or stew to sell to the Jewish peddler. For working-class customers this junk was a found treasure. These items may have had no value to those who gathered them, but the willingness of the peddlers to buy them added bits of money to the family coffers.

Backyards, empty lots, nearby riverbanks—any piece of land could be a little gold mine of "old rags, iron, brass, zinc, and copper," items valued and purchased by the peddlers. Harris Isaac, a peddler who became a full-time junk dealer in early-twentieth-century Sleepy Eye, Minnesota, entered into just such an arrangement with the women and men of the surrounding region. He resembled his brother peddlers around the world, and they resembled their sister customers.[29]

Customers and peddlers together also benefited when the latter facilitated loans for the former's possessions in times of need, and this too solidified the relationships between them. While the peddler expected to make money on the pawn transaction, the customer turned to this strategy in tough times to make ends meet. For women with little money to tide them through bad stretches, being able to pawn a watch, a necklace, a picture frame, each perhaps purchased from a Jewish peddler in the first place, might mean the difference between food on the table and starvation. Both parties gained from the economic arrangement. The peddlers with family and friends who owned pawnshops in towns and cities served as the middlemen between the women in need of cash and the pawnbrokers who provided it to them. From the perspective of the woman who had something to pawn and needed cash and the pawnbroker who made a living by selling such goods, this arrangement worked well, and the peddler enabled it.

Women customers found all of this particularly advantageous. A woman could buy an item from a peddler during her husband's working hours, while he was away from home. He might never find out. The same woman might also collaborate with the peddler by selling him the bones she had saved from cooking or the scraps of paper and strips of fabric she had gathered, keeping the money as her own. Or she could exchange these items for something from the peddler's sack, and her husband would be none the wiser. During his hours out in the fields or in the coal mines, she could collect ginseng and earn money, or she might pawn a tablecloth. These business transactions provided her with a spot of autonomy and agency in an otherwise male-dominated world. Her husband represented the family in all other matters, but when it came to doing business with the peddler, she ruled.

In all of these exchanges, Jewish immigrant peddlers went in and out of customers' homes and became real individuals who functioned in their lives. No wonder numerous places and stretches of road around the world came to be labeled with the word "peddler." Towns formally or informally designated streets as Peddlers Lane, indicating the route the peddlers took from the warehouse to their distant customers. In the South Dakota gold fields the Peddler Trail was a three-mile path along the banks of Rapid Creek between Canyon City and Mystic, along which the peddlers walked as they went from mine to mine, settlement to settlement.[30]

Peddlers, as described by themselves and their customers, tried to get along with everyone, avoiding no class of customer, selling to all. Family lore had it that everyone liked Mike Bindursky, a Bessarabian immigrant who peddled in Mississippi, where he was known as "Mike-Do-Right." According to his children, "the young man could get past the gates of even the best plantations, in a time when other peddlers had a hard go of it."[31] The peddlers sold across deep and profound social divides, some which constituted the basic boundaries of civic and political life. In the American South they sold to African Americans and whites. The same peddlers in South Africa sold to Boer, English, and native African customers. In Australia a peddler filled his customer list with aborigines and British whites, while their rosters in the American West included Anglos, Mexicans, and Native Americans. In New England and upstate New York, as well as in eastern Canada, the Jewish peddler crossed the thresholds of French-speaking Catholics, Irish Catholic immigrants, and English-speaking Protestant farmers of Yankee origins. In Central and South America they traded with Spanish speakers and those of the local Indian languages. In the Irish countryside a Jewish weekly man moved from Catholic to Protestant homes, disregarding the religion of the customers, except for knowing that selling to Protestants meant not taking out crucifixes, rosaries, and holy pictures, while selling to Catholics meant displaying those first. It might be said that the Jewish peddlers had no interest in these differences except as they facilitated or hindered sales.

SELLING TO EVERYONE BUT ASPIRING UPWARD

While the peddler had to get along with everyone, learn their habits, master their tastes, and treat them with respect, at the same time he figured out local power relationships, and wherever he went, consistently fixed his aspirations for himself and his children to become more like the local elites than the poor people to whom he sold. Philip Rubin, the son of an immigrant from the province of Kovno in Lithuania who peddled around Burlington, Vermont, acknowledged that Jews sold to all sorts of "goyim," including "Francaisen, Yenkes, Irish and others," but of these, he admitted, "We were just as unfair towards our French neighbors as they were toward us, whom they regarded as a shrewd, but swindling and cruel, race." He had picked up on the local pecking order. In contrast with his negative views of the French customers, he recalled that his "father would come home from the farms and relate wondrous tales of these [Yankee] farmers' hospitality, of their kindness and sheer wisdom." His father held up this elite group as the one to emulate. "If we children would misbehave, would be disobedient or insist on a penny to buy candy," Rubin recalled of his childhood, "Father would set before us some Yank farmer children, usually the Hazelton's of Waterbury or the Nash's of Jericho, as examples of good conduct and insist that we must act like these."[32]

Many customers, like the Quebecois of northern New England, had had no previous contact with Jews before they met the peddlers in the mill towns and on the countryside. This held for all the native peoples of the Jews' new world who became their customers in Ireland, Wales, Scotland, Australia, New Zealand, southern Africa, North America, the Caribbean, Central and South America. So, too, the African slaves before emancipation and their progeny afterward met Jews for the first time as peddlers selling them goods they wanted.

But some customers whom the Jewish peddlers encountered in America and Canada actually came from their own old homes. Many women to whom, for example, Jewish peddlers from Poland sold in places like Fall River, Massachusetts, happened to be Polish immigrants working the textile mills, people who would surely have known Jews before migration. Jewish peddlers from Bavaria and Posen who immigrated to, say, Ohio plied their trade among German Christian immigrants, while some who took to the roads of the rural Midwest met Czech-speaking Bohemians, and Jewish peddlers from the Slavic lands working western Pennsylvania in the coal and iron mill region sold to new immigrants from those same Slavic lands. Jewish peddlers opened their bags to German-speaking Mennonites in Manitoba, and others who hailed from central and eastern Europe.[33]

The ground had shifted in this old-world relationship. Back there the non-Jews disdained the Jews, or worse. In the new places, the Jews had no fewer rights, had no less a claim to citizenship, had no lower an expectation of achieving respectability than did their neighbors from the old home with whom they reunited in Buffalo, on the plains of Manitoba, or on the farms on the Nebraska prairies. Indeed, Jewish immigrants in these places, partly because of peddling, experienced a higher rate of educational, economic, and social mobility than did their Christian coimmigrants from back home. Given their commercial occupations and the support local Jewish communities extended, Jewish peddlers experienced greater economic mobility for themselves and their children than did their old-country neighbors, who derived no greater status because they happened to be Christians.

Around the new world, peddlers and their Jewish communal allies declared that they experienced little or no anti-Jewish sentiment. Some commentators declared the total absence of any anti-Jewish activity when it came to the relationships between peddlers and customers. Robert Haberman, a Jewish communal leader in Mexico, wrote in 1923, "There is no hatred against the Jew or toward their immigration. In all the six and one half years that I have been living in Mexico, I have not run across one single case of . . . hatred against the Jews. . . . As all the commodities handled by the peddlers are necessities of life and the prices in commodities have dropped . . . the populace at large looks upon the Jewish boys as benefactors."[34]

In their written and oral testimonies peddlers retrospectively also emphasized that warm, friendly relationships blossomed between peddlers and customers. Each tried not to offend the other and saw in the transaction mutually beneficial common ground. A few examples can serve to characterize a vast compendium of such experiences. A Jewish peddler in North Carolina recalled that one woman, who bought from him and in whose house he lodged, took it upon herself to help the peddler master English. She decided to give him his first language lesson. A schoolteacher, she "introduced me into the intricacies of the English language. This lesson was followed up by many others on my subsequent visits."[35] The son of Julius Solomon, who peddled in Ohio in the 1870s, described his father as "always very proud of the fact that he never went to a house and was turned away. . . . If there were children at the farmers' home, often the evening was spent as they tried to teach him English and he tried to teach them German."[36] Yet another peddler, one who sold in the South, recalled with humor that once "when he was peddling he had been out all day, it was dark, he was very tired, very hungry, so he knocked at a door. Lady comes to the door and says, 'Are you a Yankee?' He says, 'No, I'm not a Yankee, I'm a Jewish boy.' She got a kick out of it. They became fast friends."[37]

How did the customers see the peddlers? What did they think about these foreigners who knocked at their doors? Almost universally customers expressed appreciation and bought from them. Despite the planters' fears that the itinerant Jews in the antebellum period might be covert abolitionists, they often set aside a special room for the exclusive use of the Jewish peddlers who would stay the night, such as the "room to house travelling peddlers" kept at Hope Plantation in North Carolina.[38] Mike Bindursky, the peddler who could charm his way onto any plantation, developed such good relations with his customers that at the birth of his first child in 1895, a local couple "of the Episcopalian faith" gave Mike and his wife a gift to celebrate the arrival of "the first Jewish child born" in the area of Baird, Mississippi. The couple gave the Bindurskys a deed for forty acres of land.[39]

The customers' views of the Jewish peddlers became clear when settled merchants, resentful of the peddlers' advantages, stirred political and economic opposition to them. Customers, the women particularly, stood by the peddlers. When in the early twentieth century a Redemptorist priest in Limerick, Ireland, launched a boycott of the Jewish peddlers, the female customers turned a deaf ear to him and continued to buy from the Jews. When in South Africa the Cape colony legislature debated the problem of the smous, one legislator declared, "The proper way of dealing with these people is for farmers to warn them off their land." He acknowledged, though, that "the extraordinary thing I find is that the farmers encourage these men and the farmer's wives and daughters are their customers."[40] The story of Louis Jacobs, an immigrant peddler in the countryside around San Bernardino, California, in the 1850s, also illustrates the store of customer goodwill. Jacobs peddled among the Mormons who had settled in the area. He got in an argument over a payment with a Mormon elder, David Seely. Seely hit Jacobs in the course of their dispute, striking him several times with his stick. The Mormon community sided not with the elder but with the peddler. His peers forced the elder to apologize, and the church stripped him of his ecclesiastical honors. In an informal judicial proceeding, church leaders forced Seely to pay Jacobs for the assault and battery.[41]

PEDDLER LOVE STORIES

The generally positive relationships that flourished between the peddlers and their customers extended beyond the purchase of goods and the sale of scrap and other items to the sleep-over and the sharing of life details. Romantic attractions and marriages also blossomed between Jewish peddlers and their female customers. Marcus Spiegel, the Ohio peddler who fell in love with the Quaker Caroline Hamlin, had company around the world. In neighboring Indiana in the 1850s, Simon Goldman from Bavaria met Susan Trine, who like Caroline Hamlin came from a Quaker family but "agreed to become a Jewess," although unlike Caroline she decided to keep her marriage secret from her parents.[42]

Stories like these came from all over the new world. Jewish immigrant peddlers met, fell in love with, and either married or maintained lifelong relationships with customers and their daughters in Argentina, Panama, Colombia, Peru, Brazil, French Canada, Australia, New Zealand, South Africa, and no doubt elsewhere as well. A survey of life in South Africa, written in 1927 by Sarah Gertrude Millin, a Jewish novelist, noted that as a result of the Boer farmers' hospitality to the smous, some of the Lithuanian Jewish immigrant men "in these pioneering days . . . married sometimes the big, solemn daughters of their Boer hosts."[43] Isaac Pisa, who represented the Alliance Israélite Universelle, came from Morocco to the Amazon in the early twentieth century to survey the condition of the Jewish immigrants there, and expressed dismay over the fact that his former students, now peddlers, had entered into liaisons with local women. Another observer of the Jews of Brazil, Alfred Rosenzweig, equally upset with this romantic mixing, reported with alarm that the Jewish peddlers had "spread children all around the jungle. Sometimes, when you asked a child rowing a canoe what his name was, he told you that his name was David. 'I am Jewish,' he said and then he told you that his father was." Alex Levin from Posen came to the Arizona territory in the 1850s, peddled, and married Zenona Molina, a young Sonoran woman.[44] A princess of the Colesville Indians in Oregon married a Jewish peddler, as did a woman of the Acoma tribe.

Some Jewish peddlers who operated in the Australian outback, in New Zealand, and in South America who married non-Jewish women sought permission from Jewish religious authorities to have their sons circumcised. Despite millennia of Jewish adherence to the principle of matrilineal descent as a qualification for membership in the Jewish covenant, these peddlers wanted their children to be included in the Jewish community. In all of these places the rabbis in the cities, far removed from the peddlers' hinterlands, turned down the fathers' requests.[45]

Jews came as peddlers to the many places around the world where women and men craved, or came to crave, the goods that the peddlers could sell. They spoke directly to the material aspirations of the women whom they encountered, and they interacted harmoniously with those customers who saw them as men bearing goods and nothing more. The marriages between Jewish peddlers and local non-Jewish women reveal a different vantage point from which the customers saw the peddlers. They demonstrate that the peddlers' Jewishness, foreign origins, and peculiar occupation served as neither social barriers nor sources of friction.[46]

CUSTOMER MEMORIES

The ways in which non-Jewish new-world customers recalled the peddlers and used that memory to shape their subsequent lives reflects the basically positive relationship that prevailed. A sampling of statements reflects its breadth and depth. When Hosea Hudson, a Georgia-born African-American labor leader in the early part of the twentieth century, first took a job in a steel mill, "many of the Negro leaders and the Negro newspapers" warned the workers about getting involved with northern labor organizers, "Red agitators" coming down from New York. Hudson, however, remembered the Jewish peddlers of his youth, and in his memoir he remarked that he had no fear of "the white [Communist] Party coming in from New York." He remembered, "It used to be some Jewish peddlers to come through with bags of things to sell on their shoulders and they would talk about the North. I heard that talk so much until I always looked for the Yankees to come back one day and finish the job of freeing the Negroes."[47] Ira Treadway, an early-twentieth-century African American living in Live Oak, Florida, got to know one peddler, Harry Lazarus. He remembered: "We always were lookin' for Mr. Peddler. That's what my daddy called him. . . . My mom would rush out of the house" as Lazarus approached, "wipin' her hands on her apron with the biggest grin you'd ever did see. She'd tell me to fetch daddy from the fields."[48]

Such recollections offered in the American South transcended race. Thomas D. Clark, a white southern historian, shared in his memoir the details of his growing up in Winston County, Mississippi. Born in 1903, he recalled the Jews of Winston County, peddlers among them. He described the "pack peddlers who made regular rounds through the country. I never heard an anti-Semitic remark, but countrymen were amused at the Eastern European accents and manners of the visitors." Calling them "visitors" raised their status in his estimation, and he remembered "with considerable nostalgia the emigrant peddlers who trod the miserable, muddy or dusty country roads burdened with their striped canvas backpacks of merchandise." After ticking off the names of several of them, Clark returned to the description: "They all spoke broken English and used quaint phrases. The visitations of these men introduced us to the fact that not all the people of the world spoke the same language. . . . They built up an enormous amount of goodwill. . . . When these itinerant merchants unrolled their packs . . . all the wonders of the commercial world seemed to pop up before our eyes."[49] The fiction writer and essayist Harry Crews grew up "poor white" in Bacon County, Georgia. He devoted nearly an entire chapter of his memoir, *Childhood*, to the Jewish peddler "whose name I never knew, always dressed in black." To the small child of a "little closed world," the peddler's wagon "was better than anything" Crews and his brother "could make up, filled as it was with spools of thread and needles and thimbles and bolts of cloth and knives and forks and spoons." Crews, who eventually fled to New York to escape the parochialism of Bacon County, had little romantic to say about that place, but when it came to the Jewish peddler, "I can never remember anybody saying anything bad about him or treating him badly."[50]

Women also recalled in exuberant tones the arrival of the Jewish peddlers in their communities and homes. Elizabeth Jane Dietz, from West Virginia's Greenbrier County, looked back to her youth in the 1880s, when "we had Jewish peddlers that came . . . and gave us something to look forward to." It was, she remembered, "almost like having Santa Claus come, even if Mother couldn't afford to buy much." Indeed, like Santa Claus, peddlers brought novelty and excitement into the monotony of country life. Like the jolly Christmas figure, the peddlers Dietz remembered brought a "big bundle" to people who, as she described her world, "seldom saw new things."[51]

The chorus of voices went on and on as customers or former customers recalled the immigrant Jewish peddlers. A Minnesota farmer reminisced about the peddlers who "used to keep us informed of many things that went on in the cities. They introduced us to Jewish operettas; they sang them for us and we would go around repeating the songs. . . . The peddlers seemed wonderful to us and thrilled us. . . . Some would stay and help a little on the farm."[52]

Not limited to the United States, such memories could be gleaned from South Africa, Australia, Ireland, and elsewhere, but one example will serve. Alberto Lleras Camargo, president of Colombia in the 1940s, saw fit to recall the Polish Jewish peddlers of Bogotà and the surrounding small towns, the *polacos:*

> They brought about a revolution in commercial methods, beginning with their way of extending credit to poor people, with their system of deferred payments, which came to be called *plazos polacos.* . . . Little by little the townspeople, who had previously gone barefoot, started to wear shoes. The servants, that huge and disperse ancillary class, whose condition differed little from that of the slaves of the earlier period, could now, despite their indigenous origin, dress with something a little better than the cast off clothes of their masters. The hemp sandals started to disappear. The *polacos* were demanding creditors, and some of them practiced usury with considerable success. Yet I doubt whether a town, or indeed a country, has so radically changed and improved its physiognomy as much as this one has since the appearance of the *polacos* in the 1920s and 1930s.[53]

Jewish immigrant peddlers changed their customers' lives, and by extension altered the histories of the countries where they sold. They tapped into and cultivated new standards of consumption that accompanied the spread of capitalism. Their customers likewise changed the Jews. They encountered, according to their own words and those of their customers, little hatred as non-Christian foreigners. Rather, wherever they went, regardless of continent, country, region, and time, women and men willingly let them into their homes and in a larger sense into their communities, seeing them as heroes by virtue of their having brought previously unknown or unattainable wares. They did not constitute a problem to be solved, nor did Jew and non-Jew see themselves separated by an impenetrable wall of difference. Mostly they respected those differences, considering them no barriers to the Jews' citizenship and access to civic participation. The world the peddlers and their customers forged together constituted a new chapter in Jewish history, one that made the new world different than the old.

Peddling transformed the lives of the people whose thresholds the Jewish immigrant peddlers crossed, stimulating in the women and men tastes for new goods and aspirations to higher standards of living. Jews had come to these new places as strangers and outsiders. Yet they became teachers, connecting the women and men whose homes they entered to cosmopolitan consumption, to new standards of clothing, personal hygiene, and home decorating. They exposed Christian customers to Jewish practice.

No one-way street, the teaching went the other way too. From their customers the peddlers learned the languages of the land, ones they needed in order to put down roots in their new place. Customers instructed peddlers in the workings of local society, its preferences and taboos. They also, through their examples, made it amply clear that not all Christians harbored ill will toward them, that not all hated them or sought to convert them. That lesson had great historic implications for the course of modern Jewish history.

Perhaps one story might bring together the various strands of new-world Jewish peddling and the symbiotic relationship that flourished between peddlers and their new host society. This one took place in the United States, in New Orleans in the 1860s. Joseph, a young Jew from Lyon, came to Louisiana from Alsace in the 1850s, and like most of his peers, he took to the roads, peddling. When he applied for citizenship, the judge, without asking, wrote his name on the official form as "Joseph Lyon," a reasonable Americanization of Joseph of Lyon. The newly named new American, the former peddler, asked the judge whether he could choose his own American name. The judge told him that he could pick whatever name he wanted. This newly sworn-in citizen dubbed himself Joseph Israel. When the judge asked the peddler why he had chosen that name, Joseph replied, "Because I have been in this country for 10 years; I came as a poor Jew, and I have been accepted. . . . The fact that I was a Jew didn't detract from being accepted, and to show my appreciation for having been accepted as an equal, I want to change my name to Israel."[54]

In opting for that name Joseph Israel articulated a sense of comfort, acceptance, and security in his new home. The Americans to whom he sold, who had bought from him, who had welcomed him into their homes, fed him, and lodged him, inspired confidence in his Jewishness. He believed that the people he had met along the road respected rather than deprecated him for being a Jew. But such paeans to their new land aside, the peddlers did not ignore— nor can we—the times and places around the world when and where they experienced hatred, violence, and efforts to restrict them. These moments also shaped the history of Jewish peddling along the new world's many roads.

Moroccan Peddler in London, c. 1800. Mezzotint and watercolor on paper, 5⅝ ×
4 ¼ in. (14.3 × 10.8 cm). Gift of Dr. Harry G. Friedman, F 5895.

Photo by John Parnell. The Jewish Museum, New York, NY, USA /Art Resource, NY

The Peddler's Wagon. Wood engraving by Charles Green Bush. Reprinted from *Harper's Weekly*, June 20, 1868, p. 393.

Library of Congress, www.loc.gov

Young peddler with pack, c. 1890, Easton, Pennsylvania. Peddlers and Peddling, PC-3411.03.

Courtesy of The Jacob Rader Marcus Center of the American Jewish Archives, Cincinnati, Ohio, AmericanJewishArchives.org

Abraham and Straus, Brooklyn, New York, late 1800s. Peddlers and Peddling, PC-3411.02.

Simon Rabinowitz, Malden, Massachusetts. Peddlers and Peddling, PC-4892.01

Albert Fine peddling near Guelph, Ontario, 1908. Ontario Jewish Archives, item 555.

Courtesy of the Ontario Jewish Archives

Sam Krieger and Charles Wolfish peddling at Proton, Ontario, c. 1909. Ontario Jewish Archives, item 3793.

Courtesy of the Ontario Jewish Archives

Leon Koffler seated in a horse-drawn buggy, 1914. Ontario Jewish Archives, fond 37, series 4-3, item 4.

Courtesy of the Ontario Jewish Archives

Felix Shavinsky as a peddler, 1910.

Cuba Family Archives for Southern Jewish History of The Breman Museum

Side-by-side images of peddlers in Lee M. Friedman's "The Problems of
Nineteenth Century American Jewish Peddlers," *Publications of the American
Jewish Historical Society* 8 (1954–1955).

American Jewish Historical Society, New York, NY, and Newton Centre, MA

Israel Goodman of Old Town sold dry goods from the Old Town–Bangor
area as far north as Fort Kent. Later Goodman had retail establishments in
Old Town and Danforth.

The Canoochee Hotel, Stillmore, Georgia, served kosher meals for peddlers, c. 1890s.

Peddlers at a south Georgia turpentine farm, 1906.

The Peddler's Shadow, Los Angeles Herald,
September 22, 1907.

Courtesy of the *Los Angeles Herald*

A JEW PEDDLER OF THE '50s

His Four Degrees of Business
1st.   Mit a pack on his back
2nd.   Mit a horse and wagon
3rd.   Mit a store
4th.   Mit a bank or bankrupt

A Jew Peddler of the '50s, from *The*
Autobiography of Charles Peters
(Sacramento, Calif.: LaGrave,
1915), 138.

אידישער ער פארמער
THE JEWISH FARMER

Vol. III, No. 1. | New York, January, 1910 | Price 3 Cents

די אמעריקאנער צייטונגען וועגען דער אויסשטעלונג

נען לכבוד דער אויסשטעלונג אין דעם
הומאריסטישען וואכענבלייכען זשורנאל
דושאדזש, ווי אויך דיא בעמערקונג אונ־
טער דעם קארטון.

נעקאמט איבערגעבען, וואם זיי האבען גע־
זאגט וועגען דער אויסשטעלונג. דאך קע־
נען מיר זיך נים איינהאלטען נים איבער־
צור זקען דעם קארטון, וואם איז ערשיע־
נען איז דער קארטון.

דיא ענגלישע צייטונגען און זשורנא־
לען האבען היבש געשריבען וועגען דער
אידישער אגריקולטור אויסשטעלונג, נאר
צוליעב מאנגעל אין פלאץ האבען מיר נים

PROSPERITY FARM.

POTATOES

DRY GOODS

—FLOHRI—

(COPYRIGHT, LESLIE JUDGE CO., 1909.)

דישע פארטערם אין דיא פעראייניגטע
שטאטטען אליין, און מים ליצומען אנדער
ווערט דיא צאהל אלץ גרעסער. זיי זעהען
אייז אז זיי קענען האבען מעהר ערפאלג
אין פארמעריי ווי אין דיא נעדיכטבע
נעטעמטם". — פון לעסלים זשורנל.

נעקרוינט מים ערפאלג. מים א יאהר צען
ציק איז דא געווען א הייפעלע אירישע
פארמערם, צווישען אן צושפרייט איבער'ן
גאנצען לאנד און האבען היינט נים נו ער־
וואוטטם, וואם פארגען וועם פון זיי ווערען.
איצט האבען מיר איבער פינף טויזענד אי־

דאם גייע לאנד פון מילך און האניג.
"די קאנווענשאן און אויסשטעלונג
יעדע דא אירישע פארמערם האבען נים
לאנג אבנעהאלמען אין ניו יארק האבען
געוויזען, אז דעם אירע'ס אריינגערמען
אויס'ן פעלד. פון אגריקולטור האט זיך

The Glazer family in Kalkaska, Michigan, c. 1905, from
Michigan Jewish History 19, no. 1 (1979).
Courtesy of Jewish Historical Society of Michigan

The Shwayder brothers standing on a trunk.
Courtesy of Beck Archives, Special Collections, University Libraries,
University of Denver

4

Road Rage

Jewish Peddlers and the Perils of the Road

The 1904–1905 volume of the *American Jewish Yearbook* pointed out that during the past year "no startling tragedy" had befallen the Jewish people. After documenting some acts of violence against Jews in some expected hot spots—Poland, Bessarabia, Morocco—*Yearbook* editors pointed to one event of that year in one of the Jews' new-world homes that startled them. They considered what transpired in Limerick, Ireland, "less shocking" than the others, "but more surprising by far." In this Irish city a "thunderbolt from the blue [was] launched by Father Creagh," a Redemptorist priest who instigated a campaign against the small community of Jews who "had been residing in peace for twenty years, until last January," when he "made an onslaught from the pulpit before a congregation numbering three thousand persons." What did the priest have against the Jews? Creagh condemned the Jews, mostly peddlers, "who are largely engaged in the sale of goods on the installment plan."[1]

Creagh employed passionate and classically anti-Jewish language in exposing the misdeeds of the weekly men, the Jewish peddlers, who since the 1870s had been migrating to Ireland, mostly from Lithuania. Creagh thundered to his congregants that unlike their forbears in the distant past, the Jews in Ireland no longer had to "kidnap and slay Christian children, but they will not hesitate to expose them to a longer and even more cruel martyrdom by taking the clothes off their backs. . . . They came to our land to fasten themselves on us like leeches and draw our blood when they had been forced away from other countries." For the next two years, Creagh, sustained by some of Ireland's nationalist activists, particularly Arthur Griffith, editor of the *United*

Irishman, called upon the Irish Catholics of Limerick, particularly the women, to boycott the Jewish peddlers, neither to buy from them nor to pay for goods already purchased. Local shopkeepers, irritated by the competition from the Jewish peddlers, embraced Creagh's boycott and appealed to women in the name of group solidarity.

Words spilled over into action. In the next two years low-level violence was directed a few times against local Jews. A young man roughed up Limerick's rabbi. An unruly crowd broke windows of some Jewish-owned shops. A sizable number of Limerick's Jews found the city too dangerous for comfort and fled to Cork. Later historians referred to this period as the "Limerick pogrom," and while it paled in comparison to uprisings in Kishinev and Odessa and the other great massacres, Jews throughout Ireland and elsewhere, like the editors of the *American Jewish Yearbook*, worried what the campaign might portend.[2]

News of Creagh's sermons and the boycott spread. Stories about Limerick flooded the Jewish, Irish, and British presses. Irish public opinion divided over the boycott, the Jews, and the nature of Irish society. Some Catholic clerics and some nationalist leaders, like Griffith, agreed that the Jews, as peddlers and the purveyors of material goods, threatened the well-being of the people of "holy Ireland."[3] Tied to English Jewish moneyed interests, so the rhetoric purported, the peddlers went house to house enticing Irish women to buy novelty goods they did not need. By stimulating a yearning for a higher standard of living, the weekly men disrupted family stability, pitted wives against husbands, encouraged poor women to spend the limited money their husbands earned on trifles. Each time a woman bought from a Jew, she enriched him and robbed an Irish shopkeeper of his livelihood. That shopkeeper, unlike the Jewish peddler, plowed his profits back into the local economy, while the peddler hoarded his. One priest, traveling by car, scoured the countryside within his parish looking for women engaged in transactions with peddlers. He caught one woman in the act and demanded to see what she had just bought. When he saw her new blankets, according to an article in the *Irish Mission*, the crusading priest grabbed them, "threw them out the doorway, and told the man to leave the village, and never enter his parish again. He chastised her, asking, 'do you not know that you must not deal with Jews?' "[4]

Not all in Ireland, despite its majority Catholic population and nationalism's strong appeal, supported or condoned the boycott. The Jews turned for assistance to Michael Davitt, a popular nationalist leader. Seeing him as an ally since he had published just the year before *Within the Pale*, an exposé of the pogrom that had devastated the Jewish population of the Bessarabian city of Kishinev, the Jews of Ireland asked Davitt to speak out against the whole

campaign. He did what they asked. The Jews of Limerick also found a defender in Thomas Bunbury, the Church of Ireland's bishop of Limerick. As a
Protestant and a representative of the Church of England, Bunbury used the
boycott to highlight the backwardness and barbarity of the Irish masses in
general and the retrograde behavior of the Catholic Church. A flurry of letters
in local Irish newspapers from Protestant readers pointed that the Limerick
boycott resembled a medieval drama, and that such an attack on Jews should
have no place in a modern liberal society. It demonstrated to the writers the
unsuitability of the Irish for independence and the perniciousness of a priest-
ridden culture.[5]

The two-year boycott of the Jewish peddlers, with its occasional acts of
violence toward the Jews, took place in a dense matrix of social, religious,
and political relationships, challenged by contemporary developments. The
Jews who came to Limerick, like those who went to Cork, Dublin, Wexford,
Belfast, and numerous other Irish communities, chose places of new economic prospects in a changing society. Irish families previously had few material possessions, but by the later part of the nineteenth century, they had
gained access to more money. Emigrating kin sent remittances, which enabled
recipients to upgrade their material standard of living, stretching their visions
of desire and their definitions of the good life. More Irish families became
owners, as opposed to tenants, of small pieces of land, and steadily abandoned
thatch-covered cabins, with mud-covered floors, in favor of houses with roofs,
windows, and floors. They shifted from tillage to the more lucrative grazing of
cattle.

Such improvements ratcheted up of standards of living. This reality had attracted the Lithuanian Jewish peddlers to Ireland. But many Catholic clerics
and nationalists considered the migration shameful, treasonous. They believed
that the increasing joy Irish families felt in material consumption undermined
the Jansenistic strain of Catholicism that since the famine of the 1840s and
1850s had dominated Irish culture. This theological orientation exceeded
mainstream Catholicism's suspicion of material acquisition. The Jansenists
understood the new Ireland of the late nineteenth and early twentieth centuries,
the one that had welcomed the Jewish peddlers as purveyors of goods, to have
jettisoned a deeply rooted communalist ethos that abjured personal acquisition
and any desire to set oneself off as better than one's fellows. Instead, these
ideologues declared, Ireland had turned to materialism and individualism.

As standards changed, and as the Jewish peddler migration swelled,
"preachers, publicans and journalists" helped invent an idyllic image of rural
Ireland of bygone days, when young Irish women did not rush across the

ocean to earn money, when families and communities were indifferent to material comforts, and when the poor lived in harmony with one another. These
writers, orators, and clergy valorized in political, religious, and artistic venues
an Ireland of old when only the Irish, imagined as a homogeneous group, inhabited "mother Eire."[6]

Jews constituted the largest group of immigrants to Ireland. Other newcomers came—Italians, for example—but unlike the Jews, these immigrants
were Catholic. Jews differed too in commercializing the countryside,
introducing women in particular to the emerging economy of individual
consumption.

The new sense of what constituted an adequate way of life spread across
Ireland, reflecting increases in roads, emigration, education, literacy, and access to the ideas of the outside world. Ordinary people who a generation earlier had slept on straw pallets on earthen floors now could stretch out on a bed
with a mattress. Those whose mothers had owned one dress now desired a
diverse wardrobe. The woman whose priest demanded that she return her
blankets to the peddler retorted that she, "a poor herdsman's daughter," reveled in the reality that she could own "clothing and bed covering," and she
could get these things because of the Jews. Her relationships to the Jewish
peddlers resembled, as she said, those of "a good many of her class," who
without the Jews would have to do without adornments for body and home.[7]

The Jewish peddlers who happened upon Limerick, like those who showed
up in other spots around the new world, ventured into lands whose social,
economic, and political relationships had nothing to do with them. In Limerick
the divisions between Catholics and the Protestants, nationalists and supporters of British rule, men and women, emigrants and those who remained at
home, shopkeepers and poor farmers, underlay local society. What, after all,
did Jews fresh from Lithuania care about Catholicism, the Church of Ireland,
the British Empire, Irish nationalism, or the internal struggles between the
hierarchs of the Catholic Church in Ireland and the Redemptorists, with their
fierce commitment to independence? To the Jews, none of this mattered.
Jewish immigrants opted for places undergoing rapid changes in their fundamental class, national, racial, and gendered environments, which made them
promising for commerce. Those changes benefited the Jews but also exposed
them to antipathy as exemplars and beneficiaries of changes that many feared.

The episode in Limerick, so surprising to the *American Jewish Yearbook*,
constituted the single most blatant act of organized antipeddler action
that took place in the Jews' new world. It might be considered the standard
against which to measure others. Nowhere else did such a respected

individual, someone of Creagh's stature, use such a powerful institution to preach a boycott against Jewish peddlers and in no other place else did such action last as long or involve as much nastiness and mayhem.[8]

OUTRAGES ELSEWHERE IN THE NEW WORLD

The Limerick affair had lesser equivalents around the Jewish peddlers' new world. Similar transformation elsewhere also unleashed controversies over peddling and the Jewish presence. The arrival of the Jews, and their weekly circumambulations of the countryside, in Ireland or Quebec, Cuba or South Africa, stirred up conflicts and made the Jews in general, and the peddlers in particular, social and political issues.

Anti–Jewish peddler incidents popped up, although in milder form, worldwide. In all such episodes, rhetoric about the Jewish peddlers as non-Christians, foreigners, and purveyors of capitalism and mass consumption served the purposes of some local players. Such rhetoric brought with it scurrilous, racialized language, sometimes resounding with classic anti-Jewish imagery. Some such nasty talk spilled over into physical assaults and some property damage. Like the antipeddler action in Limerick, the episodes in other places reflected on-the-ground political and social divisions. The flare-ups that involved Jewish peddlers sprouted out of a convergence of forces simultaneous with, but independent of, the arrival of the peddlers.

As we have seen, most immigrant Jewish peddlers had positive encounters with their customers. Yet the history of Jewish peddling in the new world also included moments of physical violence, spurts of political agitation, jealousy by local merchants, and public mockery. Peddling carried risk and danger beyond exposure to inclement weather, accidents, and long hours of trudging the roads. The very nature of peddling and the Jewishness of the peddlers opened them up to danger. Everywhere peddlers went they stirred up local controversies, riling up some residents of the surrounding area who had reasons to want to keep the peddlers out. When the immigrant Jewish peddlers took to the roads, they stepped onto someone else's turf, disrupting racial, religious, class, and gender realities. Those disruptions inspired calls for protective actions against them. Sol Levitan, an immigrant peddler from Russia who eventually became the state treasurer of Wisconsin, recalled that numerous small towns of the state posted warning signs on their outskirts that proclaimed, "No Peddlers Allowed."[9]

What lay behind "No Peddlers Allowed"? What perils did the peddlers face, complicating the otherwise benign exchanges between them and their customers? What predominated in the history of new-world Jewish peddling, the warm welcome on the path to integration and citizenship or hostility, mockery, and exclusion? What immigrant Jewish peddlers endured, be it the brandishing of weapons by armed thieves on the road or the actions of local shopkeepers who used their political clout to try to keep the peddlers out, affected non-Jewish peddlers no less than the Jews. Licenses imposed on peddlers had nothing to do with the religious background of the peddler and everything to do with settled merchants' fear of losing business. Being a peddler, rather than being a Jew, proved to be the problem. But on the other hand, much of the rhetoric used against Jewish peddlers highlighted their Jewishness. Those who had problems with peddlers, whether cultural or economic, dipped into a full trove of centuries-old anti-Jewish slogans and phrases. Father Creagh expertly demonstrated that.

REVISITING MAX WEBER

Much anti-Jewish peddler talk and action took place in Catholic countries. Catholicism had a centuries-long tradition of warning its communicants of the spiritual dangers of excessive enjoyment of material goods. Max Weber's early-twentieth-century masterpiece *The Protestant Ethic and the Spirit of Capitalism* pivoted on the premise that Catholicism's theologically based condemnation of materialism meant that capitalism could arise only after the Reformation had loosened the church's hold on Europeans. While theorists have long debated this theory, the greatest opposition to Jewish peddlers erupted in two intensely Catholic societies, Ireland and Quebec.

The Quebec story closely resembles Ireland's. Jews constituted the largest foreign immigrant group who came to Quebec, and, as in Ireland, the only sizable population of non-Catholics. While many Quebec-bound Russian and Romanian Jewish immigrants gravitated to Montreal and its garment industry, large numbers fanned out into the countryside, selling as peddlers to farmers. The Catholic Church dominated rural life, exerting its influence in everyday matters, providing the Francophone farmers with a deep sense of belonging. Quebec Catholicism embraced French ultramontanism—much like Jansenism, a theological and political ideology that rejected liberal democracy, modernity, and the choice and consumption celebrated by individualism.

Just as many Irish emigrated to the United States during the era of the Jewish immigration and the heyday of Jewish peddling, substantial numbers of Quebecois headed to northern New England to work in the textile mills, logging camps, and other regional industries dependent on unskilled labor.

Like their Irish counterparts, French Canadian immigrants sustained kin and communities back home, sending remittances, raising the standard of living, putting more money in circulation. The cross-border flow of cash and the increased value of land and labor enabled new kinds and levels of material consumption, allowing the poor to aspire to own more goods and actually to acquire many of them.

Into this new rural environment came the Jewish peddlers, their sacks bursting with consumer goods, their foreignness and their religion so blatant. In Quebec anti-Jewish rhetoric emanated from the rural areas where the peddlers plied their trade, and where the Quebec Catholic clergy wielded substantial clout. Priests and writers for Catholic publications consistently posited the Jews as harbingers of a corrupt modern civilization that "impoverished and degraded man and robbed life of its poetry and truth." They admonished the Quebecois not to buy from the peddlers, who sucked the lifeblood out of the people. They exhorted the women to ignore the Jews' alluring goods and sharp tongues. The founding of L'Association catholique de la jeunesse canadienne in 1893 made the threat posed by the Jews to Catholic Quebec a cardinal concern, and a 1905 editorial in its newspaper, *La Croix*—the cross—declared that the Jews "threaten to overrun us. . . . These penniless immigrants for the most part have no aptitude for productive labour. In order to stay alive, they will have to exploit us in their usual way." That "usual" way meant peddling. Words like that segued into calls for political action, demands on the government to levy special taxes on peddlers as a way to dissuade them from coming into the province.[10]

The national state, Canada, as some in Quebec saw it, lay in the hands of outsiders, English-speaking Protestants, who wielded political and economic power. Like Irish nationalists, the Quebecois saw themselves as victims of English imperialism and viewed the Jews, as agents of Anglo-Canada, as English in spirit. In Quebec as in Ireland, the religious and spiritual opposition to the peddlers stemmed in part from the association of the Jewish peddlers with the hated extraneous force that had subjugated and exploited the French, depriving them of their rightful independence. In Ireland many Jewish peddler goods did in fact come from England, and in Quebec many came from Toronto or the United States, both associated with Anglophone hegemony. Those who viewed the peddlers as agents of the hated Anglo imperialists turned on the peddlers as easily identifiable symbols of the outrage perpetrated against their nation.

Ireland and Quebec shared this burning anti-English nationalism fused organically with Catholicism and its discomfort with material possession. The antipeddler actions of these places resembled the antipeddler activities that flared in various parts of Central and South America. In the 1920s and 1930s highly charged antipeddler rhetoric led to street-level agitation, as protest meetings called on governments to curb the peddlers by imposing higher and higher fees on their licenses and to curtail the admission of Jewish peddlers.

Mexicans, Cubans, Colombians, Brazilians, Peruvians, and Uruguayans all at times demanded that their governments limit the entry of Jews and make it impossible for them to peddle. Unlike their counterparts in Ireland and Quebec, they did not link their opposition to Jews to religious matters or to yearnings for a simpler, purer mythic past. Rather, they pointed to the reality that Jewish peddlers acquired goods from within the Jewish economic chain, one that extended to the giant behemoth of the north, the United States. With this mercantile clout behind them, critics claimed, the Jewish foreigners could undersell local merchants. State officials complied with the wishes of their own business class, who launched these protests. After all, these businessmen participated in national politics, unlike the Jews, who did not, and at times could not, attain citizenship. President Óscar Benavides of Peru decreed in 1936 all itinerant trade illegal, stipulating that all merchants have fixed locations from which to do their business.[11]

The countries of Latin America, like Ireland and Quebec, had complicated histories of business development, the spread of capitalism, and the creation of mass consumer societies. Those complications underscored Weber's ideas about capitalism and the emergence of the "Protestant ethic." In his view the two went together inasmuch as capitalism depended on the acquisition of wealth, fueled in no small part by the sale of goods. The sale of goods depended on the willingness of individuals to part with their money to buy things, some unnecessary for basic survival. In Protestantism, he asserted, the acquisition and display of goods betokened a state of grace. When, to put it simplistically, people earned enough money to buy wares and show them off in their homes and on their bodies, they demonstrated to themselves and to others that God had smiled on them.

It should then follow that Jewish peddlers met no hostility, confronted no concerted political action, or heard no nasty words in the Protestant parts of the new world to which they emigrated. But in fact in every place, regardless of predominant religious denomination, someone considered these immigrant Jews a threat to some value or cornerstone of social and political life. Outbreaks of rage against Jewish peddlers flared where Lutheranism, Calvinism, or other Protestant religions held sway, just as they did in Catholic cultures.

A widely reported demonstration against immigrant Jewish peddlers took place in solidly Protestant Wales in 1911, in the coal mining area around

Tredegar, in the Monmouth Valley. Jewish peddlers used Tredegar as their base for their journeys in and out of the villages where miners lived. The more successful peddlers by 1911 already owned stores in Tredegar, and like their peers around the new world, the Jewish peddlers outfitted themselves in these shops, getting the goods they carried to their customers in the valleys. "Trebellers" doubled as money lenders as in Ireland, providing cash to the impoverished coal mining families.

On the night of August 19, a Saturday, when the peddlers would be back in town, two hundred or so young men, described by some as singing Welsh hymns, went on a rampage, attacking the Jewish-owned shops. The rioting and looting raged for a few nights as outbreaks flared in other towns in the region, all directed at the Jewish-owned shops that supplied the peddlers. The looters made off with loads of goods, including watches and jewelry, the very items that the peddlers would have carried into the countryside. The attackers vented their rage on the Jewish-owned stores, but the peddlers felt the pinch. They feared venturing out on their customary circuits. As long as the riots raged and the specter of violence floated through the valley, they could not go out to collect the money owed them or make new sales.

Great social and economic transformations underlay the action in Tredegar. Rural Wales had since the middle of the nineteenth century inexorably changed from a land of farming and grazing to one of coal mining. The lives of its poor people altered as onetime farmers, either small owners or tenants of landowners, now worked for coal companies, drawing meager wages. Periodic strikes and actions against the companies took place, always followed by suppressions of the strikes by local authorities. Meaningful improvements in the conditions of labor and life were not forthcoming. A particularly intense set of strikes had broken out in late 1910. The coal operators hired strikebreakers, many foreigners. Local governments called up their constabularies, and by November the home secretary in London, Winston Churchill, sent in the army to quell the strikes. The ten-month strike, punctuated by a series of riots, arrests, and prosecutions of strikers, came to an end in August 1911, the same month when the attack on the Jewish shops that outfitted the peddlers commenced.[12] The Jewish merchants and their peddler foot soldiers became the strike's collateral damage. Being foreigners, handlers of cash, successful newcomers who prospered amid the continuing poverty of the miners, the Jews were perfect targets of local outrage.[13]

Governments in other overwhelmingly Protestant countries attempted to keep out or severely restrict the access of Jewish peddlers. Sweden provides a case in point. In the middle of the nineteenth century Sweden witnessed the influx of Jews, mostly peddlers from Lithuania, and Swedish lawmakers put up obstacles to keep them out. Swedish immigration laws specifically mentioned Jews and peddlers, hoping to discourage them. The law stipulated that only citizens could obtain peddler licenses, although by 1879 Jewish immigrant peddlers, mostly from Lithuania, had received permission to apply for special permits that allowed them to ply their itinerant trade. Swedish farmer and merchant associations lobbied hard to erect increasingly higher barriers to the entry of peddlers, and to make it even more difficult for them to secure these licenses. Fewer than half of the Jews who applied got the licenses, and while no major conflagration took place—no windows were broken, no Jews assaulted—this deeply Lutheran country considered the immigration of Jewish peddlers a threat to its social, cultural, and economic order.[14]

England and the English-speaking parts of Canada, Australia, and South Africa likewise had their share of words and deeds, uttered and undertaken by one element or another, against the Jewish peddlers. In South Africa the Cape Parliament in 1908 held a set of hearings on the problem of the hawkers. One witness after another testified that the peddlers "come to the farmers and force them to buy, and then would prosecute them to compel them to pay, very often whether they were able to pay or not." The legislators scrutinized and condemned hawkers in general, some of whom happened to be Indians. But Jews figured prominently as the objects of these hearings, as those whom the Select Committee on Asiatic Grievances hoped to deter. The representative of the Hawkers' Association, a Mr. Jacob Isenstein, pleaded that he and his fellow smous had followed all the rules. They applied to the Municipal Council, as the law required, for licenses, but had been denied. Mr. Isenstein noted that since "the majority of the bodies representing the Municipalities of Cape Town and districts are composed of shopkeepers, and these shopkeepers will not grant hawkers' licenses," the rejected hawkers just evaded the law. Isenstein suggested that the lawmakers ask Mr. J. Wenetzky, Mr. J. Arenson, Mr. D. Shapero, and Mr. Lipschitz, as well as Robinowitz and Meyerowitz, who had just come from Russia. While the word "Jew" did not in fact come up, their Jewishness and foreignness could not have been ignored.[15]

Less neutral depictions of the evil connections between Jews and peddling wafted through South African politics and journalism. A correspondent for the *Cape Times*, describing in print his trip to Bushmanland in the 1890s, remarked on the Jews' prevalence there. He told his readers, "Not a day passes but there is . . . a Jew with his cart or wagon coming to the squatters tent or hut, and making himself at home there for several days." The Jew, according to this writer, came to those poor people, "eating their food without paying for it, or doing or giving anything in return, and as they as a rule give unlimited credit and 'tick' to the Dutch and half-caste squatters, they thus have them altogether in their power."[16]

AMERICA: LIKE EVERYPLACE ELSE

What about the United States, the place to which the vast majority of the emigrating Jews went? Weber's *Protestant Ethic* had much to say about America, drawing from the writings of Benjamin Franklin, especially his *Autobiography* and Poor Richard's aphorisms. Weber considered the United States the epicenter of consumer capitalism, the paradise for the embrace of worldly success and the acquisition of material goods. A long line of other commentators have associated Americans with materialism, consumerism, and the worship of things. Alexis de Tocqueville in the 1830s made much of American materialism in *Democracy*, commenting that "the taste for material enjoyments must be considered the first source" of what moves Americans. The American celebrates the goods he has, Tocqueville noted, and "imagines a thousand others that death will prevent him from enjoying if he does not hasten." As a people, Tocqueville's Americans "dream constantly of the goods they do not have."[17]

Like many other observers of American life, Tocqueville connected Americans' love of goods to their fierce commitment to individualism. Surely such a place would not provide a fertile field for antipeddler action. But Sol Levitan's comment that towns in Wisconsin planted signs on their borders warning peddlers away belies that logic. Throughout the country, across decades, communities, under pressure from local businessmen, did what they could to impede the peddlers' roads. Whether in the Deep South, the Great Plains, New England, the upper Midwest, or the Far West, state governments and local jurisdictions placated storeowners, backbones of the local power structure, by imposing licenses with stiff fees on itinerant traders, then repeatedly raising fees, forcing peddlers to renew their licenses often, and trying to restrict licenses to naturalized citizens.

Jews paid close attention to changes in the licensing laws, noting when and where they became harsher or enforcement more efficient, and brought communal institutions to bear to mitigate the severity of such legislation. A correspondent to the *Jewish Messenger* in 1858 shared with readers the news that New Hampshire had "lately passed an oppressive law relative to peddlers which has caused the removal of several Israelites, reducing their number." A South Carolinian requirement that peddlers be bonded with the state treasurer in order to operate within the state's borders forced established Jewish merchants, those who supplied the peddlers' goods and credit, to serve as the legal bonders for the peddlers. Several successful Atlanta Jewish businessmen marshaled their political clout in 1891, petitioning the Georgia House of Representatives to repeal a law that replaced statewide licensing with a system that required a peddler to get an individual license for each county he entered. Levi Cohen, Joseph Steiner, and others charged that "these poor strangers," rather than being criminals who evaded the law, "had been *molested* or to say *robbed*, by some so-called bailiffs."[18] One of the most widely read Yiddish-language guidebooks for Jewish immigrants or would-be immigrants stated, in boldface type that appears nowhere else in the book, "A person who is found trading as peddler without a license or contrary to the terms of his license, or who refuses to produce his license on the demand of any officer or citizen, is guilty of a crime. Maximum penalty 1 year in prison."[19]

Incidents in which anti-Jewish rage segued into antipeddler rage, and the converse, when anger at peddlers who happened to be Jewish folded into hostility toward Jews collectively, appear in the record only during the Civil War. Under the banners of both the Union and the Confederacy, wartime tensions made the otherwise innocuous peddlers seem threatening to one side and the other. Union order number 11, issued by General Ulysses S. Grant in December 1862, expelled all "the Jews, as a class," from the "Department of the Tennessee." "As a class," the Jews, the general declared, had been "violating every regulation of trade established by the Treasury Department" as they went from place to place selling goods. Once the area, covering Kentucky and Tennessee, had been reopened to northerners after occupation by the Union Army, Jewish peddlers, among others, "swarmed" in, according to the Order. Grant, on his way to Vicksburg, sought to impose order to the territory he commanded. The Jewish peddlers, seemingly oblivious to boundaries, undermined his efforts. Order number 11 seemed a perfect solution. General Henry Halleck, Grant's commanding officer, encouraged him, saying that neither he nor President Lincoln objected "to your expelling traitors and Jew peddlers."[20] On the other side of the blue-gray divide, some residents of Talbotton, Georgia, in 1862—the same year of Grant's order—decided that the three Jewish families who lived in the town and the peddlers who used it as their base had brought economic ruin upon the community. The town passed a resolution ejecting the resident Jews and barring the peddlers from Thomas County. According to prevailing wisdom, the Jews circulated counterfeit money. Why did the locals pinpoint the blame on the Jews? According to the *Daily Morning News* of September 12, "the itinerancy of all between certain ages relieves them from the burden of the war, both in money and service." These people, the article claimed, "are not identified, in the strictest sense, with the permanent interests of our soil and institutions."[21]

Though acts of politically inspired violence and efforts to bar Jewish peddlers were widespread, they represented rare exceptions rather than the norm in the history of new-world Jewish peddling. But despite the rarity of such action, peddling posed many hazards for the Jewish immigrant men who went out on the road.

THE PERILS OF PEDDLING

Ironically, the most frequent danger peddlers encountered had nothing to do with their Jewishness, their foreign origins, or the political and social upheavals roiling the countries and regions where they had gone. Rather, they faced the hazards of being men on the road with money and valuable goods. Usually unarmed, they often traveled alone on sparsely traversed roads. Their money, if stolen, could not be traced, and their wares could be easily fenced by those emboldened to rob them. Moses Pincus peddled in England in the 1840s and suffered bodily injury from robbers on the road who were attracted by the forty-five watches, four clusters of pearls, silver snuff box, silver cup, and lace sewn with silver that he carried, along with some cash. These goods, valued at £73, 12s, caught the eye of a thief, who saw the open box and could "see my pearls and watches." Poor Moses Pincus fell victim a second time to a robber and lost his box and all his cash. His travails had their sad equivalents all over the new world, making robbery an occupational hazard of peddling, an assumed part of life on the road.[22]

Peddlers slept in the homes of strangers and had no reason to feel confident that their goods would be there in the morning. In fact, they could not be certain even that they would wake up the next morning. One former peddler recalled in his memoir of his days in the Hudson River Valley in the 1850s, "I went to bed, but could not sleep. I knew that I was in a wilderness, that I might be killed and all I possessed taken." The memoirist Isaac Frank recalled his mild anxiety translating into sheer terror when, "sure enough, about 12 o'clock two men, each having a gun, came into my room (imagine how I felt) and went into the next room. Then all was quiet. Could not go to sleep that night, for I did not know what might happen." (No one interfered with him.)[23]

Hardly paranoid or overexcitable, Frank was justified in his fears. Reports circulated through the Jewish world about the murders of Jewish peddlers, with no place exempt as a real or potential setting for homicide. The year

Frank came to America, the *Jewish Chronicle* reported the murder of two Jewish hawkers at Clark's Station, in the gold fields of Australia's Victoria Province. Just a few years later yet another vulnerable Jewish peddler fell victim to murder at Carr's Plains near Glenorchy.[24] Such robbery-murders connected the late eighteenth century with the early twentieth and knew no geographic boundaries. In Cuba, South Africa, Mexico, Great Britain, Canada, and every region in the United States, lone Jews were robbed on the road and murdered for their goods.

Stories of the robbery and murder of Jewish peddlers filled the pages of local newspapers, which considered these crimes matters of grave public significance, as they demonstrated the absence of law and order. When these murders took place, the full force of the state came to bear to identify the assailants, bring them to trial, and punish them if found guilty. As white men, the peddlers deserved protection, and outrages against them constituted outrages against local norms. Newspaper headlines detailed crime against Jewish peddlers and subsequent punishment in widespread communities: "Hillman Guilty of Murder" (Woodbury, New Jersey), "Overton Was Hanged" (Middlesboro, Kentucky), "Louisiana Negroes Executed" (Hahnville, Louisiana), "A Day's Hanging" (Elkton, Maryland), "Two Brothers Hanged" (Franklin, North Carolina). Governments subjected those who had killed Jewish peddlers to the most severe of punishments, as defined by the law. They did not consider the life of a Jewish peddler, a foreigner with minimal roots in the local community, to be of negligible value. Irving Engel, the son of a Russian immigrant peddler, recalled that when he was a boy growing up in Cottondale, Alabama, "there was much excitement in the family, because a Jewish peddler had been robbed and murdered. . . . The murderer was apprehended, convicted and sentenced to be hung. The Sheriff got in touch with my father and offered to send him a ticket of admission to the hanging." His father declined the generous invitation, but the son wondered about the sheriff's motivation, musing, "Perhaps it was merely based upon the Sheriff's assumption that one Jew would like to witness the hanging of the murderer of another Jew."[25]

The murder of Jewish peddlers riled up local communities populated exclusively by non-Jews. These Christians responded with outrage even when local men, individuals with roots in the town or region, stood accused. The 1849 murder of Nathan Adler at the hands of the three Baham brothers in Cayuga County, New York, provides a case in point. The young German man, "professing the Jewish faith," carried goods in his trunk, including jewelry, valued at about $400. Adler had passed through the town of Venice and stopped at the Baham home several times. Mrs. Baham had bought from him, and like many customers of peddlers, she owed him money. When Adler did not show up at a designated rendezvous with his brothers, they began to worry that Nathan had met foul play and notified the authorities. Shortly thereafter a search party organized by the sheriff's office found his battered body. In the course of the investigation, law enforcement officials arrested the Baham brothers, indicted them, and tried them for the murder. Neighbors reported to the authorities that the Baham brothers had been flashing wads of money. One neighbor after another testified against them in court, and local opinion concurred that they deserved to be punished, despite their insider status as sons of a local family. A locally produced and published account expressed sympathy for the victim, a Jew of "prepossessing appearance and agreeable manners." The Bahams went to their deaths on the gallows. A local publisher put together a substantial account of *The Particulars of the Murder of Nathan Adler on the Night of November Sixth, 1849, Venice, Cayuga County, N.Y.* The somewhat sensationalistic booklet not only included all the testimonies given to the coroner but showed that the life of an immigrant Jewish peddler counted for something among the ordinary folk of upstate New York.[26]

The victim's Jewishness did not escape public scrutiny or press discussion, although sympathy favored the unfortunate peddler. "Liquor and Jealousy," blared the headline of the *Raleigh News and Observer* on July 14, 1894, "Lead Two Brothers to Murder a Jewish Peddler at the House of Lucy and Pinkey Brewer in Franklin County."[27] The *Examiner and Democratic Herald* of Lancaster, Pennsylvania, in 1839 told of the discovery by two boys of a body on the outskirts of the town. The body bore all the marks of a grisly murder, with a "wound . . . in the neck of about two inches in length, severing several muscles, the juglar [*sic*] vein and the artery of the face. In addition . . . there were three wounds on the chin and chest, together with violent contusions on the forehead and the bridge of the nose was broken. There were four direct stabs in the back of the neck, one in the abdomen . . . two in the right thigh. His hands were shockingly lacerated, consisted of a long deep incision on each hand. . . . There were several stabs in the hands, showing a disposition to hold the hands up, while the thrusts were made at him." The article concluded with a "P.S. . . . The deceased Was a Hebrew or Jew, a Pedlar of Dry Goods, Jewelry and German Silver . . . Lazarus Zellerbach," who had carried $1,000 in cash along with his goods. The victim "is said to have been a quiet man and could scarcely have been led into a quarrel."

The reporting on the Zellerbach murder highlighted the dangers to peddlers. It identified the victim as Jewish. It gushed with the sensationalistic details and clearly painted the portrait of a brutal killing. It also informed the public that the mayor of Lancaster was offering a reward of $300 for the apprehension of the killer and the governor another $250. Henry Musselman was arrested as a suspect, and like the murderers of the North Carolina Jewish peddler, he was found guilty by a jury; a few months later he went to the gallows.[28]

Unfortunate peddlers got shot, axed, stabbed, and beaten to death, but not because of their Jewishness. Culprits who confessed to their crimes and explained why they committed them did not cite their victims' Jewishness. Even when reports of the murders, trials, and executions invoked "the Jew peddler" to identify the victim, the fact of his having been a Jew or a peddler did not exculpate the guilty or mitigate the severity of the crime in the eyes of the state, the press, and the non-Jewish public, all of whom considered the murderers of Jewish peddlers deserving of the punishment mandated by law and the peddlers men whose murders merited retribution.[29]

IMAGINING THE JEWISH PEDDLER IN THE NEW WORLD

Jewish peddlers, men who took it upon themselves to learn the intricacies of local culture, not only must have recognized the dangers they faced but must have known that popular culture mocked them, making their Jewishness central to the mockery. The Jewish peddler, often the "Jew peddler," emerged as a stock figure in the common discourse. Usually referred to in the singular, to imply that one Jewish peddler resembled all others, he provided commentators in the press, whether writing in a humorous or serious tone, as well as dramatists, songwriters, novelists, and other creators of popular entertainment, a character to ridicule. The "Jew peddler" stood outside the norm. Sinister and shadowy, exotic or absurd, he made a good subject for mockery, with his odd accent, his clothing, his lack of a fixed abode, and his distinctive bodily features: in this milieu, a prominent hooked nose was a sure sign of Jewishness, a long beard a likely trait as well.

The character of the "Jew Peddler"—or in England, "Jew Pedlar"—ran through English-language literature and theater, cartooning, and folk humor. Carrying a sack or a bundle of some kind, the Jewish peddler represented trickery, otherness, and greed. Having opted for a "pedling way of Life," as invoked by one pamphleteer in the 1750s in England during debates over a naturalization bill that would have legalized Jews' residence, he stood outside the norm. The "pedling way of life," and the Jews' natural gravitation to it, emphasized how the peddler differed from other, normal men. The "pedling way of life" linked modern Jewish peddlers to the medieval image of the eternally wandering Jew, forced to roam the earth because of the racial blame he bore for the Crucifixion. Peddler imagery in England, the United States, the Cape Colony, and indeed most places emphasized the immigrant peddler's mangling of the common language, the clothes that marked his otherness, and his vigilant pursuit of monetary gain, no matter how obtained.[30]

Words used to describe peddlers and deeds undertaken against Jewish peddlers had a kind of universality that erased the vast differences between, say, late-eighteenth-century England and early-twentieth-century Cuba. Images in one place resembled those in others: peddlers appeared as shadowy figures who went in and out of towns and regions, unaccountable to local rules, outside of the spatial moral order, and dependent upon their verbal skills to get people, mostly women, to buy unnecessary and useless items.[31] The particular tropes employed to describe Jewish peddlers did not differ much from those used for other, non-Jewish peddlers. In American rhetoric and popular culture, Jewish peddlers and Yankee peddlers were depicted as equally sharp, devious, avaricious, and at times comical, demonstrating that Jewishness was not essential to the mockery and negative rhetoric.[32] In the United States, Irish peddlers also found themselves to be the brunt of ridicule.[33] In the Cape Colony the word *smous*, the itinerant seller of household goods, was applied to non-Jews as well as Jews, and throughout Latin America and the Caribbean, Arab peddlers found themselves subjected to the same discrimination and pressures for exclusion as did Jews. Attendants at public meetings in Cuba, Argentina, and Brazil clamored against peddlers and did not distinguish between Arabs and Jews. The assembled crowds claimed that both harmed local people and both had to be curtailed.[34]

While all peddlers endured such stereotypes, the mockery of the Jewish peddlers came with a special twist, part of a long centuries-old history of being outsiders in someone else's land. While the creators and consumers of these tropes in the new world, many of them customers of the peddlers, may simply have just found such depictions funny, the slights existed in a global context in which the Jewish peddlers by the simple act of traversing the countryside selling goods inspired discussions about basic cultural values, shook up social relationships, inspired fears of change, and represented perceived threats against the local vested interests of those who really belonged in these places.

In the societies where peddlers worked, elites—whether religious, political, or intellectual—expressed deep misgivings about the spread of mass consumption beyond the level of simple necessity. Even America, the quintessential consumer society, produced its own strain of an anticonsumption ideology. Some writers, orators, ministers, and organizers of social movements advocated for the simple life, one characterized by saving rather than spending, essentials rather than luxuries; such voices deplored the veneration of things over ideas. Much of the anticonsumption rhetoric came from the top down, as elites considered it wrong for the poor to aspire to improve their material lot, to have goods previously limited to the better-off classes. Be it based on a desire to preserve their own privilege, a need to distinguish themselves from their subordinates, or a fear that the poor, once set on the road to consumption, would be dissatisfied with their subordination in the political realm as well, elite political and cultural commentators depicted the Jewish peddlers as exploiters of the poor, sowing the seeds of discontent among their poor customers.

Jewish peddlers stumbled into societies where fault lines divided the poor, who viewed the chance to acquire new goods as an enhancement of their lives, and the well off, often the employers, who saw danger in the yearning of the poor for those goods. Whether the critics of consumption really sought to protect the poor from unscrupulous merchants mattered less than that they laced their critiques of materialism with critiques of Jewish peddlers as distributors of unnecessary goods to the masses. Whether writing about Mexican laborers, Afrikaner farmers, or African-American slaves, those who fretted over the buying habits of the poor depicted the Jewish peddlers as the exploiters of the underclasses. They claimed that Jewish peddlers sold shoddy goods to people with few means, that they convinced unsophisticated women and men to waste money on cheap trinkets, cheap furnishings, and cheap clothes. A 1912 piece in the *African Standard*, a newspaper serving the white, English population of British East Africa, contemplated the possible impact of the never-realized plan to develop a Jewish colony in Uganda. The writer pointed out that the Jews who would come there would be fit only "for hawkers and petty traders," and predicted, "It is pretty safe to say that within six months of their arrival five out of every ten of them will . . . be swindling the natives and that the other five will have gone back to their native country with enough money to start an 'old clo' [clothes] shop."[35]

This editorial accused Jewish peddlers of cheating those least able to afford the mess of glittery nonessential goods. It made two other points that ran through the global commentary on Jewish peddlers. The first involved reference to "the natives." Critics often considered that Jewish peddlers' enterprises broke down natural social boundaries. The peddlers in the American South, in the West, in coal country, in the sugar, rubber, and cotton regions of South America and the Caribbean, and in southern Africa, threatened the status quo by allowing African Americans, poor whites, coal miners, unskilled laborers, and the "natives" of whatever region the chance to possess goods resembling those owned by their social and economic superiors. The Cuban and Jamaican plantation workers could, after the arrival of the Jewish peddlers, own ties and watches and go to town wearing such accoutrements of affluence. They adorned themselves with a few material signs of prosperity just as their employers did. The slaves in America's cotton belt could, with the peddlers' forays onto the plantations, furnish their cabins with bric-a-brac not so different from that found in the planter's house.

The Jewish immigrant peddlers did not do this barrier busting for ideological reasons, to bring about social change. They did it because these women and men had some money to spend and hankered for these goods. But the desire of the subordinated for material objects and the satisfaction they experienced threatened the structure of local life, which maintained the centrality of class and the power of the elite over the poor. The *African Standard* editorialist probably had no particular concern for the well-being of the "natives," but he had a clear stake in the maintenance of colonial power, which rested on the truth that indigenous people needed little beyond the basics.

The comment from British East Africa made a second global point. The writer assumed that the Jewish peddlers, having connived to sell cheap goods to the natives, would take the money and run, making no commitment to the place. The relationships the Jewish peddlers forged with local people grew out of their desire to make money, not out of a loyalty to the community, the editorialist declared. Here today and gone tomorrow, these transient figures came into a region, went house to house, showed up weekly for some period of time, and then, with no meaningful ties, left as abruptly as they had arrived.

As strangers, Jewish peddlers inspired fear; as transients, they inspired resentment. Their wanderings rendered them, according to prevailing community sentiment around their new world, outside of the local moral universe. Unaccountable to anyone, they stayed just within the limits of the law, coming and going according to their own timetables. Since they lacked roots, local matters mattered little to them. They would never settle down and become community members and taxpayers.

The reporters for R. G. Dunn had much to say about Jews in general and peddlers in particular, and the Jews' transience figured prominently in those reports. Even when Dunn reporters considered individual Jewish peddlers sober, industrious, responsible, well liked by customers, and steadily successful, they raised the red flag of transience. In tens of thousands of individual narratives Dunn notetakers emphasized that peddlers invested in no property other than the goods on their backs and their wagons. To Dunn reporters this portended that when the peddler achieved what he wanted, he would be gone.

Transience inspired suspicion. Guardians of the local order wanted peddlers gone. Sir William Pitt, serving at the end of the eighteenth century as the
Portsmouth garrison commander, was unhappy about the "great number of
suspicious itinerant Jews . . . in the Town of Portsmouth." Impressed, in contrast, by the settled Jews of Portsmouth, "many of them very respectable
Tradesmen," Pitt had little good to say about the itinerants, who "have since
been found out & removed from hence by the activity & vigilance of the
Magistrates." Their coming into and going out of the town—their being at
once present and absent—troubled him.[36]

Jewish peddlers' immigrant status fueled anxiety. They differed from local
people in religion, language, dress, and occupation. In general, the places that
experienced the least immigration became the hottest spots for antipeddler
sentiment. To Ireland, Wales, Sweden, and Quebec few immigrants came
other than the Jews. Other places, such as Australia, South Africa, and the
countries of Latin America and the Caribbean, attracted some immigrants, but
from a limited number of places, and Jews and the Chinese tended to be the
only non-Christians.[37] On the other hand, the places most receptive to peddlers
and the least likely to subject them to violence—namely, the United States and
the English-speaking regions of Canada—attracted the greatest diversity of
immigrants. In the United States in particular, the choice destination for most
Jews, the Jews' foreignness did not make them particularly noteworthy. They
came to a place bursting with immigrants from every European country and
region. To Anglophone ears, their Yiddish differed little from the Czech,
Hungarian, Polish, Italian, Greek, and Lithuanian spoken by other immigrants. Jewish peddlers took their place alongside a vast array of other immigrants filling other economic niches.

But even in the United States, anti-Jewish peddler and antiforeigner rhetoric and, at times, political action, such as Grant's expulsion order, reflected a
multistranded fear. The peddlers, in the "nation of immigrants" and elsewhere
around the world, inspired fear on a number of counts, and each of these shadowed the Jewish peddlers as they made their rounds of the countryside.

The peddler as stranger outside the norm served as a foundational image.
Literature abounds with these figures, and in nineteenth- and early-twentieth-
century America, the "Jew peddler" appeared not only on the stage and in
sheet music but at costume parties, as a popular masquerade. Local newspapers from small communities across the United States, reporting on social
events, included masked balls and other costumed frolics, detailing the attendance of guests as pirates, as witches, as princesses, and as "Jew peddlers."
The men and women who donned the garb of the Jewish peddler must have

thought that they were being quite clever and funny, but they also tapped into the deepest feelings about the peddlers. No one really knew them, and unlike the pirates and the princesses, goblins and ghosts, Jewish men laden with their sacks were seen regularly in the community. They might be considered familiar strangers, at once quotidian and mysterious.

With no local roots, Jewish peddlers could be accused of the unexpected, of anything dangerous to the social order and the community's well-being. When some local boys in Birmingham, Connecticut, found "a green substance" in the water, later discovered to be poisonous, local people, knowing that "the cause for this outrage cannot be ascertained," logically surmised "that the poison was placed in the water by a Jew peddler who passed the day previous and at whom several boys who were in the back yard threw stones."[38] A rumor spread through St. Louis, Missouri, and the adjoining area that a Russian Jewish peddler, Wolf Pickner, had introduced cholera. "Little is known of Pickner's history," and "how long he has been in this country is not known," reported the local newspaper, revealing the global trope about Jewish peddlers who slipped in to places, unbeknownst to everyone else, and then slipped out. He died while in St. Louis of cholera, and the headline of the *Chicago Tribune* blared, "The plague Introduced by a Russian Jew Peddler." The subsequent sentence confirmed the bond between Jewish peddlers and the transgression of social boundaries: "A Negro the Second Victim."[39]

With no local ties, Jewish peddlers often found themselves accused of crimes. They usually had not committed those crimes, but they were guilty—everywhere—of peddling without a license. Among themselves they devised strategies to evade license fees. Some peddlers tried to get away without paying the rental fees for the horses and wagons they used. During their weekends off the road, when peddlers spent time in each other's company, they may have swapped strategies on how best to break the rules. David Saltz, who peddled on Maryland's eastern shore in the 1890s, might have told his fellow Jewish peddlers who clustered on the Sabbath in Annapolis how he tricked a policeman and escaped paying for the rental on his wagon and horse. Other peddlers may have regaled one another with war stories about arrests, appearances before judges, and the like.[40]

But they probably did not distribute cocaine, as a writer for the *New York Times* suggested in 1908, going so far as to assert that "there is little doubt that every Jew peddler carries the stuff." Typical of much American anti-Jewish peddler discourse, the article declared that the peddlers dealt this drug primarily "among the negroes," who called it "heaven dust." Specifically pinpointing the "negro" field hands in the cotton plantations as the Jewish cocaine dealers' best customers, the article once again emphasized Jewish peddlers' violation of accepted racial borders.[41]

Such accusations made sense. Individual men, roaming countryside back-roads, with no known abode and no local ties, the peddlers made perfect suspects for murder, rape, and robbery. One man who lived in late-nineteenth-century Pennsylvania recalled an "old maid, employed as a housekeeper. . . . One time the maid started to get very stout," and when her pregnancy showed, she "insisted a Jew peddler had raped her."[42] Elsewhere in Pennsylvania a 1904 newspaper reported the discovery of the body of a murdered woman, found on her McKeesport-area farm. "The culprit," the *Daily News* reported, "could not be found but as a Jewish peddler, a stranger in town, was last seen on the premises . . . he was apprehended in Altoona." The peddler, probably with minimal English and traumatized by his arrest, failed to give a good account of his whereabouts at the time of the crime. After keeping him in jail for several months, "in spite of the vouching for him of the President of the Russian Jewish Congregation, Nathan Levy," town officials released him when "the real murderer was found and indicted."[43]

Such accusations reflected the pervasive belief in peddlers' dishonesty. The peddler wanted to make a sale and stopped at little to do so. He lied about the product's value, jacked up its price, and kept false records of customers' debts. Such stereotypes circled the globe and became the stuff of popular culture. In one of the early twentieth century's most beloved children's books, L. M. Montgomery's *Anne of Green Gables*, set in Prince Edward Island, Canada, the eponymous heroine, the plucky orphan Anne, makes a purchase from a peddler, a "German Jew." He softens her up for the sale by telling her his sad story, that he desperately needs money to bring his wife and children out of Germany to rejoin him. Kindhearted Anne falls for his line and purchases a bottle of black dye, which she hopes will cover up her flaming red hair, the bane of her existence. But the crooked peddler has sold her green dye instead. This widely read story echoed a theme heard round the world, of the peddler as the amoral stranger who wreaked havoc everywhere he went.[44]

The peddlers' purported transgressions went beyond selling bottles of green dye after promising black. Local people, usually those with political power and eager to maintain the status quo, accused Jewish peddlers of pur-veying subversive ideas. In early-twentieth-century Costa Rica, as elsewhere in Latin America, critics of Jewish peddlers worried that newly arrived Polish kloppers were spreading Communism among the local poor, making them restive and dissatisfied with prevailing economic arrangements. After all, kloppers, or semananiks, entered their customers' homes, engaged in small talk, charmed the women to make the sale. The Jewish peddlers, assumed to be terribly smart and devious, could easily lace those conversations with dangerous ideas.[45]

Local elites saw, in the mundane details of peddling, sinister forces that threatened local power relationships. Peddlers engaged positively and respectfully with all customers, treating subordinate people no differently from the better off and powerful. The peddler saw the poor and powerless as no less able to buy goods that their social betters. As no customer, whether wealthy or poor, white or black, colonial or indigenous, had any inherent reason to buy from the peddler, it behooved him to cultivate goodwill among all who opened the door to his knock. He had to address each potential buyer in a pleasing manner, in her own language. The peddler, in fact, had to allow the customer, no matter how subservient in the local society, to feel in control of the transaction.

Peddlers shaped the dynamic of the relationship despite the barriers fundamental to the local social and political codes. In societies built along sharply demarcated lines of race, where one group wielded power over the other, such respect shook up standards of acceptable behavior. In fact, the peddlers' critics got it right. When the Jewish peddler, a white man, addressed the African-American customer in the South as "mister" or "missus," when he doffed his hat to black people as a symbol of respect, he crossed the line of social etiquette, threatening the social order of deference. Jewish peddlers lodged with African-American customers, and allowed African-American women to try on the clothes they carried in their wagons.

In a social system in which whites had power and imposed upon black people an array of restrictions, the peddler disrupted rules that served an important purpose, demonstrating the power of the color line. The peddler offered a different message, that lines could be traversed. By interacting with African-American customers as they did, peddlers violated taboos deeply anchored in local consciousness, as they allowed African Americans to set the terms of their relationship.

When slavery prevailed, owners expressed concern that Jewish peddlers encouraged slaves to run away, that they talked up abolitionism. Advice columns in magazines for slaveowners strenuously suggested, "Negroes should in no instance be permitted to *trade*," and proposed that planters operate stores for simple goods rather than allowing peddlers to come in and display their wares. By cutting out the peddlers, the planters would, according to the advice, prevent their property from hearing ideas inimical to the system. Such isolation would also keep them from being stimulated by the display of luxurious wares.[46] A few times local white men roughed up Jewish peddlers, condemning them for disrupting the racial balance. So, too, in South Africa and Southern Rhodesia (now Zimbabwe), local elites considered the Jewish peddlers dangerous because of their overfamiliarity with the African people to whom they sold. A police report from Matabeleland, in Southern Rhodesia, complained that itinerant Jewish merchants constituted a "discredit to the country, and it is largely owing to the manner in which these people treat the natives that the latter is losing his respect for the white man."[47]

The peddlers' shallow roots in the places they sold made them suspect. The Jews did not honor the local code, the argument ran, and their transactions among society's lower classes stirred up those who had previously accepted disparities and deprivations. Slavery ended in Jamaica in 1834, and two years later Daniel Hart, a Jew, ran for the Assembly to represent the city of Kingston. He did spectacularly well among the newly emancipated slaves, garnering 82 percent of their vote. Howe Peter Brown, the second marquess of Sligo, governor of Jamaica, sneered at Hart as a "Jew Pedlar . . . tho' with a little money." Hart may or may not have been a peddler in the past; the words "Jew" and "pedlar" fused organically for this white, Christian member of the ruling elite, who feared the emergence of a new Jamaica, with its majority population of emancipated slaves. Hart, the "Jew Pedlar" who sought the vote of the newly enfranchised, symbolized the fragility of the world that he knew and benefited from. By invoking the "Pedlar" bogeyman, the governor asserted Hart's lack of commitment to the place.[48]

Not all the places to which peddlers went divided by race. Peddlers sold goods in numerous racially and ethnically homogeneous societies. They developed routes among German Mennonites in the Canadian prairies, fishermen of Scottish background in the Maritimes, or small farmers in Sweden. But even these places, and indeed the peddlers' entire new world, were splintered by gender, and Jewish peddlers disrupted conventional relationships between men and women.

Because peddlers sold to women, dealing primarily in goods that fell into women's domain, they established relationships with them; in this realm women held nearly all power, a far cry from ordinary social reality. Women could not vote, serve on juries, or hold office. Most jobs barred them, and if they worked, they received lower wages than men. They were represented to the outside world by their fathers and then their husbands. Upon marriage women experienced what the law defined as "civil death." Married American women until the 1850s and English ones until the 1870s could not own property. Most married women either could not or did not work outside the home, nor could they take out loans in their own names. In the United States until the 1920s, if a woman married a noncitizen, she lost her American citizenship. Men did the basic work of the society: farming, mining, and logging, and steel making. Women who worked—in textile mills, for example—were paid less than men, and men in general dismissed women's wages as "pin money." Women played secondary roles in the family and local economy, doing reproductive rather than productive work. They endured endless pregnancies, and even when information about contraception became available, laws forbade them from learning about it. Men—as fathers and husbands, ministers and political authorities, publishers of newspapers and enforcers of the social order—had all the power.

But when it came to engaging with peddlers, inviting them into their homes, choosing what to buy, how much money to put down, how much to pay each week on the balance, and allowing the peddler to lodge for the night, or not, women decided. The quotidian act of buying new blankets, as that woman in Limerick had, or of dipping into savings to purchase a picture to mount on the wall, made women economic actors. They, on their own, took on debts that their husbands, the chief breadwinners, would be legally responsible for covering. The women, officially and formally powerless, negotiated contact with the immigrant Jewish peddlers, who brought the outside world into the intimacy of the home.

While this conformed to prevailing ideas about the home as women's domain, it still upset the balance of expectations. By virtue of their exchanges with the peddlers, women modernized and upgraded their homes. They used their families' resources to introduce cosmopolitan standards, as they adorned themselves, their kitchens, their parlors, and even their husbands with new things that appealed to them. What husbands thought about this mattered little.

Peddlers did even more to upset domestic gender roles. When peddlers encouraged women to collect herbs and save the detritus of their kitchens, the rags, paper, tin cans, and old bones, they provided women with independent economic activity. When a woman accepted money for these items, she got cash that her husband had not earned. She did not have to tell her husband about the money. If the women exchanged the ginseng or feathers or other stuff for a peddlers' wares, then she could expand her cache of material possessions. She alone decided. At times, depending upon the particular country, women also borrowed money from peddlers. Most Jewish peddlers in Wales doubled as money lenders, dealing especially with women. Joseph Edelstein's Irish novel *The Moneylender* tells the story of a Lithuanian immigrant Jewish peddler whose money-lending activities set in motion a tragic narrative, as the borrower cannot repay what she owes.

Money lending, like women's purchasing goods from peddlers, compli-cated the simple paradigm, observed nearly everyplace, under which men had power and women did not. Peddlers enabled women to undercut men's exclu-sive claim to power. Not surprisingly, men perpetrated nearly all outrages per-petrated against peddlers. Men thronged the streets in front of the Jewish-owned stores of Tredegar. Father Creagh preached to, and received an endorsement from, his confraternity of three thousand men. He launched his boycott with sermons delivered to this male church society.[49] Male newspaper editors and writers castigated peddlers for cheating and lying, and male officials passed the licensing laws and tried to enforce them. Men, not women, seem to have committed the murders and the mayhem against peddlers. *Havaner Lebn*, a Cuban Yiddish magazine, reported on "A Jewish Peddler Attacked in Suárez": a group of Cuban men had killed the Jewish merchant, but "a Cuban woman had mercy on him and made a ruckus and telephoned the police."[50]

Not that all women welcomed the peddler. Everyplace in the new world, some failed to find common ground with these stranger merchants who knocked on their doors. Wiliam Lee Provol, author of a fine peddler narrative, *The Pack Peddler*, describes life on the road in the countryside beyond Syracuse, New York. Like many Jewish peddlers, Provol filled his bag with rosaries, votive candles, holy pictures, and saint statues to sell to Catholic customers. Some considered the act of a Jew trading on their religion as re-pugnant and sacrilegious. " 'You contemptible little Jew,' " one Irish woman declared "with great flourish." With "a steely glare, her voice rose first to a yell, 'What do you mean making fun of our religion? Begorra! You should be in Hell instead of on the streets blaspheming our faith.' "[51]

Peddler jokes and humorous stories that blurred the line between fiction and news consistently connected peddlers with women and raised the specter of illicit sexual encounters between them. Stories in print and in the oral rep-ertoire maintained that peddlers easily seduced naïve women, who fell under the crafty Jews' spell. Benjamin Franklin's *Pennsylvania Gazette* printed an article about an episode in New York's Westchester County, where "A Jew peddler" reportedly entered a house where a woman, alone in the premises, said that without her husband's permission she could buy nothing. The clever peddler, however, took advantage of her, according to the article, sexually and commercially. "The peddler . . . finding that the woman was entirely alone, offered to make her a present of a piece of calico upon condition of her giving up her charms to him." He made her an offer she could not refuse, "for the thought of sporting with a young man, and having a new gown in the bargain made her readily yield to his desires." The peddler, "after taking a repast in the banquet of love," met the woman's husband on the road. The peddler lied to the man, claiming that the wife had bought the calico. The husband, fearing the debt incurred to the peddler, suggested that they go back to the house and that the peddler take back the calico. The peddler thus got his pleasures without having to part with his merchandise, which he could then sell to yet someone else.[52]

Much antipeddler rhetoric, in sermon and in print, emphasized gender matters. Father Creagh announced his anti-Jewish peddler campaign to the men at the confraternity, but directed his words also to the women who dealt with peddlers face to face. He exhorted them, initially through their husbands, to stop hankering for the luxury goods purveyed by the Jewish peddlers, and instead to patronize stores owned by their fellow Irish Catholics. His henchmen, the priests who drove around the countryside, spied on women consorting, commercially or otherwise, with Jewish peddlers. *La Libre Parole*, a Quebec newspaper that helped stir up sentiments against Jewish peddlers, pointed out that they flourished in the province because the "petites Canadiennes," the young Canadian girls, could not resist the cagy Jewish peddlers' appeals. In every town and village, peddlers could be found seducing the young women with the fineries they extracted from their sacks.[53] These comments echoed a global sentiment. Women embraced the peddlers. Foolish women, unaware of the larger consequences of their actions, encouraged the peddlers. The blame for the Jews' presence in these once orderly places fell on the women.[54]

This had little to do with the peddlers themselves or even the goods they carried. Beyond class and race, even beyond the gender, this reaction boiled down to an incontrovertible fact. The peddlers by their presence mounted a formidable challenge to local businesses. They could sell for less, offering customers a better deal than sedentary merchants did. The merchants knew that all too well.

Unlike the shopkeeper, a peddler had little overhead, at most the cost of a wagon and horse, and oats for his beast of burden. Peddlers kept prices to a bare minimum, profiting by volume. They went to the customers, rather than waiting for customers to come to them. Their selling strategy promoted flexibility. They went wherever they saw new or better markets, speedily abandoning routes and territories for new and more promising ones. Shopkeepers with real stores had to stock their shelves with merchandise bought in bulk to last a length of time, making it difficult for them to pick up and leave at will. Non-Jewish merchants depended on formal credit institutions, like banks, which charged interest and profited through foreclosure when loans could not be repaid. Jewish peddlers received goods and credit through the Jewish credit network, which thrived when peddlers succeeded and offered credit on generous terms. Jewish peddlers operated in concert with Jewish shopkeepers, warehouse owners, and other wholesalers, all linked in an economic network that worked to get goods to customers. The higher echelons of that network benefited from the peddlers' good fortune. Peddlers and storekeepers, borrowers and lenders, worshiped in the same congregation, married among themselves, and depended upon one another to fulfill Jewish functions, including but not limited to constituting a prayer quorum, a *minyan*, celebrating holidays, burying the dead, and paying the salary of a ritual slaughterer or somehow procuring kosher meat. All these shared experiences meant that community interdependence operated in tandem with economic interdependence.

Peddling's essential nature challenged the fixed-location merchant. The peddler entered customers' homes, able to hold up the curtains against the windows, showing the skeptical woman how beautiful they looked on *her* windows. He spread the tablecloth on *her* table, and hung the pictures in their frames on *her* wall. The peddler ushered women into the world of consumption directly in her zone. No husband hovered about telling her what she could or could not buy, which item she did not need, which cost too much. Even when women purchased goods for men, they did so in their spaces, without husbands intruding. The neckties, belts, and suspenders that Jewish peddlers purveyed all over Latin America and the Caribbean, they sold to women in their home, while husbands labored in mills and plantations. The peddlers allowed women to transform their husbands, least outwardly, into respectable-looking men of substance.

Men dominated shops, particularly in smaller towns. Male shopkeepers behind the counter spent their days in the company of other men, those buying goods or those congregating there to spend leisure time. In American country stores men gathered, played card games, talked politics and sundry other topics, chewed and spat tobacco, smoked, and told ribald jokes, providing a chilly environment for the women who ventured in. Women concerned with respectability hesitated to come into the store, this male venue.

Peddlers, on the other hand, spent their days with women, cultivating strategies that appealed to them, always specific to the particularities of the place. The peddler entered the woman's space with no tobacco dribbling down his chin and told no dirty jokes. He did not greet her with leering eyes or catcalls. If he had, he would be met with a slamming door. Local merchants knew this too well, and much new-world antipeddler action was driven by businessmen, owners of stores, bent on eliminating peddler competition as a matter of simple economic self-preservation.

The Limerick shopkeepers who constituted Father Creagh's confraternity had many reasons to listen to his sermons. Religious zeal no doubt inspired them weekly to flock to hear the charismatic priest, who exhorted the men to pursue the deeper life of the soul. Because they were shopkeepers, however, they may have been particularly attracted to Creagh's message that the Jewish peddlers, foreigners, non-Catholics, threatened Ireland's spiritual values. The peddlers sold the same goods that filled the shelves of Limerick's stores, and in the contest the peddlers seemed to be winning the customers. The local shopkeepers in league with Father Creagh castigated the local women for not buying from "their own," for lining the pockets of the Jews who took money out of the pockets of Catholic, Irish merchants.

Store owners, town by town, city by city, organized themselves to keep the peddlers out. Little differentiated Costa Rica, Cuba, Oklahoma, Louisiana, South Carolina, Key West, Florida, and hundreds of thousands of new-world places where those challenged economically by the peddler strategized on how most expeditiously to eliminate the itinerant menace. Sometimes they invoked the peddlers' Jewishness, but even when they did not, they made concerted efforts to impede the peddlers, many of whom happened to be Jewish. Jewish peddlers, for example, came to Key West and the surrounding area in the 1880s. By the decade's end a Merchants' Protective Association formed, bent on amending the city charter to mandate an annual license fee of $1,000 for all peddlers, an enormous sum for the late nineteenth century.[55] Jewish migration to Cuba began later, in the early twentieth century, and by the 1920s enough Jews had arrived and fanned out into the countryside to sell that businessmen founded *ligas*, leagues, that pushed the city of Havana and the island's provincial towns to levy hefty license fees on the peddlers, whom liga members accused of stealing their business. In Cuba, as in Mexico, Peru, Brazil, and elsewhere, such businessmen's leagues demanded that states enforce their own laws and arrest, jail, and fine offending peddlers.[56] The *Southern Israelite* of 1934 reported on the rise of the Jewish population of Costa Rica, Jews' concentration in peddling, and their successes, which had stirred up "the jealousy and envy of a small group of Costa Rican merchants and landowners, and this group is responsible for the wide anti-Semitic attacks which are being made in a number of local Spanish papers."[57]

In all these places the business community represented the civic and commercial backbone of the local society. Merchants paid the largest chunk of local taxes. Aligned with politicians, they constituted powerful political blocs.

They had the ears of city councils, mayors, and other officials. Indeed, store-keepers often held these positions, their business interests and their civic interests dovetailing perfectly. They handily enlisted the local press to join their campaigns, arguing that foreign Jewish peddlers had no local roots, no commitments to the place, yet came in, undersold, and threatened those who did have roots and stakes in the place.

These custodians of civic order found the large number of Jews who peddled without licenses particularly vexing and used the fact of their illegal sales to justify political assaults on peddlers. A British government official in Northern Rhodesia, Arthur Glyn Leonard, gloated in his 1891 *How We Made Rhodesia* how Polish and Russian Jews, who could be identified by their "crackjaw names," "had to pay a fine of five guineas, which they could have avoided by paying a shilling for a trading license." Leonard, like his global peers, saw itinerant trade and the flaunting of licensing laws problems in need of a solution.[58]

Some merchants particularly wanted to see the Jewish peddlers gone. Owners of mines, plantations, and logging camps made money from running their own commissaries, which charged high prices to the workers. Some took payment for goods out of wages and provided credit at exorbitant rates of interests; defaults on payment got workers deeper in debt to the company store.

Jewish peddlers crossed the thresholds of miners', loggers', and workers' homes, selling at low prices with easy terms of interest. Powerless men who did not have the economic and political clout of the employers, the peddlers interacted with customers without threatening the purchasers of their goods with the loss of their livelihood. The peddler came hat in hand into the miner's home, hoping to persuade his wife to buy. She had power over the peddler rather than the other way around.

The mine, logging camp, and plantation owners saw clearly that peddlers enticed women away from their stores. They, like businessmen in town, tried to keep the peddlers out. Sometimes they forbade their workers outright from buying anyplace other than the company store. Joseph Austrian, a Jewish peddler from Bavaria who sold in and around the mining areas of Michigan around Mackinaw in the 1850s, recalled that one day, "when delivering a large load of goods, to the miners in that part of the place called 'Shantytown' . . . I had to pass through a gateway near the miner's store." Austrian went house to house among the predominantly Cornish population who worked the mine. The owner of the mine, John Slawson, "made his appearance and angrily berated the women for having bought anything outside the Company's store, and threatening to discharge their husbands, the miners, if they did not confine their purchases to the store at the mine." Austrian, the immigrant peddler, threatened Slawson's economic hegemony over the Cornish women standing between them.[59]

According to their critics, Jewish peddlers had come in to their communities as foreigners, and had succeeded economically. While not all peddlers were successful, and few fared spectacularly, the image of the Jewish peddler who came with seemingly nothing and managed to rise galled those resented them. One Quebec commentator in *L'Indicateur de Québec á Levis* noted in the 1890s, "Most of these Jews have been in Quebec only a short time. When they first came into our parishes they had nothing but their bare hands and their two feet, some sacks on their backs and quite a colony of lice." But matters had changed: "Today I can state that one of them has considerable wealth."[60] Olive Schreiner, born in the East Cape and renowned as the author of *Letters from an African Farm*, traveled back home to South Africa on a ship full of "German Jews . . . some going out for the first time and some returning to the Cape." She found them quite dignified, quite different from the smous, "the little sniveling weasel-like creatures who come out third class and as soon as they land supply themselves with a wagon and a couple of mules . . . hawking false jewellery and damaged clothing among the Dutch farmers, and growing rich on it."[61] That phrase, "growing rich on it" linked the Cape with South and Central America, North America, and Ireland, the belief prevailing everywhere that Jewish peddlers made handsome profits off the backs of the local poor, to the detriment of the local shopkeepers. State officials around the world, in the destination places to which Jews went, commented as well on the Jewish peddlers, asserting that they added nothing to the national treasury. They produced nothing and did nothing to enhance government efforts to modernize, grow the nation's wealth, or add to the common good. The Jewish peddlers, officials lamented, used their money for themselves, plowing it back into the Jewish community.

In societies where most people made a living with their hands, whether farming, mining, or producing items, particularly durable goods, Jewish peddlers seemed to do no work. But what they did do, they made money at, and, as others saw it, enriched themselves at the expense of those who labored in conventional ways. The *Bulletin*, an Australian publication of the 1880s, declared that "even the Chinaman is cheaper in the end than the Hebrew. . . . The one with the tail is preferable to the one with the Talmud every time." The publication noted, "We owe much to the Jew . . . in more sense than one—but until he works, until a fair percentage of him produces, he must always be against democracy."[62]

Agriculture and industry, productive enterprises, enhanced the economic vitality of a town, a region, a country, and contrasted starkly with the perception of peddlers, who in the words of William Faulkner in his 1929 novel *The Sound and the Fury*, written of a place, Mississippi, which had seen many Jewish peddlers, "It's just the race. You'll admit that they produce nothing. They follow the pioneers into a new country and sell them clothes." The character who utters these words goes on, "I'll be damned if it hasn't come to a pretty pass when any damn foreigner that can't make a living in the country where God put him, can come to this one and take money right out of an American's pockets."[63]

THE CALL TO ABANDON PEDDLING

Even friends of the Jews who spoke up in their defense found fault with their peddling. They distinguished good Jews from peddling Jews, indicting peddling as a cause of suffering. They suggested that if Jews gave up the back-pack and the road in favor of farming, anti-Jewish prejudice would melt. William Davis Robinson, an evangelical preacher, issued in 1819 a *Memoir Addressed to Persons of the Jewish Religion in Europe on the Subject of Emigration to, and Settlement in, One of the Most Eligible Parts of the United States of North America*. That year riots had broken out against Jews in Alsace, Bavaria, and other German-speaking lands, and Robinson foregrounded his call for emigration against that backdrop. He predicted that "emigration and subsequent settlement . . . are the only sure remedies to the evil here complained of," and he considered the relatively new United States the best place to which the Jews might "fly for an asylum, where they will be exempt from persecution and personal opprobrium." The "only difficulty" he foresaw entailed the "habitual propensity of the Jews to follow other pursuits than agriculture." While he did not address peddling directly, he asked rhetorically, "Where are the Jewish parents who would not feel delight in beholding their children pursuing the honourable and useful labours of agriculture, in preference to the wretched and menial occupations in which they are now generally engaged?"[64]

In 1881 Jews were the target of an even greater and more widely reported upsurge of violence. The pogroms of 1881 galvanized world attention and highlighted the plight of the Jews of Russia. General Gregorio Luperón, a political figure in the Dominican Republic, offered his country as a haven for Jews who were "being persecuted." He suggested to an international Jewish aid organization that "there is a country, the Dominican Republic, a vast and fertile country," and promised the Jewish aid officials that "there your co-religionists will be received with open arms." He even promised that his country would offer citizenship "and land for farming purposes, land, which immediately after possession had been taken, will become the property of the settlers." While Luperón said nothing about peddlers, neither did he proffer his invitation to those who would take up the peddler's pack and bring neckties and watches, needles and thread, glasses and picture frames to rural Dominican people. Luperón's hospitality stopped at the road upon which the peddler would embark.[65]

After yet another outbreak of pogroms in the first decade of the twentieth century, particularly the one in the Bessarabian city of Kishinev in 1903, advocates for the Jews had another chance to express their concern and deprecate peddling. Michael Davitt, the Irish nationalist to whom the Jews of Limerick turned to defend them against the calumny of Father Creagh and of Arthur Griffith, also found the Jews' economic profile problematic. He blamed the Christian world for the Jews' perverse concentration in trade, but still defined trade as abnormal and unproductive. "Christendom is prejudiced against this race," he concluded in his *Within the Pale* of 1903, a report on the pogrom in Kishinev, "because its sons are generally non-producers of wealth, and mere exploiters of the fruits and necessities of direct industry." But, he went on, "if the race generally are exploiters and extortioners, who made them so?" The fault lay with the "centuries of deliberate oppression in every Christian land (Ireland honourably excepted)." *Within the Pale* argued for the nascent Zionist movement, and foresaw that the migration of the Jews to Palestine would liberate them from their concentration in the "small huckstering class."[66]

From the Celtic fringe to the antipodes, advocates for Jewish rights and governments championed the Jews as victims of Russian anti-Semitism. Some states declared, through Jewish aid organizations, their willingness to offer places of refuge to Jews but excluded from their humanitarian gesture those who might peddle. Officials of Queensland in 1907 informed the Jewish Colonization Association that it "would welcome the settlement of Jewish agriculturalists and Jewish agricultural labourers," in that province in the north of Australia, but "pedlars and petty traders would not be received."[67]

The century of migration came to an end in 1924, when the United States enacted severe immigration restriction. Officials in various Latin American countries thought that the restrictive legislation would make their countries attractive to potential Jewish newcomers, increasing their white population and incorporating Jews whose skills, credit networks, and literacy would improve

society. But they did not want peddlers. Plutarco Calles, elected president of
Mexico in 1924, made that clear, after conversations with representatives of
numerous international Jewish aid organizations. He announced that the
"Government of Mexico is prepared to welcome most warmly the immigration
of Jews from Eastern Europe to engage . . . both in agricultural as well as industrial pursuits."[68] The *New York Daily News* dubbing Calles's declaration
"Mexico's Invitation to the Jews" reported that after a meeting of government
leaders with representatives of the American Jewish Congress and the Hebrew
Immigrant Aid Society, Mexico guaranteed "to grant a large tract of arable land
for Jewish settlement . . . the remission of all land taxes . . . a reduction of railroad fares, and . . . other facilities for the settlers." If some did not or could not
farm, Calles envisioned a government plan that would "provide the means for
employing tens of thousands of Jews in various branches of industry," noting
that "it would be . . . a distinct benefit to Mexico to manufacture within its
own boundaries many items which it now has to import from other countries."
But as with the Dominican Republic, the largesse of the Mexican government
did not extend to the men who would willingly go out as semananiks, as
cuentaniks, to bring goods to the nation's rural dwellers.[69]

JEWISH CRITIQUES OF PEDDLING

The rhetoric of governments and individuals who expressed concern about
the fate of the Jews, particularly those in Russia after the 1880s, mingled sym-
pathies with disdain for peddling. Their attitudes resembled those of the global
Jewish elite: rabbis, newspaper publishers, philanthropists, and operatives for
aid organizations. These Jewish notables, all settled and well off, conveyed in
no uncertain terms their view that peddling reflected badly on the Jews and
inspired anti-Semitism. As they saw it, wherever and whenever itinerant
Jewish merchants took to the roads, they harmed all Jews, complicating the
process of integration. Invariably described as unskilled or, as in the words of
the Industrial Removal Office, a Jewish aid organization founded in New
York in 1899 to ameliorate the poverty of newly arrived Jewish immigrants,
"men without trades," peddlers haunted the consciousness of Jewish communal leaders, who feared that wherever the peddlers went they stirred up resentment and spawned antipathy to all Jews. Jewish philanthropic associations
cooked up schemes to "save" the Jews from peddling, and in sermons, newspaper articles, speeches, and other intrafaith communications sought to prove
that Jews peddled only out of duress, and would never have embraced such a
despicable occupation had the Christian world not forced them into it. Had

they not been denied the right to join guilds and own land—and had they not been exiled from their land, the Zionist argument ran—they would have eschewed the life of the road.

The problem of the peddlers, according to the Jewish elite, grew out of their own success. As Jews came to, say, Mexico, and did well in peddling, others followed, having learned that the occupation promised rewards there for Jewish men seeking new homes and livelihoods. But this, as Jewish leaders saw it, led to overcrowding in the field. As Maurice Hexter, executive director of the Federated Jewish Charities of Boston, reported to the Emergency Committee on Jewish Refugees in 1924, referring to conditions for Jews in Mexico, "Many have taken to peddling. A number are selling goods on the installment plan. . . . The growing number of Jewish peddlers has overcrowded the field. They go around in groups and compete with one another. They have aroused the opposition of the storekeepers from whom they take away trade. Each new peddler takes bread out of the mouths of the older ones."[70] This talk about the pernicious implications of peddling extended beyond the Ashkenazi world of European Jews. The Alliance Israélite Universelle, founded, funded, and run by French Jews for the benefit of the Jews of "the Orient," encouraged young Jews from Morocco to equip themselves with real skills before heading to Brazil, Peru, Venezuela, and elsewhere. But Jews already in those places reported to the Alliance that only those bound for agriculture should come, "because itinerant vendors have no chance here on account of the many Arabs who are to be seen selling Christian beads and crosses and every article that is saleable." Fear pervaded the Jewish world that peddlers would spread the bacillus of anti-Semitism to the new world.[71]

That fear underlay Jewish antipeddler talk and action. Jewish officials in Brazil, such as Rabbi Isaiah Raffelovitch, worried in the 1920s lest the influx of "a large number of *luftmenschen* [those with no means of support; literally those with their heads in the air] who should swell the already too large number of peddlers is to run the risk of increased anti-Semitism."[72] He sounded like Isaac Leeser decades earlier in Philadelphia, who wrote in 1863 in *The Occident*, in a piece entitled "On Persecution," that "we," the Jews, "become much too often the objects of animadversion; and since comparatively few only have any knowledge of our people, except when they conceive us to be by taking some itinerant Jewish *gaberlunzie* [peddler], to borrow a Scottish word, as the real type of the . . . Jews."[73] Such talk by Jewish officials dogged Jewish migration into the terrifying days of the 1930s, as frantic Jews from central Europe sought places of refuge. Planners for the Joint Distribution Committee, which oversaw global Jewish migration, opined in 1937, after

Hitler's rise to power, passage of the Nuremberg laws, and the deepening outrages against Jews in Poland, that peddlers had given rise to anti-Jewish hatred
around the world. The committee hoped to direct the refugee stream to more
attractive enterprises, ones that, it believed, others would not find repugnant.
Such comments went back in time. In 1882 the Hebrew Emigrant Aid Society
had announced that it would not use any of its Mansion House Funds to assist
those Jews who had peddled or planned to do so in America.[74]

Around the world Jewish welfare associations experimented with creating
trade schools for younger immigrants so that they would shun peddling
and labor instead as mechanics and artisans, producing wealth and creating
new kinds of Jews, self-liberated from the scourge of peddling. The Jewish
elite of Jamaica in 1855 established an "apprenticing fund" to help immigrant
Jewish children learn a trade, which its leaders considered "far better than
to encourage a system of hawking and peddling . . . which is all they can do"
at present.[75]

A near obsession dominated Jewish elites about agriculture. Why not, they
asked vis-à-vis the United States, Canada, Australia, Brazil, Argentina, and in
fact nearly every settler society to which Jews went, assist Jews to farm, and
in the process "exterminate peddling," in the words of the Jewish Alliance of
America, an 1890s effort to promote farming.[76] Why not, Jewish newspapers,
aid organizations, and elite commentators proposed, divert Jews from peddling, normalize them, and make them agriculturalists. In 1886 a prosperous
Jew living in Melbourne, Australia, sang the praises of his land in London's
Jewish Chronicle, suggesting to the Jewish poor of Europe that in that land
"down under," "the resolute tiller of the soil" would find fertile fields, but not
so "the individual with proclivities towards traffic in brass jewellery, second-
hand sponges, rehabilitated clothing."[77] To many of the advocates of Jewish
agrarianism, the transformation of Jewish immigrants from peddlers to farmers would redeem them from, in the words of Adolph Levy of the Jewish
Agriculturalists' Aid Society of America in 1901, "the pusillanimity and shy-
ness which is so sadly noticeable in the Jewish peddler" and introduce them to
"self-reliance, courage and confidence in one's own ability."[78]

Some Jewish observers believed that peddling harmed the Jewish family.
With the man gone for days on end, wrote social workers and other providers
of Jewish social services around the world, wives had to fend for themselves.
Jewish social service agencies had to remedy the damage brought on as peddling fragmented families. Children had no father present on a regular basis
and women bore the sole responsibility of caring for their large families and
often could not handle the pressure.

Not only did peddling purportedly challenge the stability of Jewish families, but other commentators worried that it exposed the new Jewish immigrants to the temptations of shedding tradition, losing Jewishness. Rabbis,
among others, fretted over the fact that Jewish men, on their journeys through
the countryside, met and fell in love with non-Jewish women. Romances led
to marriages and long-term relationships, which in turn led to the birth of
children. Given that Jewish status passed from the mother, not the father, the
children of these immigrant Jewish peddlers and non-Jewish women were not
Jews; often they were referred to as "lost" to the Jewish people. Israel Zangwill,
author of the enduringly significant play *The Melting Pot* and a major player
in British and world Jewish politics, addressed a New York Jewish gathering
in 1898 and placed the blame for the diminution of Jewish religious observance on the fact that "the peddler in the country, the itinerant merchant who
wandered from village to village, year in and year out, and finally settled
down in some growing community as a shopkeeper and merchant, had learned
to disregard the dietary laws and the laws concerning fasts." To Zangwill and
others, the back roads of the United States and all the other new-world settings
provided the Jewish peddlers with the melting pot into which they could meld
with the local population, abandoning tradition to follow the styles and cultures of their new homes.[79]

The Baron de Hirsch Fund, founded in the aftermath of the 1881 pogroms
in Russia, launched a global effort to assist Jews out of czarist lands through
agricultural projects. It envisioned the birth of a new era in Jewish history, a
transformation of commercial Jews into agrarian ones, which would redeem
"hawkers, petty traders, and workmen into sturdy sons of the soil," as foreseen
by an agent of the fund in Argentina in 1906.[80] The Jewish Territorial
Organization also pinned its hopes on farming and opened a branch in
Melbourne in 1913. Joseph Kronheimer, a wealthy tobacco merchant, funded
some Russian Jewish families on the land in Shepparton, where they would
support themselves and avoid "menial, disheartening work . . . such as hawking and bottlewashing."[81] The nearly messianic hope organizers pinned on this
project pivoted on the notion that peddling hurt Jews while farming would
elevate them. Well-off Jews in Montreal created the Montefiore Agricultural
Association in 1885 to "make organized efforts to direct the enterprise and
industry of our co-religionists . . . at the present stage of our relations with
other races and peoples," no doubt referring to the smoldering tension between the Jewish peddlers and the French-speaking Catholics of Quebec.[82]
The magazine *Der Iddisher Farmer*, "the Jewish farmer," a publication of
the Jewish Agricultural Society, a beneficiary of the Baron de Hirsch Fund,

said it best on the cover of its January 1910 edition: a drawing with a substantial house in the background, smoke wafting from its chimney, the word
"Prosperity" across its front. Sacks bursting with food, including one labeled
"potatoes," lay to the side. A hale-looking, upright farmer, not marked by any
stereotypically Jewish features, standing with a pitchfork in his hand beckons
across a fence to a miserable-looking man loaded down with packs on his
back. An enormous sack marked "Dry Goods" perches perilously on the peddler's shoulders. A bundle of clothes hangs from his left hand, labeled "Sweat
Shop," and a pack, "Tin Ware," dangles from his right hand. In contrast to the
farmer, the peddler's hooked nose marks him as a Jew. (The image seems to
have appeared first in *Leslie's* magazine but clearly appealed to the editor of
Der Iddisher Farmer, who may or may not have acquired copyright permission to reproduce it.)[83]

While enterprises like the Baron de Hirsch Fund also considered the
clustering of immigrant Jews in large cities—New York and Buenos Aires,
among others—as deleterious to the image of Jews, they saw peddling as
equally pernicious. The peddler, they believed, degraded the Jewish people
by making himself a pest to the customers upon whose doors he knocked.
But agriculture would save the Jews. It had been, according to its proponents,
the Jew's original way of making a living, when he still "dwelt in his own
land," as declared Mr. A. R. Levy, president of the Jewish Agricultural Society
of America in 1906. But history had "forced" the Jew into "commercialism."
Yet, Levy continued, in all the centuries of his "dispersion the Jew's continu-
ous prayer had been to be brought back to the soil and till it, as in days
of yore." While that prayer envisioned a return not to the land in general
but to the land of Zion, the distinction mattered only to Zionists. For other
campaigners for Jewish agriculture, any plot of land that took the peddlers off
the road would do.[84]

The desire to excise peddling from the Jews' occupational repertoire and to
present Jews as clean, settled, respectable, and respectful of local norms dominated the elite Jewish political project from the end of the eighteenth century
onward. Undertakings large and small, economic, social, cultural, or political
pivoted around the problem of peddling, as Jewish elites sought to show the
world a different kind of Jew. The Jews of Portsmouth, England, presumably
well off, educated, native-born or at least naturalized Englishmen for some
length of time, founded a literary society. One member delivered a speech
at the inaugural meeting, intoning, "Wash off the stigma cast on you, that you
are nothing but pedlars," and instead "show non-Jews you love culture and
literature, not just money."[85]

The Jewish elite worried about peddling and its proliferation in the new world, be it England, Ireland, South Africa, the United States, Canada, Australia, wherever, in part because they, the leaders, would be called in emergencies to pick up the pieces and smooth over social and political tensions when outrages against the Jews erupted. The self-appointed, well-connected representatives of the Jews fretted over any and every manifestation of anti-Jewish activity, whether verbal or physical. The Jewish peddlers, according to the elites, stirred up local animosities. They stimulated anti-Jewish sentiment among the merchants, who resented the economic competition, and the guardians of local law and order, who saw the peddlers as disruptive. When antipeddler and anti-Jewish feelings spilled over into action, the elites felt obliged to intervene. In 1843, for example, Sir Moses Montefiore, financier, philanthropist, and sheriff of London, noted in his diary that the police notified him when two Polish Jews had been arrested for peddling without a license. He had to bail them out, and more abstractly, he had to bail out the Jews of England by financing schemes to eradicate peddling and secure a more positive image for them in the eyes of the English people.[86] When General Grant issued his order expelling the Jews because of the activities of the peddlers, leaders of the B'nai B'rith and of the Board of Delegates of American Israelites headed for Washington to plead the case of the Jews with President Lincoln. When people in Wales and Ireland raised questions about Jewish peddlers and their money lending activities, the chief rabbi of Great Britain had to intervene and mediate. And when violence flared in Limerick after Father Creagh delivered his sermons, officials of the Board of Deputies of British Jews and the leaders of the Dublin Hebrew Congregation had no choice but to come to Limerick, investigate, and devise strategies to dampen the flames of unrest and end the boycott.

In their intervention they not only defended the Jews against the calumny heaped on them but pointed out to the Jews the perils of peddling. In doing so they participated in a global strategy aimed at getting the immigrant Jewish peddlers off the road, hoping to transform them into settled, respectable merchants and citizens.

They really did not have to do that. The Jewish peddlers had no desire to stay on the road. They turned to the occupation not because they liked it but because they saw in it the fastest route to achieving economic security. They, too, wanted to become settled and respectable merchants and citizens. And for the vast majority, in fact, life on the road proved to be a short sentence, a brief stint before settling down. The intervention and advocacy of elites was superfluous for another reason: despite the chorus of condemnation around the

world, characterizing Jewish peddlers as alien, subversive, greedy and devious, their customers stood by them. Women bought from them, even in times
of conflict; when offered the choice between local shopkeepers and Jewish
peddlers, they opted for the latter. The priest on that woman's doorstep could
not dissuade her from buying her blankets and other goods from the peddlers.
Customers like her—their patronage, loyalty, and support—made it possible
for the peddlers to stop being peddlers and cease their time on the road.

5

The End of the Road

Life After Peddling

Sigmund Eisner, age sixty-five, died on January 5, 1925, in the town where he had lived for decades, Red Bank, New Jersey. He had arrived from Bohemia in 1881 so poor that he had to borrow a dollar from a cousin to get started, beginning his American life as an on-the-road peddler. He passed away a wealthy merchant, a clothing manufacturer whose factory churned out uniforms for the Boy Scouts of America. Many soldiers of his adopted land wore the shirts and pants produced in his plant.

His story had all the makings of the quintessential American success story, a proverbial "rags-to-riches" tale, almost too good to be true. It also encapsulated a Jewish historical narrative, demonstrating the liberating power of freedom, how old-world poor Jews thrived in the free air of the new. His life history extolled the virtues of the place and the group.

Eisner's experience does more than detail one successful man's life. It offers a window into the role of peddling in shaping new-world Jewish life, demonstrating the possibilities available to Jewish immigrant men who took to the road as pack peddlers. Eisner, the oldest of seven children, left Bohemia to pursue America's "wider scope for his energy and ability." He came to Keyport, New Jersey, where a relative lived, and, according to a slim tribute book printed in his memory, "He started humbly indeed. A peddler's pack and a little merchandise," provided by his kin, "were the weapons with which he set out to achieve success." While peddling he met his wife-to-be, and they settled down in Red Bank, where he and the cousin opened a small clothing manufacturing business. Sewing among his few employees, Eisner initially

155

still went out on the road in a horse-drawn wagon. He sold the factory's clothes directly to customers in their homes. Business flourished. By 1898 the partners secured a handsome contract from the United States government for uniforms to clothe the young men who went off to fight in the Philippines and Cuba during the Spanish-American War. Although Eisner had resided in the United States less than twenty years, by the time the country plunged into its "splendid little war," Eisner had won this lucrative business deal and served on the Council of National Defense.

In the years to come, as business blossomed, so did his civic engagements. Named his town's water commissioner, he also participated in creating Monmouth County's Organization for Social Service and sat on boards of the State Reformatory for Boys and the Monmouth County Memorial Hospital at Long Branch. As befit a prosperous local merchant, a custodian of the local order, he occupied a seat on the board of the Second National Bank and Trust Company and helped direct the investments and loans of the Citizens Building and Loan Company. He contributed money to the Red Cross, the Boy Scouts (which also awarded him a contract for uniforms), and other helpful local and national institutions. He joined the Masons and the Lions Club, manifestations of his social integration. Three of his four sons studied at Philips Exeter Academy, a prestigious boarding school, and graduated from Harvard College.

Eisner's rise from pack peddler to contractor to the United States Army and revered local civic activist did not compromise his Jewish commitments. A trustee of Congregation Beth Miriam of Long Branch, he considered his involvement in this Reform synagogue "a source of pride and happiness." He expended large sums and much energy on behalf of American Jewish Congress, the Joint Distribution Committee, and the Zionist Organization of America. No one less than Rabbi Stephen Wise, probably his generation's most famous rabbi, delivered the eulogy at Eisner's funeral.[1]

While the name Eisner does not resonate as broadly as those of other former Jewish peddlers who became wealthy in America, names like Guggenheim, Lehman, Seligman, or Straus—either the family associated with Macy's Department store or Levi Strauss (spelled with one more s), who made his fortune off of the denim pants he sold to the miners among whom he peddled during the California Gold Rush—he had an exceptional American experience.

But not limited to America, counterparts to Eisner could be found among Jewish immigrant peddlers who went to dozens of new-world countries. Simon Noll came to the George District's Longkloof Valley in South Africa in 1888, like so many others from Lithuania. He went out on the road as a peddler, starting at age sixteen. Successful enough, he opened a shop in a regional town,

Dieprivier, and bought land, planting it with thousands of trees for an apple orchard. His store attracted so many customers that the railway bus service located a stop in front of it to accommodate the region's eager shoppers. His shop dominated local retail, and the town was ultimately renamed Noll's Halt. The observant Jew, who always shuttered his store on the Sabbath, provided free land to the community to build its church and school. His daughter studied at that school as a girl and later became its teacher, educating Noll's Halt's children. The town fathers named Simon a justice of the peace, and by his death at age seventy-four, he could boast that not only had two of his daughters received teacher certificates, but two of his sons had become doctors and another a chemist.[2]

The global Jewish peddler success story also had a Latin American iteration. Surveying the influx of Polish Jews who arrived in Mexico in the 1920s and 1930s, a local Jewish communal leader commented, "Since the war, many thousands of Jews of the poorer classes have come to Mexico. . . . It is remarkable to observe how these people, generally from Poland, Russia, or Lithuania, starting out as peddlers with a small stock in trade . . . after a few months or years, by constant hard work, saving, and endless sacrifice, are able to establish themselves with a larger stock in trade in some doorway or market place, and not long afterwards open a small store, which gradually expands into a respectable business." Beyond that, the observer opined, "quite a number of immigrants, from these beginnings, have in less than fifteen years developed large retail or wholesale business establishments." From the window of his office he saw "not less than twenty Jewish owned establishments."[3]

Noll's story, Eisner's, or those of the unnamed Jewish immigrants to Mexico echoed in the life experiences of almost all new-world peddlers who with time left the road to occupy stable positions, mostly in businesses. New-world Jewish enterprises grew out of peddler antecedents, and even small, humble businesses founded by erstwhile peddlers constituted mobility. Those who once peddled did not measure their success against Eisner's, let alone Guggenheim's or Lehman's, but rather against their own trajectories. A Romanian Jewish immigrant living in Michigan's Upper Peninsula communicated in 1906 with an official of the Industrial Removal Office, the Jewish agency that worried about the negative effects of peddling. He informed its executive director, David Bressler, with pride, "I came from New York to Marquette [Michigan] as a painter, but only worked at my trade a short time when I dropped it and went peddling and finally into business for myself. I merely mention this to show the possibilities open for the right kind of man who comes here." Being a painter had led him, as he saw it, nowhere, while peddling had opened doors.[4]

Details of the painter-peddler-businessman's life lay shrouded in obscurity. But by virtue of his prominence, Eisner's story can provide a framework to see how peddling enabled new-world Jewish business success and civic integration. That he, like so many others, had once sold door to door from a pack on his back provided Jews in America with an argument for inclusion and reason to congratulate themselves on hard work and industry. Likewise, that he started as a lowly peddler allowed some non-Jewish Americans to take pride in their country's liberality.

Stephen Wise turned his eulogy for Eisner into a statement about America, as he saw it in the mid-1920s, using the funeral oration to praise the deceased, champion the Jews, and advocate for a liberal America that he saw facing real threats. The political context shaped the eulogy. Eisner died a few days into 1925, the first year after the United States Congress severely limited how many immigrants could enter the country. Quotas were based on national origin, and relatively few slots were assigned to the lands where the world's Jews lived and which they wanted to leave. Wise delivered his words about the former peddler in January of a year in which circulation figures of the *Dearborn Independent*, published by Henry Ford, swelled to 900,000, second only to the *New York Times*. In its pages the automobile magnate warned about plots against America being hatched by an international Jewish conspiracy. Even in Sigmund Eisner's New Jersey, in 1925 the Ku Klux Klan, a racist and anti-Semitic organization notorious for its burning crosses, political activism, and inflammatory publications, was increasing in membership and spreading the message that Jewish wealth and depravity threatened America, a Christian nation.

Wise paid attention to that context as he described Eisner as a lad who "came to this land and to these hospitable shores whilst yet the gates were wide open, forty years ago." He arrived "a poor boy." "Poor boy?" the rabbi asked rhetorically, tackling the xenophobia and anti-Semitism of the 1920s. "Poor only in worldly substance. . . . He brought with him precious things from the old world and the old life. He brought with him the habits of industry and thrift; he brought with him out of the old world ideals of undeviating integrity and rectitude." He transported the best of the "old Jewish family life."

Eisner's non-Jewish neighbors made the same point as they celebrated him, his Jewish origins, and his peddling past. The Borough of Red Bank passed an official resolution lauding the man who "came into our midst in humble circumstances, but with honorable and worthy impulses." The First Presbyterian Church issued a statement praising this Jewish benefactor of local endeavors.

The town's paper, the *Long Branch Daily Record*, shared with its readers an account of Eisner's rise from penniless immigrant to ownership of "the immense business of the Sigmund Eisner Company," a concern employing so many townspeople.

The *New York Bulletin* joined the chorus of those who honored the man, simultaneously warning about challenges faced by the nation. The *Bulletin* reminded readers that Eisner had been "forced to do what many another Jew was forced to do, get his peddler's pack, sling it across his back and walk through the city, town and village to sell his ware." Despite hardships, Eisner, with hard work and unbounded dreams, prospered. His life, the *Bulletin* writer asserted, should be held up to all "who complain that there is no opportunity, no chance of success?" Yet readers of the *Bulletin* needed to keep in mind that in 1925, "the klan is powerful," threatening the possibility that another Sigmund Eisner could replicate this trajectory.[5]

Even shorn of its specific American political context, this personal history of a Jewish immigrant peddler who died a substantial man of property and civic virtue offers a template for the history of Jewish peddling around the new world. Jewish immigrants who came to the new world as peddlers arrived with skills, contacts, and experiences that equipped them to transform peddling into bigger and better opportunities.

But their successes had deeper and more complex roots. The Jewish immigrant came to sell to people who had little access to material goods. Many came at the frontier stage of many undeveloped places. The Jewish peddlers honeycombed the United States, moving increasingly westward with customers. Those who went to Canada followed the path of the Canadian Pacific Railway, and like their peers who chose South Africa and Australia, moved in tandem with the surge of the white population to areas they defined as free, wide open, and fit to be settled. Jewish peddlers benefited from the expansion of population and capitalism in remote regions of long-settled countries. Jewish peddlers in Sweden, Ireland, Scotland, and Wales benefited from the commercialization of agriculture, construction of roads and railways, development of mining and other extractive enterprises, and creation of industries that allowed women and men to want and to buy things. People who lived in places with few stores to satisfy material yearnings embraced immigrant Jewish peddlers, who succeeded as a result of newly awakened desires for goods. Their customers' isolation laid the ground for the peddlers' achievements. So, too, peddlers' readiness to sell to poor people, whether on farms, on rubber, sugar, banana, and cotton plantations, in coal mining regions, in textile and steel mill towns, helped inaugurate these regions into the cash economy, ensuring that Jewish immigrant peddlers would find people eager to buy.

Jewish peddlers did well, moving into more substantial businesses because so many migrated to places that encouraged the immigration of white people. While officials of many of these countries did not encourage peddlers, they did welcome Europeans and, as such, Jews. Jews headed for Peru, the United States, Australia, or New Zealand, engaged in whatever businesses they chose, and aspired to achieve more.[6] Despite anti-Jewish rumblings, for example, when South Africa initiated a literacy test in 1917 to weed out undesirable newcomers, it declared Yiddish a European language, issuing a linguistic passport of acceptability to Lithuanian and other eastern European Jews.

New-world places promised Jews access to economic resources, never reneging. No laws impeded them as they took to the roads, and when they settled. Anti-Jewish prejudice existed, but Jews, as white men, faced few limitations and pursued goals of their choosing. Their adherence to a minority religion presented scant obstacles in securing state protection, engaging in commercial transactions, and moving about freely.

The experience of Sammy Marks, born in Lithuania in 1899, illustrates the benefits of whiteness. Marks came to South Africa in the 1860s, started as a peddler, hawking knives and cheap jewelry, and quickly carved out a remarkable career in business and in the life of his adopted country. Marks moved speedily from peddling to other businesses, most important dealing in diamonds and gold, the two treasures buried beneath the soil of the land beyond the Cape of Good Hope and two commodities precious to Europeans. Marks expanded his interests in multiple directions, always seizing new opportunities, acquiring and expanding his wealth. This onetime peddler forged a close alliance with President Paul Kruger of the Zuid-Afrikaansche Republiek (ZAR). To Kruger, Marks represented the limitless possibilities of Africa for white people. In tribute, Marks at the end of the Anglo-Boer War commissioned a massive bronze statue of the Boer leader to loom over Pretoria's Church Square. Marks, who had once sold small items from the road, actively participated in the political life of the country, serving in the Senate and using his wealth to endow local charities. He also amply funded local Jewish institutions.[7]

Whiteness alone did not ensure peddlers' success. Immigrant Jews peddled in Sweden, Ireland, Wales, Scotland, and Quebec, where race did not serve as a dividing line. Rather they benefited from the emigration of women and men who sent back remittances to those left behind. Now awash in cash, these lands beckoned Jewish peddlers who supplied the receivers of these gifts from abroad with wares unattainable before. Jewish peddlers who first sold door to door did well enough in these lands, transforming into settled merchants.

Jewish peddlers also succeeded, most modestly, others spectacularly, because of Jewish credit networks. Jewish merchants motivated by philanthropic and practical impulses extended credit and equipped new immigrants with goods. Polish Jewish immigrants in Cuba, for example, relied for credit on a Jewish web of relationships that stretched from hinterland towns to Havana and to the United States. A Jewish communal worker from the United States, Harry Vitales, went to Cuba in 1925. Upon his return he reported to Jewish manufacturers and leaders on the promising sales opportunities in Cuba for Jewish immigrants, particularly in such fields as shoes, stockings, men's clothing, leather goods, ties, zippers, and belts, all items the semananiks carried around the island. Investing in Jewish peddlers in Cuba, he suggested, constituted good business and was good for Jews no longer able to enter the United States due to quota restrictions. Why not Cuba, Vitales asked rhetorically. He knew that peddling had brought success to nearly all who had done it; for some few it had been the proverbial goose that laid the golden egg. Many of the Jewish manufacturers in New York and the communal operatives who read the report had themselves once peddled, and if not they, then fathers, uncles, cousins, or friends.[8]

Peddling enabled some Jews to buy land in their new countries. While R. G. Dunn reporters in nineteenth-century America considered Jewish peddlers poor risks because they owned no real property, some peddlers, once settled, invested in real estate. Around the new world some made fortunes in land development. Buying up unused and undeveloped land, peddlers facilitated the growth and exploitation of unsettled regions. In the United States, Canada, South Africa, and Australia they used money earned in peddling and from small first and second off-the-road enterprises to help extend railroads, lay roads, and plant communities for further settlement. Otto Mears, born in the Latvian province of Kurland, came to the United States a young orphan before the Civil War. He headed west, peddled for ten years, particularly among the Ute Indians, then operated a freight and packing business, and ultimately became a major developer of western roads and railroads.[9] Alfred de Mattels, a Sephardic Jewish peddler, came to Haiti, starting out "with a pack on his back." He became "the largest real estate proprietor in Port-au-Prince," having first gone into the jewelry business after stepping off the road.[10]

A few Jewish immigrants, once through with peddling, purchased plantations, extensive cotton, coffee, sugar, and rubber holdings worked by servile or semiservile laborers. As peddlers they had come onto plantations to sell to landowners and workers, slave and free, learning details of the system in the course of selling. When they had saved enough, a handful tried made fortunes this way. Gabriel Meyer peddled around Pine Bluff, Arkansas, and by the 1870s owned no fewer than nineteen plantations.[11] Leon Godchaux, an Alsatian Jewish peddler who, like other Jews from that French-speaking region, went to Louisiana, eventually owning a sugar plantation so large and lucrative that locals called him the state's "Sugar King."[12]

For some Jewish peddlers, money earned by peddling brought them into banking, particularly locally. Solomon Meir made his way from the Hunsruck region of the Rhineland to peddle in Noble County, Indiana, in the 1850s. The 1860 census showed that Meir, now a shopkeeper, owned $2,000 in personal property and $1,000 in real estate. Ten years later his worth stood at $45,000 and $14,000, respectively, and instead of listing his occupation as dry goods merchant, as in his first postpeddling census, he now described himself as the owner of a private bank.[13]

Only a few former peddlers became even remotely as wealthy as Sigmund Eisner or Sammy Marks, let alone Meyer Guggenheim, the Lehman brothers, the Seligman brothers, Lazarus Straus, or Levi Strauss, but around the world untold numbers acquired serious wealth. Isaac Schwayder went from Poland to Manchester, England, and then to Colorado, where he peddled in the mountain towns around Central City, using as his base a store owned by Abe Rachovsky, himself a former peddler. Isaac then opened his own store and could easily have rested content. But in 1910 he and his brother Jesse decided to venture into luggage manufacturing, forming the Schwayder Trunk Manufacturing Company. Inspired by a biblical narrative of physical strength, the brothers came up with a new, catchy name: Samsonite.[14] Isaac Bernheim also began his career in America as a peddler, arriving in 1867 from Bavaria. He headed for Kentucky. After peddling he worked as a bookkeeper for a wholesale liquor company, Loeb, Bloom and Company, and then with his two brothers opened their own distillery, which became one of the largest in the nation.[15]

A roster of names of peddlers who did very well, carving out lucrative niches for themselves around the new world, could also include Joseph Littauer, founder of one of the America's largest and most successful glove factories in upstate New York, in the town of Gloverville; Marcus Goldman, who peddled for two years before establishing Goldman, Sachs, and Company; and Samuel Zemurray, who began as a peddler but topped off his career as founder and owner of the mammoth United Fruit Company.

A list extended to the children of peddlers, beneficiaries of fathers' years on the road, would include Abraham and Simon Flexner, an educator and a physician, respectively; Julius Rosenwald of Sears and Roebuck fame, a pillar of early-twentieth-century American philanthropy; Joseph Fels, a soap manufacturer, known for the brand that carried his name, Fels Naptha; art critic and connoisseur Bernard Berenson and his sister, Senda, creator of women's basketball; Jacob Blaustein, founder of the American Oil Company; the sculptor Louise Nevelson, a diplomat and Jewish communal activist; Judge Joseph Proskauer; and members of the United States Congress Sol Bloom, Abraham Ribicoff, and Arlen Specter. English barrister and legal scholar Norman Bentwich and playwright Israel Zangwill, author of *The Melting Pot*, had peddler fathers. So did C. P. Taylor, a Scottish dramatist, who wrote dozens of plays for the stage, radio, and television. Dublin's Lord Mayor Robert Briscoe was born to a father who came to Ireland from Lithuania and also peddled.

Even children of relatively unsuccessful peddlers surpassed their fathers. William Lee Provol can exemplify the progress from immigrant peddler father to successful new-world son. Provol's parents migrated to Sweden from Poland, then moving on in 1881—father first, then the mother and children— to Syracuse, New York. The father earned enough peddling to bring over his family but never made more than a living. His son William, born in Sweden, helped out at times, peddling farm to farm. Success proved elusive for the father, but not for the son. William as a young man decided to try the fur business, did well, and opened stores in San Francisco and Salt Lake City. He donated money to various causes and helped found the Loyal Order of Moose, a national fraternal and service organization. Provol's mobility from son of a barely successful peddler to substantial businessman did nothing to make him disavow impoverished immigrant origins; he dedicated his 1933 memoir, *The Pack Peddler*, to "The Memory of the Vast Army of Courageous Pack Peddlers by the Son of One of Them."[16]

William Provol's father probably considered himself a failure, a peddler who achieved little, but his son's achievement of status and comfort may have served as a counterbalance. Like the younger Provol, sons often avoided replicating their fathers' work experiences. More important historically than exceptional and extraordinary stories of fame and fortune, nearly all Jewish life histories in the new world tell an almost monotonous tale of men peddling as new immigrants, then using their earnings to open a sedentary business, thus enabling daughters and sons to rise in the business world or secure educations that lead to the professions. Sara Millin, the daughter of a South African immigrant peddler, wrote in 1937 that "the universities are full of Jews. Those pedlars ... have fulfilled their ambitions vicariously." Statistics bore out Millin's observations. In 1917 the roster of first-year medical students at the

South African School of Mines and Technology abounded with Jewish sur-
names. A report at the time declared, "We cannot refrain from mentioning the
very large proportion of students of the Jewish section of the community;
which is remarkable. It is," the observer went on, "notable also, that the bulk
of these is not drawn from wealthy families, but are carrying on the arduous
and prolonged study of medicine under difficulties." While some students
may have had smous fathers, given the sizable number of Jewish immigrant
peddlers, most had probably been men who had migrated from Lithuania before putting packs on their backs.[17]

Peddlers everywhere became shopkeepers or graduated to other sedentary
occupations. In their town or city lives, they achieved higher standards of living than they had endured as peddlers. Likewise, once peddlers settled down,
they lived better than most of their non-Jewish neighbors. In Dublin no Jews
lived in the city's tenement districts. Rather, former weekly men, and even
some still peddling, occupied three- and four-room terraced single-family
homes. In Dublin, Limerick, Cork, and Glasgow's Gorbals neighborhood of
the late nineteenth century, many small shopkeepers, onetime peddlers, employed domestic servants.[18]

By avoiding tenement life and employing some domestic help, former peddlers resembled the native-born middle classes more than the working class.
Former peddlers sought to emulate the educational and cultural practices of
the better off of their towns and cities. In settings divided by race, religion,
and ethnicity, erstwhile peddlers looked "up," modeling themselves against
the most prestigious groups, the white, well off, and cosmopolitan. In South
Africa, Ireland, and Quebec they identified with those of English background,
sending their children to English schools. In Ireland, for example, the children
of the Jewish weekly men were schooled no differently from Protestant children. The denizens of Clanbrassil Street and elsewhere in Dublin's "Little
Jerusalem" mocked Catholics for their poverty, religious practices and beliefs,
and resemblance to the Lithuanian peasants their parents described from back
home. Catholic rural people provided the weekly men with much of their livelihood, but the Jews, children and adults, peddlers and shopkeepers, called the
local people *laptsehs:* gullible, oafish, and easily hoodwinked.[19]

The peddlers, even if they did not earn spectacular sums, did save enough
to send money back home, and that fulfilled the purpose of their migrations.
Making enough money to bring over wives and children constituted a level of
success. Louis Singer, born in 1871 in White Russia, proclaimed himself his
family's "pioneer in America." He peddled in West Virginia, moved to the
Mesabi Iron Range, and settled down in the peddler supply business. Reflecting

back on his life, he detailed each family member he brought from Europe. With pride he noted, "I brought over 2 brothers, 2 sisters and their children, and to Duluth I brought over Nathan Singer and family and his brother B. Singer and his family, then cousins Evans family and Joselsons and family and some friends." He received harrowing letters from family members trapped in Belarus after World War I and during the great pogroms of 1917 through 1921. He and his wife traveled back home "to bring them all to this country."[20] Isaac Bernheim used some of his money to bring running water to his old home in Bavaria, while Abraham Kohn saved enough to bring over all his brothers and his mother. Jewish peddlers who went first to Sweden, Ireland, and the British Isles probably measured their peddling success according to whether they earned enough to continue to the United States. Many of those who first hawked wares in England, Scotland, Wales, and Ireland came to America in command of English, skipped the peddler stage, and got right onto some sedentary business.

In every city and town where immigrant Jews settled, some former peddlers entered the ranks of the largest merchants, the most extensive real estate owners, and the most generous benefactors of local endeavors. The masses of Jewish peddlers who went into businesses experienced nothing resembling such meteoric trajectories but realized the basic aims of their migrations. In mid-nineteenth-century Cincinnati, within three years of arrival in the country, eight immigrant Jewish peddlers had become wholesale and retail clothing merchants, five owned dry goods stores, and others appeared in the city directory as a silversmith, a hatter, the owner of a coffeehouse, a boardinghouse proprietor, and an entrepreneur in the fuel and lumber business. None labored in industry. All worked for themselves. The wholesale and retail merchants succeeded mightily, while the others held their own, a not inconsiderable feat in the mercurial nineteenth century, where downward, rather than upward, mobility haunted many Americans.[21]

The cessation of peddling meant the chance to marry or bring wives and children to the new world. For Jewish peddlers who married local non-Jewish women who did not convert to Judaism, peddling's end spelled the end of their connection to Jewish community life. In Australia, South Africa, Cuba, Brazil, New Zealand, and probably everywhere, they and their children melded into the larger population, as the men essentially had to cut their ties to the Jewish world. Jewish communities did not countenance intermarriage. Children of Jewish fathers had no standing within the matrilineal Jewish system. For these men, an uncountable number, who had peddled and fallen in love with local women, the moment they stopped peddling amounted a farewell to organized

Jewish life and to the rituals and services which belonging to a community offered.

In a few documented cases, like that of Marcus Spiegel, whose wife, Caroline Hamlin of Ohio, converted to Judaism, men did not have to choose between the women they loved and Jewish community membership. Their number defies quantification, but individual life histories regularly tell such stories, and while the conversions may not have conformed precisely to Jewish law, the women participated fully in local Jewish communities. The author of one peddler family history from late-eighteenth- and early-nineteenth-century England, described a pattern he observed. While the typical peddler who "had saved a little money . . . would marry his patron's daughter, or the daughter of an itinerant colleague, or would send for his wife from abroad," some "would induce one of the Gentile lassies among his customers to share his humble fortunes and embrace the religion of his fathers." The married peddler "would set up a shop of his own, preferentially in the center of the district in which he had worked as a pedlar, and the peripatetic trinket-seller would bloom out into a jeweler and silver-smith." The writer, Israel Solomon, emphasized the positive relationships which flourished between Jewish peddlers and their customers, particularly the "lassies." But his words indicate that those "lassies," once married to Jews and converted to Judaism, still remained close by their Christian parents, relatives, and friends. The Jewish jewelers and silversmiths had non-Jewish relatives and their wives' friends close by. This social proximity linked Jews and non-Jews in a distinctively new-world way.[22]

Most, though, did not marry outside the Jewish community. Those who had arrived single turned their attention to matrimony when they decided it was time to abandon the road. They faced the question of whom to marry. Where, they asked themselves, would they find a suitable Jewish wife? Some, particularly central Europeans, returned home to make a match. So, too, some who emigrated to Latin America from North Africa and the Ottoman Empire also went back to their original communities to select from among the growing number of unmarried young women left behind in the wake of the male exodus. At times the new couple embarking on the journey back to the new world recruited single women, sisters, friends, cousins, all of whom would face little trouble in finding husbands among the bachelor peddlers ready to settle down.

Others sought brides close by. Connections made through business often eventuated in marriages. Zender Falmouth, the peddler outfitter in late-eighteenth-century England, married off all his daughters to peddlers to whom he supplied goods.[23] For some peddlers Sabbaths spent in town became times to meet daughters and sisters of shopkeepers and other settled Jews.

Others encountered future wives when they traveled to some large community to replenish their stock. Abraham Flexner's mother and aunt had come from the Rhineland to Louisville to live with relatives, including an uncle who operated a wholesale china business. According to the son, "at their uncle's home" the young women "met many of the young Jewish merchants or peddlers, who used to spend the Jewish holidays and weekends in the large city." From that pool she found her husband-to-be.[24] Samuel Rosenwald, an immigrant who peddled out of Baltimore, selling to customers along Virginia's Winchester Trail, got his goods from the Hammerslough Brothers. They introduced him to their sister Augusta, whom the peddler married. The wholesaler brothers gave the couple a wonderful wedding gift, a clothing store in Peoria, Illinois, to manage.[25]

Former peddlers could make attractive marriage partners, according to young Jewish women and their parents. Sophia Heller looked back on her life in Milwaukee and Chicago in the mid-nineteenth century, recalling that "P.G."—Philip Goldsmith, whom she was to marry—"had $1,500 in cash invested, with nice credit, which he had earned through peddling."[26] Her father and mother liked that as well. Jewish communities around the new world during the age of peddling operated as informal marriage markets, as parents, owners of stores, craftsmen, peddler suppliers, and junk shop owners evaluated peddlers as potential spouses for daughters and sisters.

Sometimes coincidences brought unmarried peddlers together with other Jews who knew of women in search of matrimony. William Frank, a Pittsburgh-based peddler, sat down on a train going from Harrisburg to Philadelphia and met another Jew, Samuel Dreyfoose, a newlywed. "I told him," Frank recalled, "that if I could meet a desirable girl, I would marry also." His travel partner immediately suggested that "if I would stop at Lancaster, he would introduce me to his wife's cousin, who was living with them." Frank agreed, and the two met and married. William left peddling to make a good living as a glass manufacturer.[27]

Married peddlers faced different challenges when they settled down and reunited with wives and children than did bachelor peddlers. Husbands and wives, fathers and children had to get to know each other all over again after long separations of time and space. For wives and children who had remained in Europe, North Africa, or the Ottoman world, the husband-father might have become something of a stranger. Even those wives who had emigrated with husbands might see their peddler husbands only two days out of seven, and the couple might have to readjust to each other weekly. Women accustomed to being alone and independent for large chunks of time may have found their husbands' permanent return constricting. Sometimes this grew out of business concerns as much as domestic ones. Mike Goldwater, an immigrant from Russian Poland to California in the 1850s, peddled in Arizona in the early 1860s after several failed businesses. His wife, Sarah, refused to move to Gila City, the base of his operations, remaining instead in Los Angeles, where she developed a flourishing business in his absence. When he returned, she demanded sole control of her finances, going so far as to file a legal statement declaring, "From this date and after this date I intend to carry on and transact in my own name and on my own account, the business of tailoring and merchandising. . . . I will be personally responsible for all debts contracted by me in said business."[28]

Memoirs and family histories attest to high fertility rates among the wives of former peddlers. Most births seem to have taken place after the move into sedentary business. One memoirist of Jewish life in Swartland, South Africa, in the 1920s, recalled that his father had arrived from Lithuania and took up peddling, with his wife and four children still in Europe. When he could afford to bring them over to Malmesbury, he opened a store, and the couple proceeded to have another three children. "Many of the other families had 7 or 8 children," the son wrote, and most such families were headed by a smous father, now turned proprietor of a small shop.[29]

Wives of peddlers had spent time, years often, making financial, familial, and even communal decisions. With the husband on the road and no way to communicate, women responded to crises as they came up and carved out independent roles in the local Jewish community. The return of the traveling husband forced each individual woman, each in her own way, to bend her activities and curtail her authority to his, based on his definition of proper gender roles. In their initial years of settling down, if they had opened a dry goods store as so many did, they typically lived above or behind the store, making work and home overlapping spaces. Likewise, in initial postpeddling years, Jewish families operated modest businesses in retail or manufacturing, and wives generally worked alongside husbands. The men at times continued to peddle while wives managed the store. But as enterprises grew and as the number of children increased, paid employees took over where wives had once worked. Wives of now-middle-class shopkeepers no longer routinely and by necessity played active roles in the family economy, or if they did, they acted as advisers and not daily participants.

Instead, they played increasingly more formal roles in the Jewish communities and in their various benevolent activities. Their Female Hebrew Benevolent Associations all over America, for example, became powerful players in Jewish communal life. Women's groups raised money, spent it as they saw fit, and pushed back against the authority of the male communal leaders who assumed that they, as men, had the right to control the community and its purse strings.

With or without family discord, peddlers typically succeeded well enough to step off the road. Few peddlers failed so badly that they could not ever save enough money to open a business on their own. Some children, though, remembered peddler fathers who had a difficult time transitioning out of peddling. The Shubert brothers became major impresarios of the American theater. But their childhoods in Syracuse, New York, like that of William Provol, reflected the reality that their immigrant father, who went house to house in and around Oswego, Canandaigua, and Binghamton, had so little success that his boys occasionally peddled with him and their mother took in boarders.[30] Some elderly Cuban Jews, reminiscing decades after retirement, reported how hard they had found their economic circumstances after peddling, and one remembered about his father, an immigrant from Belarus, "Of course he was . . . a peddler, an occupation to which he returned more than once."[31]

Reports issued by Jewish charitable organizations gave further evidence— by omission—that peddling was likely to keep its practitioners from becoming dependent on communal philanthropy. A report of 1914 noted that of the Jews aided by the United Hebrew Charities, "the larger proportion of the loans made . . . was granted . . . to needle workers," many suffering from lung diseases.[32] The same year, Rabbi David da Sola Pool, in *Jewish Charities*, extolled peddling as an avenue for the mobility enjoyed by Levantine Jews in the United States. Acknowledging that the publication's readers looked down on peddling, he observed that Jews from Rhodes and elsewhere in the Ottoman Empire had in America speedily moved from peddling to substantial sedentary occupations.[33] Jewish charities bemoaned the fate of the ubiquitous urban pushcart peddlers, who often turned to communal funds and swelled the ranks of the Jewish poor. On-the-road peddlers, though, did not as a rule share that dependent fate.

And when peddlers decided to get off the road and open businesses, they rarely relied on benefactors or Jewish community coffers. Their savings sufficed. Some did need a bit of help, and immigrant Jewish peddlers particularly in Latin America banded together, forming loan societies in order to assist each other to open shops. These peddler *kasses*, informal banks, functioned like rotating credit associations, as peddlers pooled their money, each in his turn borrowing from the common pot. These peddler cooperatives, such as La Corporación Comercial, founded in 1929, and Cooperativa Comercial Israelita del Uruguay in 1936, funded peddlers to become storeowners.[34]

Most Jewish peddlers, wherever they came from and wherever they went, left the road for businesses, starting with small-scale enterprises that dealt in the familiar dry goods, housewares, and clothing lines. Jewish-owned dry goods stores became fixtures of local life on multiple continents. Millions of Jews made a living this way. It happened everywhere. It took place in Sweden and Rhodesia, in Newfoundland and Australia.[35] Moisés Nae Assa recalled that his father came to Cuba's Oriente province in 1923, "began as a peddler in the north and in 1927 opened a store called the Zeppelin." José Miller Friedman's father, a Lithuanian, came to Cuba the next year, peddled and then opened his shop, La Economía in Yaguajay in the northern province of Las Villas.[36] At the other end of the world Nehemia Dov Hoffman, who eventually launched South Africa's first Yiddish weekly newspaper, shared his trajectory in his *Sefer Hazichronot*, his book of memories. He set out from Johannesburg as a peddler, when "peddling was . . . a good business, and the 'green' Jew made money in those days." Upon reaching "Hottentots Cliff," in the Karoo Desert between Ceres and Calvina, he decided to stop and open a general store; soon after, he "brought out my family from Russia."[37]

The small Jewish-owned store, marketing a jumble of goods, or specializing in some item—jewelry, watches, clothing for men or women, furniture, picture frames—constituted a transnational Jewish reality. Belzoni, Mississippi—the "catfish capital of the world"—Swansea, Wales, Nababeep, in Namaqualand (now in the Northern Cape Province of South Africa), Hokitika, New Zealand, Curaçao, and literally thousands of other places shared the presence of Jewish-owned dry goods stores opened by immigrants, graduates from peddling. H. Marks peddled among the miners and others who flocked to New Zealand in the 1860s. Within a few years he operated his Beehive Store.[38] The son of the proprietor of the Confidential Store in Curaçao recalled that his father, an immigrant peddler from Poland in the 1930s, situated his "first shop . . . opposite the Anna Church . . . a very small shop where he sold all sorts of things, then he opened the next one, the one called Confidential, where he sold pots and pans, household goods, cloths, this and that."[39]

Wherever this happened—and it did so everywhere—Jewish peddlers, then storekeepers, did reasonably well. A Jewish communal leader in Brazil in the 1920s, Jacob Schneider, commented that Jewish immigrants to that country experienced great hardships, that they "have to struggle hard in order to find independent existences. . . . They . . . start as hawkers." He continued, looking forward, "they succeed in establishing themselves as shopkeepers." Schneider, eager to spur on more Jewish immigration to Brazil, particularly after the

United States had restricted their influx, may have sounded a bit too positive, but empirical data, life histories, and communal biographies all tell the same story, regardless of time or place.[40]

Jews made their way to hundreds of thousands of spots around the new world, and peddling and then shopkeeping generated the movement. T. Thomas Fortune, a journalist and civil rights activist, commented in 1913 in the *New York Age* that after the Civil War, "the Jews invaded the Southern States." They came initially, wrote the former slave, "with their merchandise in packs on their backs and began to open stores in the cities, towns, and crossroads as fast as their wholesale Jewish merchant connections in Baltimore, Philadelphia, and New York could ship the goods they ordered."[41] Peddling and its almost inevitable successor, shopkeeping, drove Jewish settlement into the hinterlands of dozens of countries, on every new-world continent. The farther removed from the metropolis Jewish men peddled, the farther out were the places they got off the road. They planted themselves in communities far removed from large cities.

Likewise, the immigrants' progress from peddling to store ownership generated centripetal dynamic. New York, Chicago, London, Buenos Aires, and Johannesburg drew Jews who once had peddled deep in the countryside. When the time came to settle down, they moved to these big cities, places abounding in business opportunities for someone with capital, places where many other Jews lived and Jewish communal institutions thrived. Of the millions of Jews who lived in the major new-world cities, inestimable numbers had once peddled in some rural region and then had moved to the cities to start businesses and families. One Scottish Jewish memoir writer remembered that his father and uncles had all peddled around the Shetland Islands and set up some stores there, but "eventually . . . left Shetland to live in Glasgow where there was a large Jewish community." While in Shetland, the son recalled, they maintained fine relationships with their customers, acquired from peddling and store proprietorship days. Customers embraced the "bonnie things" which before they "had only seen in picture books." But when these Jewish purveyors of "bonnie things" contemplated their future and that of their children, they wanted the metropolis with its synagogues, Jewish and general educational institutions, and the other accoutrements of community life.[42]

Jewish shopkeepers, onetime peddlers, used their stores like stationary versions of their old peripatetic occupation. As peddlers they had lugged an array of goods, almost whatever men and women on their routes wanted. So, too, their dry goods stores carried a wide range of items, ever responding to local needs and attuned to big-city novelties. As on-the-road peddlers lent money to customers, so, too, many small stores functioned as protean banks. Ironically, after years of sleeping in customers' homes, some Jewish shopkeepers provided a kind of parking lot, where rural people who had come to town could sleep in their wagons. Farmers and their wives who had previously collected bones, feathers, tin, fur, and herbs for the peddlers now made the reverse journey, bringing this stuff to the Jewish shopkeepers. The Wallace brothers came to North Carolina in 1859 from Hesse-Kassel to peddle around the town of Bamberg. In three years they opened a store in Statesville. They sold the usual dry goods store items, ran a small private bank, and launched a brisk business with customers who brought herbs and roots. Their enterprise grew into a drug business on a national scale.[43]

An inestimable number of these stores catered specifically to working-class and poor customers. While some—again uncountable—operated in Jewish neighborhoods, large numbers sold to non-Jews: Americans, Irish, Welsh, Cubans, South Africans, Australians, whoever constituted the local population. Legions dealt in secondhand and low-end goods, as women and men who labored on plantations, mines, logging camps, and factories came to these stores to meet their material needs. In Brazil's Bahia Province, in the city of Salvador, former Jewish peddlers established stores that sold to the poor, as they did in Mexico, Cuba, Jamaica, Rhodesia, and indeed in Pennsylvania, Georgia, Dublin, and everywhere. These stores cropped up in immigrant neighborhoods, particularly ones where only a few of their cohort entered small business. Former peddlers ran stores in Slavic neighborhoods in Buffalo, New York; Johnstown, Pennsylvania; and Chicago. Droves of peddlers decided to open shops catering to African Americans, and the peddlers who had once gone into black homes and allowed customers to try on clothing now did so again in their fixed-place stores. A historian of the American South, E. Merton Coulter, a thorough and unabashed defender of racial segregation, wrote of these former peddlers, "The end of the war saw an invasion of Jews to reap a harvest in trade; the ante-bellum Jewish peddlers . . . now settled down and opened stores. Sticking to their business and treating the freedman as an important businessman, not eschewing to call him 'Mister,' they," the Jews, "secured a great amount of the Negro's trade." Coulter considered this transgressive behavior, dangerous to the social order. The Jewish merchants saw it as good business. Jewish shopkeepers and their children invariably in the early postpeddling years made their homes above or behind the store, making them among the few white people to live on these streets.[44] Former peddlers traded in used goods and operated pawnshops, mainstay institutions in poor neighborhoods. Yakov (Jake) Sender had peddled in

Maryland and Pennsylvania. On his travels he met a young Jewish woman, American-born, and decided to stay in Harrisburg, where her family lived. Together Jake and Nettie opened a used furniture store, selling goods they advertised as "Used but not abused."[45]

Just as peddlers had not hidden their Jewishness from the women whose thresholds they crossed, so too when they opened stores, they made their identities clear. More often than not, they hung out shingles with distinctive Jewish names, ones that differed from those common in the area. They closed for the Jewish holidays, moments on the calendar with no Christian equivalents. They often placed advertisements in local newspapers and posted signs on their doors announcing to the public that because of a Jewish holiday, Rosh Hashanah, Yom Kippur, Passover, they would shutter their shops. They affixed *mezuzot* on the doorposts to their stores, decorative cases with a piece of parchment inside, inscribed with a Hebrew verse. The proprietors' unmistakable accents marked them as different. Throughout the United States locals referred, without negative valence, to "the Jew store."

All over the new world some small stores, operated by onetime Jewish peddlers and their wives, transformed into bigger, grander ones. They became department stores, grand emporia, on busy commercial streets, in some cases the most important one in the city or town, designed with ornate architecture, fixed up with elegant accoutrements, and in the newest styles. Many retained their founders' foreign-sounding names, such as Gimbel, Altman, Kaufman, Filene, Stein, Thalheimer, Sanger, Lebo, Schuster, Poliakoff, Hutzler, Hecht, Pitzitz, or Loeb, as well as the partnership of Nieman and Marcus, among others. The women and men of Walgett, in Australia's New South Wales, could shop at W. R. Cohen's Department Store, founded and operated by a Polish Jewish immigrant, a former peddler. That these Jewish department store owners, once on-the-road peddlers, did not hesitate to mark their commercial enterprises with their clearly Jewish names reveals something about the confidence they felt in themselves and in their customers, who accepted them for who they were, Jews and merchants.

Others chose names that reflected marketing visions, based on their knowledge, acquired on the road and off, as to what customers wanted, beyond the goods themselves. A onetime peddler opened the Style Shoppe in Rolling Fork, in the Mississippi Delta, playing to the aspirations of the women looking for something more than just the utilitarian and mundane. Shoppers in Long Branch, New Jersey, bought goods at Jacob and John Steinbach's Temple of Fashion, opened by these peddlers in 1870, a few years after they arrived from Germany.[46] The name Grand-Leader, chosen by Russian Jewish immigrant Sam Lindy after three years of peddling, allowed the men and women of Jackson, Tennessee, to feel that by crossing the threshold of his store, no matter how limited their resources, no matter how little agency they had in their workplaces, they could temporarily experience a world of elegance. (Their race mattered, however: African Americans had little more access to Jewish-owned department stores than to Gentile ones.)[47]

Some store names, like the Globe, a Jewish-owned department store in a small town in Arkansas, enabled its residents to imagine themselves part of the big world. Many Jewish-owned department stores, founded by men who once had sold from the road, opted for the names of faraway places, unreachable for the residents of small remote communities. They dubbed their stores with the names of Paris, London, New York, and Boston, sites of sophistication, symbols of urbanity. When Herman Figelman, a Romanian Jew who had first peddled in Minnesota, decided to open a department store, he moved to Helena, Montana, and named his emporium New York, a name sure to convey to the residents of the region, far removed from the East Coast, the idea of cosmopolitan luxury. All over the United States, New York or Manhattan department stores in particular cropped up, opened by Jewish men who had once sold from packs and wagons on the road.

Peddlers who had interacted with women one by one in their homes, continued to see them as their core clientele. Women, they believed, reveled in consumption and could be brought to their stores with some adroit advertising. Charles Dante from Lithuania settled, after peddling, in Dumas, Arkansas, where he situated the Globe department store. There he addressed the women of the town and its surrounding countryside with the slogan, "You furnish the girl, we furnish the home."[48]

Each department store involved an immigrant Jewish peddler who moved up to retail, usually first with a small general store, followed by a large and ornate one. Louis Pitzitz peddled goods in the South after arriving in 1889 from Poland. His first shop, a modest dry goods store in Birmingham, evolved into a major department store. By 1937 he employed 750 women and men and his store, a size not equaled by any other store in the state.[49] Nor was this just an American story. In Australia the department store bearing the name Myer—founded by Sidney (born Simha) Baevski and his brother Elcon, from Krychaw in the province of Mogilev in the Russian Pale, men who took their first steps in the antipodes as peddlers—became synonymous with elegant urban shopping. While on the road, whether in Indiana, like Adam Gimbel, or around Bendigo in Victoria, like the Baevskis, peddlers had learned that their customers yearned, even when poor, for a connection to style, quality, and cosmopolitanism.[50]

Other erstwhile peddlers, rather than selling from behind counters, ventured into the making of items they had once hawked. Some opened factories, like Sigmund Eisner's, which manufactured clothing, while others made jewelry, or eyeglasses, picture frames, and watches. In Ireland a sizable number of peddlers transitioned to the sedentary life by becoming picture frame makers. Michael Goldstone came to Liverpool from Warsaw in the 1820s, roaming the countryside, selling quill pens door to door. By 1838 he set himself up in Manchester as the manufacturer of those same pens, with a workshop on Springfield Lane. Over the next five years he branched out, adding jewelry and watchmaking to his operations, both goods peddlers took out on the road.[51] *Havaner Lebn*, Cuba's premier Yiddish publication, reported in the 1930s on Jewish life in other parts of Latin America; a 1935 feature article on "How the Jews Live in Lima, Peru" observed that while "the entire Jewish economy is peddling," some of the peddlers opened "small factories; factories which produce goods that support the peddlers."[52]

The factories employed local non-Jewish workers. Leon Birhaber's father came from Romania to Colombia in 1927, arriving in Cartagena, where he had a brother. He "began to travel," that is, peddle, when he first got there. When his sweetheart came from back home, he settled down in a town on the Caribbean coast, and "established a small industry for the 2,000 inhabitants" of the small town. The factory produced small goods, the kind peddlers could carry on their backs. This one Romanian immigrant ended up a substantial employer of Colombian workers.[53] Victor Perera told a similar new-world story about his father, an immigrant from Jerusalem to Guatemala, who "began life as an itinerant peddler." The elder Perera believed that peddling "reduced" him in circumstance and bemoaned the fate he endured by "peddling bolts of colored gingham to Indian laborers in a country so ignorant of his lineage it labeled him 'Turk.' " Yet he "eventually owned a textile manufacturing shop," becoming "one of Guatemala's leading merchants." Throughout Central and Latin America numbers also chose to make furniture. The newest peddlers then took the tables and chairs onto their wagons and sold them to residents of the countryside.[54]

Jewish immigrants, once the itinerant sellers of eyeglasses, became opticians, while those who had sold watches, began to make and repair them. Peripatetic dealers in jewelry experienced little difficulty later in making the bracelets, necklaces, and pins, marketing them retail to customers and wholesale to the newest peddlers. Joseph Harris, a Polish Jewish immigrant to England in the 1850s, took to the road hawking watches. He became a watchmaker in Manchester, selling retail as well as to the neophyte peddlers who replaced him.[55] David Davis peddled eyeglasses, among other goods, in 1820s Scotland, then becoming the proprietor of a combined optical and jewelry store in Glasgow within the decade. Such a move was a perfectly reasonable business strategy: these peddlers, who already knew the items and knew customer tastes, seamlessly shifted from marketing house to house to making the same items for other peddlers and to sell over the counters of their own stores.

No endeavor registered this seemingly organic drift from peddling to manufacturing more dramatically and globally than the clothing trade. Jews had participated in needlework for centuries, since long before the great migration. But in the places to which Jews emigrated during that long century, the making and selling of clothing shaped their lives. Their migrations coincided with a set of linked developments, particularly the invention of the sewing machine in the mid-nineteenth century. Peddlers carried clothes in their bags, used and new. Some carried samples of garments to show them to eager customers, who chose what they liked, picking style, color, and fabric. The peddler measured the customer for size, and when he returned to town put in his order with a local Jewish tailor or store owner. The peddler then delivered finished garments to the women and men on his route, who eagerly awaited their new dresses or blouses, pants or jackets.

The transition from peddling to making clothing took place almost organically and everywhere. The Swerskys and the Sidels made this occupational move from peddling in Canada's Maritime Provinces, Newfoundland, and Labrador. Emanuel Shoyer peddled in Wisconsin's small towns, and although he often had trouble collecting payment from his on-the-road customers, in the 1850s and 1860s he presided over Milwaukee's largest clothing manufacturing business.[56] R. H. Rapinsky graduated from peddling to making clothes in New York's Rockland County, as did Henry Mack and his three brothers in Cincinnati. Joseph Schaffner in Chicago, whose firm Hart, Schaffner and Marx became one of the nation's largest manufacturers of men's clothing, began in peddling. And so did Sigmund Eisner of Red Bank, New Jersey. Hundreds or thousands of peddlers did so in Mexico, Cuba, Ireland, Australia, and South Africa.[57]

Many peddlers pursued a different route, gliding over from peddling to supplying peddlers, opening warehouses catering to newcomers. Jacob Epstein, the Russian Jewish immigrant who created the Baltimore Bargain House, provided the goods for new immigrant peddlers who honeycombed the South and parts of the mid-Atlantic. A Suwałki immigrant, David Zemansky, made his way to the United States in 1860 and after a stint in New York headed for the still raw town of Chicago. There he resumed peddling before settling down and distributing goods to thousands of recent immigrant peddlers who spread out across the Midwest and beyond.[58] Zender Falmouth followed a similar trajectory in late-eighteenth-century England, as did Jack Goldberg in Griqualand West, a region that would eventually become Zambia.[59]

Other Jewish peddlers, once down from their wagons, capitalized on the reality that during their years on the road, they had been collecting refuse of one kind or another. They went into the junk business, sometimes referred to as salvage or waste. Like supplying new peddlers, the path from peddling to scrap seemed natural, and like the peddler supply business it had a global reach. Peddlers knew that someone, the junk dealers, would buy the refuse and that they in turn would sell it to someone who could recycle it into something new and different. As with any other enterprise, some barely eked out a living, while others found fortunes in other peoples' castoffs. Isaac Cohen came to Kingston, Ontario, from Russia as a seventeen-year-old in 1890. He first tried to make a living as a Hebrew teacher, but he realized that the occupation would bring him few chances for financial security. So like so many of his peers, he became a "traveler," and then a metal dealer—that is, a middleman in the scrap-iron business. One testimonial to Cohen from the 1920s noted, "By steady application to business, Mr. Cohen has developed this industry into one of the largest scrap metal firms in Canada." With a change of names, that characterization could have applied to Jews everyplace in their new world. Cohen learned a new-world Jewish economic principle: peddling begat the scrap business, and for some, the scrap business begat economic solidity, even wealth.[60]

The clustering of Jews in the scrap business, whatever the specific junk, grew in the early twentieth century, as eastern European Jewish peddlers settled down. One Oregon woman, asked about her immigrant father in an interview, declared, "My father was a peddler. That's what he did, Dear. After he got through with the horse and wagon, he was able to get a truck. And he still continued. Most of the men did that then—salvage." After rattling off the names of several of Oregon's wealthiest Jewish families, all of whom "didn't do any more," she continued, "They all started out that way."[61]

These observations reflected memories nearly three-quarters of a century old, but hundreds of community studies, corroborated by city directories, census forms, and other empirical and statistical sources, confirmed these recollections about Jews, peddling, and the trash business. In 1897 the *Toronto Mail and Empire* explored, in a series of article, "Foreigners Who Live in Toronto." The writer described the "large number of Polish and

Russian Jews . . . busied in collecting and selling from one year's end to the other." These men took themselves up with "bones, bottles, waste paper . . . or rags . . . and . . . old iron." The writer could not precisely quantify the phenomenon but nonetheless asserted that "the number of Jewish peddlers who go about the city and out among the farmers in the country is fairly large, and the quantities of old rubbish they collect and utilize is something amazing."[62] Similarly, according to *Forbes*, in its 1936 study of Jewish economic activity in the United States, Jewish entrepreneurs owned 90 percent of all scrap-metal companies in the United States. While some scrap-metal outfits may have had other origins, the life histories of hundreds of thousands of former peddlers who embraced the salvage business point to peddler proprietors.[63]

Just as the peddler supply business, junk, and dry goods retailing flowed from peddling, so too did other occupations that attracted peddlers as they built their after-the-road lives. Peddlers, particularly in Ireland and Wales, needed little training to become money lenders. They had dealt in cash with customers in their homes, and as the peddlers settled down, they set up money-lending businesses in storefronts and offices. Referred to as *percentniks*, Jewish money lenders at times doubled as merchants who sold sundry goods, offering loans to customers who could not make ends meet. They operated in league with Jewish retail merchants, often paying commissions to steer needy clients their way. This postpeddler occupation embarrassed Jewish communal leaders, who believed that it stirred up resentment against the Jews as a group, and while non-Jews also lent money on interest, often at higher rates, officials of the Dublin Hebrew Congregation, for example, struggled to curtail this seemingly vexatious postpeddling occupation.[64]

In the course of any former peddler's lifetime he probably engaged in multiple businesses. If he left the road to become a peddler supplier, he may have dabbled in real estate or ended up as a wholesaler who provisioned large stores. He might transform himself from peddler to dry goods shopkeeper, to stable owner, to contractor for scrap metal. A man's final business, the one that brought the greatest wealth, represented the family's pinnacle of success, built on peddling as start-up. Pearlstine Distributors, for example, a supplier of wines, sodas, snack foods, and other such items, came into being in 1982, but its history stretched back to the arrival of Tanchum "Thomas" Pearlstine, who came from Russia to South Carolina in 1854 and peddled. The Civil War proved a huge boon for the peddler, whose family joined him in the United States. Tanchum and several male relatives sold homemade buttons and buckles to soldiers in the Confederate Army. In 1865 the peddler settled with his family in Beech Hill, where he ran a small general store. In 1877 several Pearlstines decided to pursue the carriage and buggy business in nearby Charleston. By the next decade they operated a grain business in Ridgeville, which they sold after two years, plowing the profits into a wholesale grocery, grain, and hay business. The enterprise moved in 1903 to a three-story building and warehouse in Charleston, selling hardware, wagons, roofing, and fencing material. Tanchum and his sons and brothers continued to acquire new operations, and by the first decade of the new century, they reigned over an empire of wholesale and retail stores not just in Charleston but in more than a half-dozen other South Carolina towns.[65] The Polish immigrant to Curaçao, the former *klopper* whose son recalled the life in the Confidential Store, which sold "this and that," went on to sell "textile materials, nothing else." He then progressed to a much larger store, financed in large measure by a local Sephardic-owned bank, Maduro and Curiel, probably founded by former peddlers as well.[66]

Other subsequent enterprises also can be traced back to peddling. In the American South, for example, some peddlers who ventured onto cotton plantations became cotton brokers. The time spent in the region, the relationships forged with planters, and the knowledge they gleaned about the crop ushered these former peddlers into the business of ginning, bagging, and shipping cotton, taking a percentage of the profits of the sale for themselves. They also advanced cash to farmers, large and small, betting on next year's market price and guessing the size of the crop. The Hungarian-born Bernard Friedman came to Tuscaloosa, Alabama, in 1852 at sixteen years old and peddled. Within a few years he owned a store, with $300 in real estate and $600 in personal property. His store, appropriately the Atlanta Store, offered rural customers a "sleeping apartment" in the wagon yard, and he encouraged them, "Bring along your cotton." He simultaneously sold goods and arranged for the processing and sale of the cotton his clients had grown.[67]

Two sets of brothers did particularly well at this. Henry and Josiah Weil came from Bavaria in 1838 and peddled in the South. After a brief stint behind the counter of their Montgomery, Alabama, dry goods store, they turned to the potentially lucrative field of brokering cotton. Emanuel and Meyer Lehman replicated the Weils' history, seguing from Bavarian immigrants to peddlers to Montgomery shopkeepers and then to cotton brokers. They did even better. For this brother duo, cotton brokering launched them to phenomenal wealth, prominence, and fame. The Lehman brothers opened Lehman Brothers in New York in 1858, and the firm became one of America's premier finance houses. One son of Emanuel's, Herbert, served New York State as governor and then as a senator. Peddling drew the Weils and the Lehmans to lines of work that brought them great riches.

Peddling incubated other enterprises. In South Africa and Australia, many peddlers became hotel keepers. The connection between the two occupations may seem opaque, but in lands characterized by vast empty spaces, traversed by merchants, miners, government officials, and farmers going to and from market, hotels provided valued relief. Having walked or ridden through these lands, peddlers learned much about the topography. Their knowledge of the landscape and climate provided valuable cues to where best to situate lodging establishments, oases in otherwise inhospitable environments. The peddlers, who knew firsthand the desolation of these lands, figured out the ideal places to build their inns. Having themselves traversed the primitive roads, by foot or wagon, they could easily imagine that travelers would rejoice in a place to lodge for the night, offering a soft and clean bed and a cooked meal. These hotels often doubled as taverns, and travelers, the peddlers knew, equally welcomed a cold beer after a day's journey.[68]

The connection between peddling and the business of photography, or the movies, or the theater may not appear organic, at first blush, but all over the new world, individual peddlers, as they strategized their next steps, opted for these fields. In widely separated places, South Africa, Ireland, South Carolina, Colorado, Tennessee, Michigan, Utah, and Australia, among others, peddlers opened photography studios, movie theaters, and opera houses, grand entertainment establishments common particularly in nineteenth-century America. Photography suggests a relative clear line to peddling. Peddlers with wagons sometimes brought photographic equipment into their customers' homes, offering to take family portraits, a luxury for farmers and others with negligible incomes. The peddler brought the negatives back to town with him for development. Adorned with a frame, commonly crafted by former peddlers, the picture became an illustration of the solidity and material worth of the family of the farmer or miner or plantation worker who hung it on the wall. Some peddlers recognized an opportunity in setting up studios in town, places to develop and take pictures.

The movie and opera houses served the interests of both former Jewish peddlers and local residents of such places as Dublin; Traverse City, Michigan; Central City, Colorado; and Brunswick, Maryland. The launch of such palaces of entertainment proclaimed a city or town's modernity, its growth and connectedness to the big world. The peddlers who opened these cultural venues used them to make money and also to secure insider status, to win the praise of their fellow citizens. Once seen as shadowy figures with no fixed place of residence, peddlers made these temples of culture symbols of belonging. By bringing a town its first movie house or establishing its only opera house, a peddler could link his personal progress to his new home. Cinemas and theaters, bold public structures, eagerly embraced by the public, connected erstwhile peddlers to local boosterism, to assertions of civic growth and achievement.

Maurice Elliman left his mark this way on Dublin, and it evolved directly from his peddling time. He came from Latvia to Ireland in 1894, peddled for a few years in the countryside, married, and opened a fruit shop, then a carting business before deciding—with a friend, another Jewish immigrant—to bring the movies to Ireland. He first lugged a projector and a screen around the countryside, going from town to town, effectively "peddling" his movies. He exhibited short films in rented halls. In 1911 he opened a movie theater in a rented space on Pearse Street. The following year he built and celebrated the opening of Ireland's first cinema house, appropriately called the Theatre de Luxe, on Dublin's Camden Square. The notion of Elliman's movie house as "de luxe," of luxury, replicated his previous function as bearer of luxury goods into the homes of poor Irish country people. His theater allowed the people of Dublin to connect to a cosmopolitan world far larger than Ireland.[69]

Julius Steinberg, a peddler who sold in and around Traverse City, did the same for the northern Michigan town where he settled. He came there in 1868 from Suwałki, spending a few years peddling to farm families in a region famous for its tart cherries. He followed the usual steps, from foot to horse and wagon to dry goods store. In 1871 he brought over his wife and son, and he spent twenty years as proprietor of the Reliable Dry Goods, Carpet and Clothing House of Julius Steinberg, situated, like so many Jewish-owned stores, on the town's main street. In 1891 he took a chance, dipped into his savings, and did something of such note for Traverse City that it made the front page of the *Grand Traverse Herald*. He opened the doors of Steinberg's Grand Opera House, the city's first. The newspaper covered the opening with great fanfare, reporting, "Mr. Steinberg is kept busy receiving congratulations upon his enterprise in erecting so fine a building and securing for the opening night so eminent a tragedian as Walker Whiteside," a noted Shakespearian actor. By 1915 the days of opera houses and touring troupes had ended, and Julius Steinberg again saw a business opportunity. He built Traverse City's first movie house, the Lyric. So warmly did the town embrace Steinberg, the former peddler, and his contribution, that a delegation urged him to run for mayor. Steinberg eschewed electoral politics, telling his supporters that as he saw it, in politics one made enemies, while the successful merchant sought only friends, something that no doubt resonated from his peddler experience.[70]

Many of Steinberg's compatriots, however, were drawn to politics. All over the new world, especially in the United States, peddlers who had made them-selves into merchants combined business activities with public service. Using the public visibility gained as honest and civically committed merchants, many former peddlers sought local, state, and national office. Leopold Morse, an immigrant from Bavaria and a five-term representative to Congress, repre-senting Massachusetts, had endured a five-year stint on the road, peddling in and out of Sandwich, New Hampshire, in the 1840s. Sol Levitan migrated from the Russian-Prussian-Lithuanian border town of Taurrogen in 1862 and peddled, helped out by his cousin's Peddler Supply Company in Chicago. He decided to settle down in New Glarus, Wisconsin, married, and operated a general store in the 1880s. Residents, many of whom had immigrated from Switzerland, elected him a justice of the peace. Levitan, an active participant in the local Jewish congregation, also belonged to the Masons and Odd Fellows. In the first decade of the twentieth century the Levitan family moved to Madison, where Sol became a banker and plunged into the progressive politics sweeping the state. "Fighting" Bob La Follette tapped the former ped-dler to run for state treasurer, and he won. Neither being an immigrant Jew nor his history as a peddler prevented voters from trusting him with the fiscal af-fairs of the state. The political fortunes of immigrant Jews like Levitan em-bodied a process which took place throughout the country, as Americans came to accept with few reservations the proposition that Jewish men could represent them. Throughout the country, across regions, spanning the century of migration, American men went to ballot boxes and voted immigrant Jewish peddlers into office at all levels.[71]

In America, a notable cadre of peddlers moved into public service. Numbers may illustrate the political trajectory of Jewish peddlers in America, inasmuch as so many more Jewish immigrants went there than any other place. In the British Isles and Sweden, Jewish immigrants faced more complicated paths to naturalization than in the United States, and many of the Jews who went to these places tended to consider them way stations before journeying on to America. Both factors precluded political participation and civic activities.[72] The rules for naturalization varied among South American and Central American countries, but as a rule, Jews could not become citizens until the 1920s. In any case, many Jews who went to Mexico and Cuba had no intention of staying there but hoped instead to make their way to the United States, making their civic engagement rare.

Those former peddlers who did acquire Latin American citizenship and who participated politically—in Brazil, Chile, Argentina, and Colombia, as well as some in Mexico—opted for radical politics. They associated with their countries' Communist Parties. Although they came as capitalists, peddlers in South and Central America embraced left-wing politics. Simon Guberek, who immigrated to Colombia as a peddler and emerged as a successful industrialist, played an active role in the Communist Party there from its 1930 founding. Colombia's other parties, like those elsewhere in Latin America, represented the interests of landowners and the Catholic Church, offering Jews little space for participation. These parties provided no room for Jewish involvement, as they argued that the Jews in general represented a left-wing threat to the social order.[73]

Some Jews who had come to Canada, the British Isles, Australia, and South Africa as peddlers also stood for office and won, although less frequently than in the United States. Philip Blashki peddled jewelry among the miners in Australia's Ballarat gold fields in the 1850s, exchanging gold dust for goods. Decades later, in the early twentieth century, he served as a magistrate of the Victoria. But most Jews who involved themselves in politics in these places tended to be the sons and grandsons of peddlers rather than the men who themselves had sold from the road.[74]

Canada most closely resembled the United States. Across the country individual Jews who had once peddled affiliated with political parties and sought elective office. Aaron Meretsky came from Sztabin, a Polish province under Russian control, to Windsor, Ontario, in 1880. He moved from peddling to the junk business, dealing in fur on the side. He succeeded in business, and by 1910 he had entered local politics, successfully running for the Windsor city council as a member of the Liberal Party. Meretsky's tenure on the city council and other municipal boards garnered positive attention from the local press, which pointed out to readers that "Alderman Meretsky is one of the leaders in Windsor's Jewish Colony, and is full of native shrewdness. He is said to own about 20 houses in the city, and gives his business as a real estate man." Meretsky, like legions of local Jewish office holders south of the Canadian border, did not associate politics with ideology, but emphasized business and the town's general welfare. He told an *Evening Record* reporter in 1913, as he pushed the council to fund a large market building, "I am going to try and have a fine building put up, one which will be a credit to the city of Windsor." He articulated his civic boosterism, declaring, "I would like to see a market building here as good as they have in Chatham, or better."[75]

Hundreds of Jewish immigrant peddlers around the United States replayed Aaron Meretsky's experience. American politics, marked generally by relatively low ideological fervor, meant that parties had to embrace all white men who could vote, enabling white immigrants regardless of religion or national origin to participate, particularly locally. The two-party system blunted ideological differences, except for the era before the Civil War when the slavery question raged. Even then, though, those who managed the parties appealed to as many voters as possible, running candidates of various ethnic backgrounds to lure the largest possible number of men.

That political system incorporated the Jews. It became a mark of pride for Jews to tick off the number of their coreligionists, city by city, state by state, who had won the trust of their fellow citizens and gained election to town councils, boards of education, judgeships, and mayoral offices. Former peddlers abounded among the Jews who held elected or appointed positions. Having once peddled did not handicap them but rather served to show that they, like Aaron Meretsky to the north, had proven themselves as men who put the economic welfare and social order of the community chief among their concerns. Candidates running for office in the United States, in fact, liked to tout their own personal tales of rags to riches—or in the phrase of the nineteenth century, their log-cabin origins. For Jews a personal history of peddling as a new immigrant functioned as an equivalent, allowing Jewish candidates for sheriff, city council, school board, the mayoralty, or a judgeship to boast that they had arrived penniless, with no English, and by hard work and the openness of the local people, had come to exemplify the beneficence of America. Jewish peddlers who turned to public life sounded their own descant to an American anthem.

Without understating the extent of misinformation about Jews and Judaism that Americans, like most new-world people, endured, and the resentment thus engendered against Jews for their economic activities, being Jewish did not impede acquisition of citizenship, hamper physical or economic mobility, or block the Jews' civic integration. Barriers existed, particularly in elite institutions. But for the masses of Americans, someone's Jewishness did not preclude his civic respectability, impede positive personal interactions, or prevent non-Jews from trusting Jews to direct community life. Certainly some Americans resorted to anti-Jewish rhetoric, particularly in the heat of the political moment. But in the main, Jews who sought electoral office functioned as citizens who happened to be Jews, not as members of a pariah group. The reality that governors, mayors, and city councils appointed Jews, across the nation, to positions of authority and prestige—boards of education, commissions, boards, judgeships, and the like—reveals the fluidity of life in the United States and its openness to all white men, especially individuals associated with the business order. And among those Jews who benefited from this, peddlers abounded.

A few examples of this history represent a widespread phenomenon. Isaac Goldschmidt came to Hartford, Connecticut, in the 1850s. The city directory listed him as a peddler in 1854, a grocer by 1859. Elected to the Hartford City Council for the Fifth Ward in 1867, he served four consecutive terms. Marcus Spiegel, the immigrant peddler who wooed and married Caroline Hamlin, accepted an appointment as postmaster in Green Township, Ohio, in the mid-1850s, serving the area in which he had peddled. Louis Gratz, a onetime immigrant peddler who operated around Pittstown, Pennsylvania, joined the Union Army at the outbreak of the Civil War, mustered out in Tennessee, and decided to remain there. He opened a grocery store and qualified for admission to the state bar. He then served as Knoxville's city attorney. In the 1880s Samuel Rosenberg came to Portland, Maine, as a peddler, ending up one of the city's most successful clothing merchants. That helped him win election to Portland's Common Council. Abraham Kaplon, an immigrant from Lithuania, moved up the ladder from peddler to storekeeper in Harpers Ferry, West Virginia, to member of the city council and commissioner of a governmental body charged with laying roads and paving streets. In 1856 Morris Lasker, from the east Prussian town of Lask, arrived in the United States, stopping first in Virginia, then heading for Texas. Here he peddled, then served in the Confederate Army, from which he emerged penniless. He returned to peddling, and operated a series of businesses in Galveston, Texas, which succeeded beyond expectation. By 1895 Galveston voters sent him to the state legislature in Austin.[76] Not outstanding by themselves, these stories and the thousands like them, gleaned from around the United States, point to Jewish integration and the role of peddling in fostering it.

So, too, the active participation of Jewish men, once peddlers, in party politics, demonstrated the symbiosis between America and the Jews. They did not all follow the same party until the end of the 1920s, when the Democratic Party attracted the masses of American Jews. Previously they had been welcomed by both parties, and had divided evenly between them. The Ohio Democratic Party rewarded Marcus Spiegel for his efforts with a postmaster position. Abraham Kohn, the peddler whose anguished diary lamented his misery on the road, cast his lot with the Republican Party in its infancy. Party leaders in Chicago rewarded him by nominating him to run in 1860 for the post of city clerk. He won. As an activist for the Illinois Republican Party, Kohn met and befriended Abraham Lincoln. When Lincoln became president, Kohn sent him an American flag upon which he himself had sewn a biblical verse, in Hebrew and English, from the Book of Joshua, "I will not fail thee or forsake thee. Be strong and of good courage."[77]

Jewish men who had become merchants after peddling planted themselves into local communities all over the new world, especially in the United States. There, to a degree not seen in other new-world lands, they achieved and exhibited their integration by serving on boards and commissions linked to civic improvement. As merchants with a stake in local prosperity, they sat prominently on, even chaired, planning commissions, merchants' associations, local boards of trade, and the like. Benedict Lowenstein arrived in New Orleans in 1854, peddled in Mississippi and Arkansas, and within a year owned a store in Memphis, success that allowed him to call for his brothers. A prosperous retailer and wholesaler, he chaired the General Trade Committee's Dry Goods Division of the Memphis Merchants' Exchange.[78] School board service particularly attracted former peddlers, allowing them to demonstrate the depth of their local integration. Gabriel Meyer, the Alsatian immigrant who peddled around Pine Bluff, Arkansas, and by the 1870s owned almost two dozen cotton plantations, served ten years as an alderman. He championed the expansion of local public education during the twenty-one years he sat on the school board. In 1860, when Pine Bluff ran out of money and could not pay its teachers, he dipped into his own considerable resources to make up the shortfall and negotiated loans for the schools from a number of banks. In Michigan's Thumb region, Louis Glazier, a Latvian immigrant who had arrived in 1891, took the classic route, moving from itinerant merchandising to ownership of a large store, marriage, then a larger store, five children, and finally a major building downtown Kalkaska with his name on it. In the process, he achieved a visible civic persona. Some local notables approached him, suggesting that he run for the school board. Glazier turned them down, claiming that as he had so little education, he could hardly make good policies about the community's schools. But town leaders in Kalkaska, as elsewhere, considered that successful Jewish businessmen, even if they had previously peddled, would be fine custodians of public schooling. The Jews represented local stability, and non-Jews associated Jews with a commitment to learning.[79]

Local American politics bridged divides between Jews and other people, some of whom might seem not to have been their allies. Ben Stern, born in Lithuania, peddled in Massachusetts, settled in Maine, participated actively in the local Jewish community, particularly in the Workmen's Circle, and by the late 1920s ran for the state legislature. A French-Canadian Catholic priest, minister to a community of immigrants from Quebec, approved of Stern's opposition to child labor. He publicly endorsed Stern for his support of old-age pensions and his advocacy of protective legislation for women workers, issues that resonated with the community of Franco-American textile millworkers. In Quebec the Catholic Church articulated deep antipathy for Jewish peddlers, but in Maine such resentment, if it existed, did not translate into politics. The priest campaigned for Ben Stern, a former Jewish peddler who shared his political agenda.[80]

Peddlers, off the road, did not all run for office or serve on commissions, but many used their economic resources to better their communities. Across the country, and in other new-world places, men who had once peddled underwrote many communal undertakings, including donations to hospitals, parks, local chapters of the Salvation Army, YMCAs, libraries, and the Boy Scouts, notwithstanding the overt Christian agendas of some of those organizations. Isaac Bernheim endowed local nature preserves and gave Louisville an arboretum. Jewish merchants donated money to churches and church-related undertakings. Isaac Merkel, a onetime peddler and then owner of Merkel's Department Store in Plattsburgh, New York, funded the Grey Nuns of the Sacred Heart to create the Champlain Valley Hospital. Jewish men who had once been itinerant merchants also provided the money and helped organize such civic celebrations as Fourth of July festivities, perfect opportunities to showcase their rootedness. They served on committees to plan patriotic parades and other public gatherings calculated to foster economic development and blunt ethnic, class, and religious divides.[81]

Wanting to demonstrate their personal progress and position themselves as exemplars of the mercantile class, Jewish former peddlers flocked to fraternal societies, most often the Masons, Odd Fellows, Elks, or Knights of Pythias. These groups, with their special handshakes and secret passwords, lodge halls and meeting rooms, emphasized the brotherhood of all members. Here men, sometimes wearing distinctive regalia, met as equals. Potential members had to apply and could be rejected. Membership went to those with means, who fit in by appearing honorable, friendly, able to mingle, and in harmony with the lodge's values; no American Jewish community history lacks a roster of men who joined such associations. Biographies, autobiographies, and memoirs of Jewish immigrant peddlers, graduated to merchants, abound in references to membership in one or more of them. The ubiquity of such accounts further points to the peddlers' trajectory, the acceptance they won in their new home communities, and the importance they attached, as Jews and immigrants, to forging formal social relations with respectable non-Jewish men.

As men who had once walked the roads, they had seen firsthand the meaning of poverty and stigmatization, be it racial, religious, or class. They knew this personally from the home country, while in the new world they learned vicariously what being defined as nonwhite implied. Peddlers had entered the homes of people with few rights in the society, and carried on friendly business with them, continuing to do so in their stores and shops. But Jews, whether still peddling or occupying some sedentary business, had no urge to share the fate and status of their nonwhite customers or to replicate their own premigration marginality. They understood that society defined them as white, yet simultaneously they knew that as Jews they occupied a liminal space in the eyes of the Christian majorities. Jews believed that hatred against them, whether religious, racial, or economic, always hovered in the air or existed just below the surface, popping up often enough convince them of their vulnerability.

That made former Jewish peddlers in the United States different from the Jews who migrated as peddlers to Central and South America, South Africa, Ireland, even England. In those places their peers also achieved economic mobility and universally gave up peddling for stable businesses. Their children also entered the professions and the higher rungs of commerce. But they perceived hostility to Jews as more blatant, more essential, and more entwined with their new homes' political cultures than did those who came to the United States.

But former Jewish peddlers in the United States still perceived themselves as on trial. They felt compelled, based on knowledge gleaned from newspapers and other sources, and from firsthand observations while on the road, to comport themselves in such a way as not to jeopardize their status. Serving their larger communities, aligning themselves with progress, could, they believed, help them as they sought security. They could not miss the contrasts between their lives in the new world and the ordeals of their literal and figurative kin who had not joined the great migration. They knew of outbreaks of anti-Jewish violence and threats to Jewish security in Europe, the Ottoman Empire, and North Africa. From the 1819 Hep-Hep riots in Bavaria to the pogroms in Alsace in the 1830s and late 1840s to the institutionalization of anti-Semitism in Romania in the 1860s, the bloody attacks on Jews in the Ukraine, Moldavia, and elsewhere in the Russian Empire starting in 1881, through the vast slaughter of Ukrainian Jews in the aftermath of World War I and the Russian Civil War, violent anti-Semitism reared its head every decade or so. While these violent outbursts had not propelled their migrations, the Jews of Plattsburgh, Pine Bluff, or Kalkaska, as well as those of Ballarat, Johannesburg, Montevideo, or Cork, wanted to ensure that they would continue to enjoy the protection their new homes provided.

They viewed the United States as a singular society, in a category all its own. Certainly Jews who migrated to other countries, to England, South Africa, Australia, Chile, or Ireland, also left warm words about the people whom they encountered in their peddling years and expressed patriotism for those countries. Yet their rhetoric does not compare in volume, depth, or frequency to the accounts of Jewish immigrant peddlers who came to America. Moshe Lissak immigrated to England, for example, from Posen in the early part of the nineteenth century, leaving his impressions in *Jewish Perseverance, or The Jew, at Home and Abroad: An Autobiography*, published in 1851. He peddled. He "travelled from county to county, and from city to city," eventually staking out Bedford as his base of operations. In his memoir he extolled the people of the English countryside, their hospitality, and their concern for him. He "loved England." Lissak believed that most Germans felt similarly, but "it is particularly so with Jews. It seems as if the God of Jacob" assisted the Jews to adapt to English ways. Although Jews did not enjoy full civil rights, he wrote, "they feel no actual restrictions impeding their mercantile pursuits or the exercise of their religious worship."[82]

Jews who went to the United States also cared greatly about "their mercantile pursuits" and "the exercise of their religious worship." But in America they also wanted full acceptance by their neighbors and expected integration into civic life. Those Jewish peddlers whose words have survived made clear that having sold from the road did not dampen their enthusiasm for the country, and may have enhanced it, since they believed that in America the once despised occupation had enabled remarkable opportunities. Robert and Helen Lynd, authors of *Middletown*, a 1929 sociological study of Muncie, Indiana—as they saw it, the archetypical American town—captured the voice of one former Jewish peddler, who, speaking in "broken English" to a meeting of the Chamber of Commerce, declared, "It is not the Chamber of Commerce . . . but Uncle Sam who is our host tonight." In his remarks he recalled, "I was a peddler with a horse and wagon." After recounting acts of kindness by one of his customers, he summarized his life since arriving in the United States. First he apologized, "I am sorry I cannot speak better," but continuing his speech, he declared, "I honor your schools that are teaching us. But I do want to say that you have gold in America—not paving your streets, but gold of this sort in the hearts of your citizens, the gold which, too makes each of us able to go all over the world with respect and safety as American citizens."[83]

It is possible, of course, that Jews put the most positive face on their status when addressing non-Jews, in front of whom they might have felt apprehensive and obliged to praise the country and prove their patriotism. But documents circulating only within Jewish circles adopted a similar tone, even ones never intended to go beyond the authors' own families. The daughter of Gustav Kussy, an immigrant from Bohemia who started off "walking the streets of Newark and the suburbs—with the peddler's pack on his back," recalled vividly, in a private tribute to her parents, her father's pride on having become an American citizen: he "was never more proud than when he exercised his privileges as an American citizen at the polls. This was to him truly a religious duty as attendance at synagogue services." She remembered decades later that "on Election Day father walked to the polls with shoulders erect, and cast his vote. It put him on terms of political equality with the president of the United States, who also had but one vote. . . . This is what it meant to be an American!"[84] A 1940s interview project involving Yiddish-speaking immigrants in the United States focused on their experiences before and after coming to America. Many had spent time on the road and most, despite the large number who considered themselves socialists, praised the United States, seeing their peddling years as prelude to patriotism. Israel Rosen, an immigrant who came from the Ukraine in 1910, told the interviewer that "one could live in peace here without fear of government officials or anyone else." This former peddler echoed the phrase used in Middletown, calling the United States the "golden land."[85] Morris Galatzan's father, an immigrant from the western Ukrainian region of Belz, peddled around El Paso, Texas. He saw up close the straits of "low wage earning Mexican laborers" to whom he sold, and juxtaposed their plight with his joy at becoming an American citizen. "Pop never missed the opportunity to vote. He was never able to understand why so many citizens failed to go to the polls and cast their vote, a privilege he never enjoyed in Russia."[86]

Non-Jews bore witness to the successful integration of former immigrant Jewish peddlers into American life, hailing them as fellow Iowans, Wisconsinites, North Carolinians, Mainers, and the like. A 1931 multivolume *Narrative History of the People of Iowa*, a celebration of *Their Chief Enterprises in Education, Religion, Valor, Industry, Business, Etc.*, praised in effusive terms the Jews of the Hawkeye state. The history not only profiled substantial Jewish businessmen, like Moses Scheuerman, who came "as a poor boy" and then "gained his early capital by carrying a pack on his back." It made Scheuerman's Jewishness and his peddling matters of respect and pride rather than of embarrassment. "Mr. Scheuerman," the entry on this Des Moines wool merchant concluded, "is a member of the Jewish Synagogue, is a thirty-second degree Scottish Rite Mason and Shriner, and member of the Des Moines Club and the Hyperion Club." A number of such portraits valorized the Jewish peddlers and by association praised the benevolence of Iowa, its people, and America's ethnic liberalism. On Iowa's religious land-scape, the *Narrative History* waxed eloquent: "The Jews . . . the most remark-able people of whom we have a record. Their story is dramatic, often pathetic. The romance of the Jews is written large in the records of the human race." At home, the piece asks its readers to recall the state's past and their own: "Most of us whose memories reach back to the pioneer period of Iowa, or the years immediately following recall the Jewish peddler, who frequented the cabins of the early settlers. These peddlers and their packs, with their display of cheap jewelry, including tin horns, used by the pioneers to call the men-folks from the back fields, were among the first memories of the writer." Indulging in a bit of nostalgia about his childhood, the writer recalled that "his mother bought her table linens of them, bargaining in the usual manner. The children always looked forward with interest to the coming of the peddler." These Jewish ped-dlers "were men of quite remarkable character," and "many of them afterward becoming prominent business men in the growing towns and cities of Iowa."[87]

Neither a fluke nor an oddity, the Iowa booster book had equivalents in other local directories and in town newspapers that told of individual Jews who had arrived as peddlers. J. A. A. Burnquist, who compiled *Minnesota and Its People* in 1924, provided a roster of notable Minnesotans who came as im-migrant pack peddlers and who by that year, the year of immigration restric-tion, served the state as pillars of the business community and civic virtue.[88] Obituaries in local newspapers eulogized deceased Jewish merchants, embrac-ing their humble peddler origins. David Leibovitz died in 1926 in Gastonia, North Carolina. According to the local *Gazette*, Leibovitz, the town's "oldest retail merchant," owner of shoe stores there and in other surrounding towns, had immigrated from Lithuania; "a lad of eighteen he started peddling with a stock of tinware." Lebovitz took his first steps in North Carolina "ignorant of this country, its customs, its language, etc., unable to speak a word of English." The paper declared him "a loyal citizen of Gastonia. . . . He is a member of the Chamber of Commerce, and always ready to do his bit for the civic betterment of the community." The deceased, to be buried after services "in the Jewish Temple," provided Gastonians with a story "that reads like a romance."[89] On a broader geographical scale, Harry Hall's *America's Successful Men of Affairs*, published in the 1890s, joined in the chorus extolling the nation's willingness to accept and nurture the poor Jewish peddlers and catapult them to success.[90]

A core element in the American narrative, the romance the *Gazette* referred to, claimed that any man (since only men mattered) who tried hard enough, regardless of his background, could transform himself and achieve his desired goals. A narrative that harked back to Benjamin Franklin's *Autobiography* and Alexis de Tocqueville's observations, the heroic notion of the self-made man and America's power to foster personal transformations grew from deep roots in American culture. The success of Jewish peddlers like Leibovitz allowed Americans to congratulate themselves on the nation's essential goodness. The Leibovitz obituarist considered his story "inspirational. The career of these im-migrants ought to put to shame many an American boy, who is raised in the lap of luxury, and knows no care or want from the day of his birth." These Jewish exemplars won the accolades of their fellow citizens precisely because they had been immigrant peddlers who did well. The peddler who opened the Globe Department Store in Dumas, Arkansas, Charles Dante, served as mayor, and upon his retirement, the local Lions Club honored him as Outstanding Citizen of the Year. Tupper Lake, New York, did the same for Mose Ginsberg, once an immigrant peddler who had traversed the farmlands and logging camps of the Adirondacks and eventually became the owner of the town's largest depart-ment store. The town named him Tupper Lake Citizen of the Year.[91]

Former peddlers' unpublished memoirs and those of their children invoked the same theme, the tribute to America, statements thanking the nation to which they had immigrated as peddlers, which facilitated their success and acceptance. In oral histories conducted by Jewish museums and research or-ganizations, men who once peddled in the United States had nothing to say about anti-Semitism, or categorically claimed that it had not hampered them, and if it existed it was mild and sporadic. Rather, they told of positive relation-ships with customers, amid the difficult conditions of the road, followed by the joy of success that made it possible to start families and achieve stable, settled lives. Memoirists and interviewees expressed gratitude to the country that afforded them integration and material success.

Integration did not come at the expense of their Jewish commitments. Former peddlers also shared in the creation of Jewish community life. They brought the rituals and institutions of Judaism to places mostly devoid of a Jewish presence. While untold numbers slipped away from Jewish practice and community, for whatever reason, most peddlers—particularly after transi-tioning to sedentary lives—went to great lengths to engage with other Jews and participate in celebration of holidays and life-cycle events: marriage, cir-cumcision, burial. In many new-world places, peddlers, both on and off the road, established such formal communities themselves, founding congrega-tions, leading religious services, consecrating ground for the first cemeteries, and banding together to fulfill religious needs. Former peddler Woolf Ruta Cohen, who had come to the antipodes from Poland and opened Paris House

Tailors, made possible his community's first congregation, Central Synagogue in Sydney, Australia.[92] Former peddlers also became founders and leaders of Jewish benevolent societies, charities, and communal organizations, like B'nai B'rith lodges in the mid-nineteenth century and Workman's Circle (*Arbeiter Ring*) lodges of the early twentieth.

Jewish men migrated to new-world lands, distant and removed from established Jewish communities, not to escape from Jewishness or to free themselves from the highly regulated code of personal behavior of Jewish law, but to make a living. While on the road, they had difficulty observing Jewish practice, dietary laws in particular. Getting off the road made it easier for them to heed the details of Jewish practice as they chose. Settling down made it more possible to get kosher meat, and as a communal infrastructure emerged that allowed them to eat as they believed Jews should. In the small town of Port Talbot, Wales, in 1900 Mr. Deggotts, a Jew who settled in the region and "had established himself as a traveler," went on a weekly basis to the larger community in Swansea to get kosher meat, using his horse and wagon to serve the dietary needs of the small town's Jews.[93]

On the other hand, they felt more pressure, once settled, to compromise on the punctilious observance of the Sabbath. As peddlers with their weekly circuit, they actually rested, with or without synagogue attendance, on Saturdays and spent their weekends off the road, transacting no business. When they became shopkeepers, however, they faced a problem. In most places local people shopped on Saturdays, leaving Sundays for sacred time. In many locales in the United States and elsewhere, stores had to close on Sundays by law. Shuttering their shops on Saturday effectively robbed Jewish merchants of one-sixth of their potential business, if not more.

Some Jews, who became accustomed to a five-day work week, perhaps out of religious commitment and perhaps as a result of their peddling years, abstained from business as usual on the Sabbath. Nonretail businesses could better afford to close on Saturday than could those that dealt in dry goods, clothing, watches, and jewelry sold directly to the public. Even those who kept stores open on Saturdays, however, did not dispense with all aspects of Sabbath observance. Gustav Kussy, the onetime peddler who wended his way around Newark's suburbs, did a brisk business on Saturdays, according to his daughter, but "never failed on Friday night and Saturday noon to bless his children, chant the Kiddush [the blessing over the wine], *bentshmezumen* [sing the grace after the meal], sing psalm 144 Saturday at dusk, and make *havdole* [the ceremony marking the end of the Sabbath]." Kussy considered that his family's economic well-being demanded that he open his store on the

Sabbath, but engaging in business on the day of rest did not diminish his determination to mark the day as holy. His violation of the Sabbath did not dim his commitment to Judaism. Kussy did not limit his Jewish engagements to the domestic. Despite not being a strict observer of the Sabbath, he helped found Congregation Oheb Shalom and served as its secretary, vice president, and president, honors marked by the congregation with the presentation to him of a gold watch and chain. Sarah Kussy, his wife, served equivalently important positions of authority and respect in the Miriam Frauen Verein, the ladies' auxiliary. The congregation, despite its traditionalism, did not condemn the family for Kussy's business-related lax observance of the Sabbath.[94]

Geography and size mattered greatly in terms of how the former peddlers participated in the formal apparatus of Jewish life. The small communities they lived in across much of South and Central America made a full Jewish life difficult. Small populations of Jews impeded the celebration of holidays and Sabbath, the acquisition of kosher food, and the provision of Jewish educations and eventual marriage partners for children. No single source of religious authority held sway, and in nearly all of South and Central America and the Caribbean, the tiny number of Jews still divided into Sephardic and Ashkenazic factions, with their separate institutions. Even when children of the peddlers married across this chasm, the division still predominated, undermining the emergence of vibrant formal institutions. Memoirs left by peddler-merchants and their children do not pay homage to the immigrant generation's traditionalism, nor do any contemplate how the immigrants consciously improvised new forms of Jewish religious life.

Those personal narratives reveal that the Jewish peddlers who had come to Guatemala, Cuba, Mexico, and elsewhere in Latin America aspired to leave those places for the United States, where they could join institutionally elaborate Jewish communities. Yet despite their desire to emigrate to the United States, the Jews of Latin America, like those in all new-world settings, organized congregations, consecrated cemeteries, provided some Jewish learning, and also founded other kinds of Jewish institutions, charitable, Zionist, or benevolent. Wherever they stepped off the road to open businesses, they wanted to avail themselves of the services of ritual circumcisers to bring their sons into the covenant. Even Jews who married non-Jewish women and settled along the Amazon River still hoped, in vain, to get their sons circumcised. Jewish families scattered in the Cuban provinces, living in dozens of small towns, getting together for holidays. They lacked synagogues, Torah scrolls, rabbis, and kosher meat, but when Jewish festivals came around, they banded together, marking holy time and fostering Jewish sociability.

Former peddlers of Latin America did not, and probably could not, improvise, creating novel religious institutions and practices that reflected tradition and new realities. The Sephardim among them had no interest in or inclination toward the reform of Judaism, a phenomenon with roots in the Jewish Enlightenment of Germany. Furthermore, they lived in overwhelmingly Catholic countries, where religious experimentation had little appeal.[95]

The religious postpeddler experience in South and Central America differed from that which predominated in new-world places administered by the British Empire. In the latter settings, memoirists, chroniclers of family stories, and writers of community biographies emphasized instead persistent traditionalism. These biographies, personal or communal, described a nearly total transplantation of small-town Lithuanian Jewish life, the place from which so many Jews in Ireland, Australia, and South Africa came. One such document, offered by one South African Jew, looking back to life in Malmesburg, in the Western Cape, claimed that the Jews in his town had literally re-created "shtetl life." The smous and shopkeepers of this memoir partook of "daily minyanim [prayers]. Shabbat services, our Yom Tovim [holidays]." They surrounded themselves with "our Rebbes [traditional rabbis], the cheder [religious school], Kashrut [dietary laws] and life in the home—all the threads of our lives in that small Swartland town, were linked to the traditions that our old folks had brought out with them 'Fun der Heim' [from the home]."[96]

In British Empire outposts, Jewish peddlers once settled did not create new Jewish practices and forms to reflect the culture and circumstances of life in Ireland, South Africa, Wales, or Australia. Even Canada saw little innovation. Religion did not need to be tampered with or altered to accommodate changed cultural and social realities. These places instead became hotbeds of Zionism, which offered an alternative structure to Jewish community organization. But when it came to religious practice, Jews of the Empire maintained traditional forms and articulated an obligation to do so.

In their private lives the Jewish women and men of the far-flung British Empire did not necessarily adhere meticulously to the commandments regulating personal behavior. But when it came to public display of Judaism, they rarely deviated from tradition as they imagined it. This may partly reflect the fact that Judaism, as a religious system, fell under the authority of the office of the chief rabbi of the United Kingdom, seated in the Great Synagogue in London, an office in existence since the end of the seventeenth century. In the various countries of the Empire the office of the chief rabbi repressed innovation and congregational autonomy. Individual Jews, whether they had once been peddlers or not, whether they still peddled or were settled, saw Judaism as synonymous with orthodoxy. Peddlers, active or erstwhile, and their children did not strive for the reform of Judaism in light of lived conditions, nor did they wonder how to create a distinctive Irish, Welsh, or South African iteration of Judaism that could pay homage both to tradition and to the beneficent impact of the countries where they had peddled and then settled down.

Jewish communities in Latin America, the Caribbean, and the British Empire contrasted sharply with those in the United States, where Jewish ped-dlers who graduated to shopkeeping embarked on a different path. Like their peers around the world, they, outliers excepted, worked to make Judaism pos-sible. Many Jewish community histories tell of the first formal Jewish institu-tion, the cemetery, owing its origin to the death of a Jewish peddler. Other Jewish peddlers in the vicinity, perhaps all supplied by the same shopkeeper, who gathered in the same town for the Sabbath, felt obliged to provide the deceased with a proper Jewish burial. They had to pool some money to buy a plot of land, become a formal group to hold the deed, and finally inter, with proper rituals and prayers, the unfortunate peddler. Town after town in the United States became home to a synagogue so overwhelmingly made up of peddlers and former peddlers that it became known as "the peddlers' *shul*," like Beth Joseph, founded in 1905 in Tupper Lake, New York, or Ezras Achim, founded in 1910 in Indianapolis. The moniker served as a marker of class in the case of the latter place, a sizable community with multiple congregations, but in the former, no other synagogue existed in the town in the Adirondacks. All Tupper Lake Jewish men and women worshiped and socialized in the peddlers' shul.[97]

In the United States peddlers and onetime peddlers led congregations as presidents, treasurers, and trustees. In places without paid clergy, men who once carried packs on their backs, along with those who still did so, chanted the service as cantors, read from the Torah scrolls, and functioned as proto-rabbis. Their occupation, past or present, did not disqualify them from the prestige that accompanied such ritual prominence. Max Feder, the first rabbi of the congregation he founded in Davenport, Iowa, in the 1850s, appeared in the city directory as a peddler.[98]

The degree to which peddlers shaped Jewish community life, their engage-ments with the institutional practice of Judaism when they became sedentary merchants, and the positions of respect they garnered in their congregations varied little by place. Yet the United States differed in several discrete but linked ways. The former peddlers who became shopkeepers and integrated themselves into their local communities articulated a remarkable degree of comfort in their American homes, a trust in their non-Jewish neighbors that extended to their behaviors as Jews. They printed notices in local newspapers announcing that they would close their stores on upcoming Jewish holidays, emphasizing that their calendar differentiated them from their neighbors. The Suwałki-born former peddler William Saulson, proprietor of the People's Store, in Michigan's Upper Peninsula, was an active Odd Fellow, a volunteer firefighter, and the sometime chairman of the town's Fourth of July Celebration General Committee, but he declared in the town press, "The People's Store of Wm. Saulson will be closed on the following days, on account of the Holy Days." After listing the dates, he continued, "No business will be transacted on those days." Some of Saulson's customers probably knew him from his peddling days. They would remember his openness about being a Jew, and that he had never eaten the meat put in front of him. In his postpeddling career they gave him their business, and he continued to assert what his religion demanded of him.[99] Jewish congregations likewise sent items to local newspapers, detailing synagogue events, telling the majority Christian readership about holiday and life-cycle celebrations, congregational dinners and lectures, all weaving Judaism into the fabric of community life. The Jews invited non-Jews, including Christian clergymen, to synagogue dedications, the investitures of new rabbis, and other Jewish religious events. Protestant ministers and rabbis exchanged pulpits on Thanksgiving, the Fourth of July, and other civic occasions.

It may therefore not be surprising that the development of Reform Judaism in the United States, something that did not happen in other new-world settings, attracted numerous former peddlers. While Jews who had never peddled also turned to Reform, onetime peddlers played a conspicuous role.[100] Isaac Bernheim, Abraham Kohn, and Marcus Spiegel, among many others, cast their lot with the movement beginning in the 1850s, seeing it as a way to blend Judaism with Americanism. Henry Mack joined a stream of young Jewish pack peddlers, immigrants from German-speaking lands; he sold goods on the roads and pathways of the east, then moved to Cincinnati in the 1840s. He became one the city's merchant princes, making his fortune in clothing. And like nearly all in his cohort who came to the Queen City, he fell under the spell of the Bohemian rabbi Isaac Mayer Wise, who laid the foundations for American Reform Judaism. Solomon Schindler, a Reform rabbi at Boston's Temple Israel, himself had peddled in his early days in America, gleaning knowledge of the country and its people during his days of itinerant selling.

All of these American Jewish peddlers traversed a country ablaze with religious reform. New denominations, new churches, new modes of worship characterized American religion in the nineteenth and twentieth centuries, as new popular religious forms reflected changing cultural, social, and economic

realities. Women and men who envisioned better ways to stimulate their spiritual stirrings did so, innovating, experimenting, and improvising with inher-
ited practices. Abraham Kohn, when peddling in western Massachusetts, sold
his goods among the Millerites, a group founded in 1833 by William Miller,
who prophesied the imminent Second Coming of Christ. Kohn did not join
them, but he did see that in America, ordinary people, not just the clergy, created the religious institutions they wanted. No one could stop them, and so
long as they could convince enough people to join their new churches—
Baptists of various types, Mormons, Disciples of Christ, Shakers, Christian
Scientists, and Holiness worshipers, among the better-known of the new
religions—could compete in the religious marketplace with the Presbyterians,
Methodists, and other more substantial bodies. They could become religions
of no less communal stature than those with long and deep historic roots.
Americans likewise changed their denominational affiliations readily, and
churches seeking new members tweaked their theologies to fit the sensibilities
of those who sat in the pews. The men and women who listened to the
Lithuanian Jewish peddler in the Dakotas worshiped in a nondenominational
community church, a religious body made up of those who chose to attend and
pay tithes, giving the church legitimacy and sanctity, although it did not operate under the banner of any organized ecclesiastical institution.

Peddlers learned of this American appetite for religious variety from their
forays into the countryside, and many former peddlers tried to bring this same
spirit of innovation into Judaism, a religious tradition they loved but which
they believed needed change. These peddlers, turned businessmen of substance like Mack or public servants like Kohn, led their congregations from
traditionalism to Reform. Some founded Reform congregations. After years
on the road, characterized by positive encounters with American customers,
followed by their rise to economic success and integration into American civic
life, they elevated America to an almost sacred element in their cultural identities. Their embrace of Reform correlated with their embrace of America, the
place they believed had provided them and other Jews with a home. They
wanted to incorporate it into their Jewish lives. They embraced Wise's 1858
prayer book *Minhag America*, the American rite. They contributed money to
Hebrew Union College in Cincinnati, the training school for Reform rabbis
and self-proclaimed incubator of an American rabbinate, attuned to American
values of openness and flexibility. They sought to bring to life a Judaism ap-
propriate for an integrated people. They and other former peddlers provided
the financial support for Wise's Union of American Hebrew Congregations, a
body that highlighted America and its singularity.

Wise's use of the word "America" in the title of his prayer book challenged conventional ideas about the United States, articulated in Europe particularly among the traditionalists. America in their estimation constituted a place to go out of economic desperation, a place of refuge for Jews in flight from violence. But as a Jewish setting, it lacked substance, authenticity, and coherence. Wise, aided by his coterie of former peddlers, men who learned about America door by door, home by home, and farm by farm, rather thought that the migration to America constituted a new era in Jewish history. They believed that it deserved its own rite, its *minhag America.*

Former peddlers engaged with religious innovation not only through Reform. Many congregations founded by now sedentary eastern European immigrant Jewish peddlers, organized in the late nineteenth and early twentieth centuries as Orthodox or traditionalist, moved after the 1910s to the Conservative movement. These congregations affiliated with the United Synagogue of America, founded that decade, and it, like Reform, defined America, its values and institutions, as not inimical but congruent to Judaism. The Conservative movement gave the laity and even the rabbis less room to innovate than Reform. But its adherents considered that as men of the twentieth century they could play with tradition to fit American conditions. The men who created these congregations, who provided the lay leadership and determined matters of ritual, had encountered Americans on the road, had experienced decades of civic involvement, and that entitled them to redefine some elements of Jewish religious practice.

Notably, Reform and Conservative Judaism developed only in the United States of all the new-world settings, and especially in America did peddling provide Jewish men with a path toward civic integration. Peddling, both in the years that Jewish men did it and in the decades following, continued to shape their lives. It left a mark on the families and communities they created. As an occupation it enhanced their earning power, enabling poor Jews who went to new-world places to become comfortable merchants and businessmen, some achieving spectacular leaps into the highest rungs of financial success. It paved the way for men who had walked the road to move into civic life and create new forms of Jewish life. While the economic turn took place everywhere, civic integration and religious innovation proved to be distinctly American. Sigmund Eisner's life contained elements both global and American. Whether we read it as an American story or a new-world one, the details demonstrate that without peddling it might never have happened.

Legacies of the Road
A Conclusion

Peddling gave millions of Jews from North Africa and the Ottoman Empire, from the Czarist lands and the Austro-Hungarian Empire, from the Germanic states and Alsace, a chance to spread out to a bigger new geographic canvas. It structured their first footsteps in the British Isles, Sweden, and North, South, and Central America, as well as southern Africa, Australia, and New Zealand. Some of these places housed tiny, relatively inconspicuous Jewish communities before the peddlers' mass arrival. They offered the peoples of these places an instant on-the-ground immersion course in Jews and Judaism, lessons offered on the spot in the customers' homes and on their roads.

Peddling shaped the great migration, opening the pages to a crucial new chapter in modern Jewish history. Some Jews, in reaction to anti-Semitism, to the complexities of emancipation, and to continued impoverishment, sought other solutions for their ills, such as socialism or Zionism. But one-third of the Jews voted with their feet, embracing a different kind of movement. This choice took them to railroad depots and ports of embarkation, where ships carried them to new homes. Their humble but ubiquitous occupation facilitated the emigration.

In turn, this migration gave birth to new globally scattered Jewish populations, including the most important, by size, influence, wealth, and cultural production, in the United States. While America attracted far more Jews than any other land, becoming the behemoth of new-world Jewish communities, other communities arose from this mass exodus as well. South Africa, Canada, England, Argentina, and Australia over time welcomed substantial numbers of Jews, and these communities too owed their origins to the peddlers, not-withstanding the migration of other Jews who pursued other occupations.

As of the late nineteenth century, the rise of the garment industry drew masses of Jews who went directly from ships to factories in many new-world cities. But the worldwide Jewish garment industry grew, in part, out of ped-dlers' earlier activities. Hundreds of thousands of Jews came to Chicago to labor in the men's clothing industry. Many sewed in the massive plant owned and operated by Joseph Schaffner, of Hart, Schaffner and Marx. That com-pany had evolved out of Schaffner's peddling activities, undertaken when he first came to America. His years on the road provided the start-up capital for his emergence as one of the largest manufacturers of men's suits in Chicago, in the United States, and indeed in the world.

This great migration shifted the center of Jewish life from Europe, and the new-world centers emerged in the early twentieth century as powerful players in world Jewish politics, financially assisting, even rescuing, old homelands and using their growing political clout to advocate for Jews back there. Particularly after World War I, new-world Jews championed the Jews caught up in increasingly harsh, nationalistic realities, culminating in the horrors of the 1930s and 1940s. Jews in new-world places, carved out by peddlers, *smous*, *semananiks*, *cuentaniks*, *kloppers*, hawkers, travelers, weekly men, or *wochers*, provided relief and aid to their fellow Jews who had decided to stay home.

The immigration of Jews to new homes left its mark on the non-Jewish women and men whom they met. Most simply, the woman in provincial England in the late eighteenth century who had never before owned eyeglasses saw the world differently after the immigrant Jewish peddler pulled a pair from his sack. The poor people of Colombia who had owned no shoes until the immigrant Jewish peddlers arrived, afterward felt the ground beneath their feet far differently, and less painfully. The wives of Cuban sugar cane workers who bought ties and cloth handkerchiefs for their husbands from the peddlers altered the way others perceived them and their families. Women around the new world who spread sheets and pillowcases on their beds, adorned their walls with mirrors, pictures, and picture frames, bought from the peddlers and thus lived more comfortably and with an altered aesthetic. Peddlers who paid female customers to collect herbs, or to gather feathers, bones, tin, or rags, expanded the women's personal resources and enhanced their own and their families' possibilities. Former peddlers who opened clothing factories or workshops to make and repair watches, furniture, and picture frames provided employment for women and men, and that too altered them and their home communities. The Jewish peddler who showed up weekly at the home of Ida Jiggetts set her on a life course of discovery about Jews and the big world.

The peddlers acted as cultural innovators, offering alternative ways for women and men in their adopted countries to spend time and money. That a former peddler lugged a movie projector, a makeshift screen, and films around the Irish countryside and then inaugurated Dublin's first movie house offers one example. The Shubert brothers peddled with their father in upstate New York and later brought theater and entertainment to Americans across the country, helping to shape a new American vernacular culture.

The children of the peddlers who went into the teaching profession, politics, social reform movements, social work, law, medicine, the academy, entertainment, literature, and the arts also influenced the histories of their new-world homes. Their professional work in classrooms, courtrooms, or doctors' offices constituted part of the peddlers' legacy as well. Those who became accountants, dentists, sellers of insurance, or proprietors of large stores also, one by one, shaped the societies they lived in. The son of Morris Lasker, the peddler who sat in the Texas legislature, invented modern American advertising. The American-born son of Samuel Rosenwald, the peddler whose brother-in-law gave him a store in Peoria, Illinois, as a wedding gift, not only achieved fame and staggering wealth as president of Sears Roebuck but as a philanthropist poured millions of dollars into the education and health care of African Americans and into many undertakings in the Jewish world. Many American art museums display works by Louise Nevelson, and a sculpture garden of her pieces can be found in New York's financial district. Peddling brought her father, Isaac Berliawsky, to Maine from the Ukrainian province of Poltava at the end of the nineteenth century. The Briscoes, named Cherrik when in Lithuania, migrated to Ireland, where Abraham ventured out as a weekly man. Their Irish-born son Robert threw himself into the activities of the Irish Republican Army and the Sinn Féin during Ireland's War for Independence against Britain. He served in the Irish Parliament for thirty-six years and eventually held the position of lord mayor of Dublin.

This list could go on. Names could be drawn from South Africa, Australia, and the many countries of South and Central America, but even in short form it points to the reality that the peddling that catalyzed the great Jewish migration did not just change the Jews but left its impress on the political, cultural, and economic life of their destination countries. These Jewish women and men would never have been in Cuba, Mexico, South Africa, Canada, or Wales—or Texas, Mississippi, Vermont, or Maine—had their fathers not gone there to peddle. But they did, and these children of the peddlers provided their services to their fellow citizens, offering education, medical care, legal work, and the like.

How peddlers changed their host societies and their cultures might be encapsulated in one letter published in a Peruvian newspaper in the middle of the 1930s. When in 1935 anonymous flyers appeared on the streets of various Peruvian cities, attacking the "Turkish" and "Romanian" peddlers who were purportedly harming the nation, a group of local Jews, from Turkey and Romania, among other old-world places, peddlers all, responded with an open letter in a newspaper in Trujillo, *El Dia*. The peddler-writers declared that "the menace of commerce of Trujillo is not Turkish or Romanian itinerant vendors because we force no one to buy our merchandise. Everyone is free to do as he pleases." They added in their own defense, "All we do is make it easier for people to clothe themselves—those who cannot get together enough money to go to the larger establishments to buy their attire, get their clothes from us." In this service, and in the license fees the peddlers paid, these self-defenders declared, "We offer an important *Peruvian* service, making life easier in numerous households." The letter writers proceeded to attack narrow nationalism by outlining their contribution to the nation: "We are the distributors of national products, receiving this merchandise and distributing it on our own shoulders to the farthest corners, into the jungle, so that the inhabitants there might come to know these national products—to the benefit of the economy, the state, the culture. Because to wash oneself and dress oneself well is a manifestation of culture and a step forward for a people. . . . We with the system of installment payments, relieve many poor people who lack a blanket to cover themselves from the cold, who lack a dress to present themselves well." The peddlers spoke out against the "Man in the Street," the pseudonym of the author or authors of the anti-Semitic, antipeddler flyer: "They should be grateful that honest and hardworking men come to their doors and offer them what they need."[1] By coming to the doors of the poor denizens of Trujillo or Lima, or of any of the towns around the new world, Jewish peddlers, whether Turkish Jews or Romanian, Alsatian, Polish, Moroccan, or Lithuanian, changed life for those who answered, looked in the bags, and bought. They improved the lives of their customers.

The creation of new sites of Jewish life constituted one legacy of the great Jewish migration. Peddling also facilitated Jewish integration in these many places. The essence of the occupation depended on one-on-one interaction between customer and peddler. The peddler's act of crossing the threshold of some strangers' home, talking to her in her language, and striking up a positive personal relationship built bridges, rendering Jews as real human beings and not odd foreigners. Peddlers brought desired goods to people yearning for a higher material standard. Peddler by peddler, community by community, the immigrants who initially shared little with the inhabitants of the various lands, nearly all Christians, learned to communicate and establish themselves as not so different.

Peddling provided the initial mechanism by which the Jews met their new neighbors, speakers of a multiplicity of languages. It forced them to eat at the tables of Christians and compelled them to present themselves as like their customers—worried about the weather, or proud of their children—and simultaneously as distinctive, as men who hailed from exotic places like Bohemia, Galicia, Rhodes, Romania, or Morocco, who earned their living so unlike everyone else, and who would not eat the pork, squirrel, bear, or whatever other foods their hosts ate.

Peddling forced new immigrants to become students of culture, autodidactic anthropologists, who learned languages and ways of life brand new to them. A consumer's culture, the peddlers intuited, included details that translated into tastes for clothing, jewelry, housewares, kitchen goods, and furnishings. A consumer's culture also included the small gestures, cues, and assorted elements of nonverbal communication that could spell the difference between a sale and a slammed door. Jewish peddlers figured out on their own, or were advised by their suppliers, themselves former Jewish peddlers, that when entering African-American homes, they must doff their hats in respect, and greet the woman or man who opened the door as Mrs. or Mr., as "ma'am" or "sir." They learned to do this not to advance a civil rights agenda but to advance a sale, by winning over customers who in public could expect no respect from white people. Despite being newcomers, "green" in new-world ways, they had to learn, and peddling became a school on the road. A peddler memoir, written by an eastern European Jew who came to the state of Georgia at the end of the nineteenth century, plying his wares to rural, Christian fundamentalists, recalled that when he began his American peddling career, his supplier told him, "This sack will teach you to talk, will give you food to eat, will give you an opportunity to emerge from your greenness, will teach you to integrate yourself into American life."[2]

That integration did not everywhere take place easily or in the same way. The United States stood at the top of the chart in terms of speed and ease with which peddlers, during and after their itinerant lives, entered civic life. In the other new-world places the process proceeded more slowly and less dramatically. In America constitutional guarantees and political principles vis-à-vis religion and national origins mattered, as Jews, like all white immigrants, experienced a relatively smooth path to naturalization. Their foreign births did not disqualify them from assuming civic roles.

At times, in some places, powerful elements of society found modernity suspect and questioned the value and morality of material acquisition. In predominantly Catholic countries Jews as purveyors of consumer goods representing cosmopolitanism encountered opposition in rhetoric and action. In some destination societies for peddlers, like Ireland, Quebec, and South Africa, Jews shuttled between two inimical cultural and national groups, English and Irish, English and French, English and Afrikaner. There the Jews' otherness stalled temporarily their quick integration. Not so in the United States, where acquiring new clothes, the latest gadgets, showy household objects, and things of every kind did not jar with the national creed. In America the idea of the modern and up-to-date fit with the cultural veneration of progress, personal and collective. Too heterogeneous to be divided between two groups only, the United States, which made it clear that people of color had the fewest rights and resources, embraced the Jewish peddlers. Opposition to them emanated purely from the fear of economic competition expressed by local businessmen.

The United States during the great age of migration fostered the world's most dynamic economy. This, too, made the road to integration smoother and swifter for immigrant Jewish peddlers than elsewhere. But in fact, everywhere Jews went, peddled, and then became merchants, they entered, with varying degrees of speed, into the middle class and the civic life of their adopted communities. No matter where, no matter what continent or country, they assumed that peddling would bring economic stability, and that their children would lead comfortable lives, attending high schools and universities, moving to the professions, and interacting easily with non-Jewish peers.

All over the new world, when a Jewish man who had once been a peddler joined the Masons, the Lions Club, or the Elks, every time he sat on a local committee to plan an Independence Day gathering or a public library, Jews as a whole achieved local reputations as integral members of the community at large. The life histories of the peddlers mitigated the deeply rooted idea of the Jews as eternal outsiders, wanderers who had no stake in the local order, who made no commitments to others, expressing loyalty only to their own people, people who took and never gave back. When Jewish men who had once knocked on doors to sell watches, picture frames, and glasses stood for public office, and helped decide where the town should lay its roads or how to pay its public school teachers, they demonstrated their integration and their inclusion. When they, as settled merchants who had once been peddlers, contributed money to building a hospital or to some other charitable endeavor, they marked their integration and others took note.

The integration of Jews, men who had once peddled, and of their daughters and sons, transformed the societies where this process took place. This involved more than Jews knocking on the door, asking to be admitted to clubs, schools, and political parties, entering hat in hand and leaving those institutions as they found them. Jews altered social, political, and cultural realities of their new-world places. They did so differently in different places, but everywhere they shook up conventional and long-standing practices and modes of expression, introducing new cultural forms and political ideas. Sol Levitan, the Wisconsin peddler, held office and participated in the progressive movement to foster the "Wisconsin idea" of public policy. Other peddlers who went into public life also left their marks on the political cultures of their communities, although not necessarily as progressives. Rather, they articulated the premise, directly or indirectly, that an orderly society stimulated prosperity, that prosperity benefited business, and that vast class differences threatened that orderliness. They demonstrated to their fellow promoters of the social order that a commitment to civic welfare did not have anything to do with Christianity.

Ordinary people and molders of public policy in the peddlers' new world stopped thinking of their country as a home for Christians only, gradually acknowledging the presence and legitimacy of another religious community that differed from Christianity. Christians who came to know Jews, in part through peddling, learned to reconcile their own religious beliefs and commitments with the reality that Jews lived and prospered in their midst. The preamble to Ireland's 1922 Constitution acknowledged the fact of its overwhelmingly Catholic majority, invoking "the Most Holy Trinity, from Whom all authority and to Whom . . . all actions . . . must be referred." It declared the Irish people's "obligations to our Divine Lord, Jesus Christ." Yet the migration, settlement, and integration of several thousand Jews, many getting started as weekly men, persuaded the framers to declare that just as the new state "recognized" a number of Christian denominations, so too it extended its hand to "the Jewish Congregations" of Ireland. By the 1940s American public discourse had begun to refer to the nation as one made up of Catholics, Protestants, and Jews. This vision of the country as one of three faiths ignored the Jews' small number, that they constituted no more than 5 percent of the population. Their integration had so thoroughly seeped into the national consciousness that such a statement seemed self-evident and right.

Integration challenged Jews as bearers of a religion which insisted on separateness and on the division of the world into two categories, Jews and the other nations. Peddling forced the Jews to redefine Judaism, and even in places like England, South Africa, and Ireland, where former peddlers did not pursue religious reform, years on the road loosened the bonds of personal religious behavior. Although all the synagogues they created as peddlers and former peddlers clung to traditional forms, in their everyday decisions peddlers, on the road and off, felt less compelled to comply strictly to many obligations mandated by the commandments.

Many Jews in Europe and the Ottoman Empire who stayed home also underwent this process, shedding strict adherence to the dietary rules, Sabbath observance, and other dictates of Jewish law. But the new world telescoped, speeded up, and intensified the process. Peddling played a role in this. The peddler who had on the road decided to eat whatever the friendly farm women put on their tables, seems, when he settled down, to have decided that what he ate did not impinge on his Jewishness. Abraham Kohn, a former peddler, helped found the first congregation in Chicago, K.A.M., Kehillat Anshe Ma'arav, the congregation of the men of the west. He and his fellow prairie Jews, nearly all once peddlers, worshiped together, buried their dead, celebrated Jewish holidays, and did not keep kosher. Only when Kohn and his brothers brought over their observant mother, Delia, did they seek out the services of a ritual slaughterer. Until then, as they saw it, they lived as good Jews, and what they put in their mouths did not take anything away from that.

As with political and civic integration, the transformation of Judaism in the new world did not take place evenly, and the United States again proved to be sui generis as peddlers and former peddlers redefined themselves as Jews. Here, more than elsewhere, peddling facilitated the reform of Judaism, not just in terms of the founding and development of the Reform movement. Jewish religious institutions that defined themselves as traditional rather quickly deviated from their counterparts in their native lands. Women took a more energetic and visible place in new-world synagogues than they had in premigration communities. By dint of new-world necessity, even traditionalist synagogues assumed social functions that had not existed before. Back home, the synagogue had provided a place for male worship; in the new world it served as a hub of Jewish social and cultural life. New-world, peddler-inspired Judaism offered more latitude for the less observant. Men like Gustav Kussy, the onetime peddler, who operated his Newark store on the Sabbath, help found an observant congregation and held various honored positions in it, demonstrating flexibility born of necessity. Kussy's synagogue, Oheb Shalom, began as traditional, but gradually inched toward innovation. It soon joined the Conservative movement, which was open to changes based on American idioms.

For the most part, new-world Judaism, and American Judaism particularly, shed a sense of exclusivity born of centuries of oppression and inherent in the system. That so many new-world Jews had peddled and had experienced positive interactions with non-Jews played no minor part in this new iteration of traditional attitudes. Caroline Spiegel, the young Quaker woman who met her future husband when he peddled in Ohio, then converted to Judaism and moved with him back to Chicago, became actively part of his extended family, participated in synagogue women's activities, and eventually helped found and then led one of Chicago's first formal Jewish women's organizations, the Johanna Lodge of the United Order of True Sisters.

Jewish men on the road as peddlers watched their customers pray and discussed the Bible, the origins of Jewish rituals, and Jewish history with them. They came to recognize non-Jews as more than despised goyim, with whom they should avoid contact other than in matters purely commercial. The Jewish peddlers peppered memoirs and shared stories with their families about customers as warm and hospitable people who respected Judaism, people with whom they could talk and spend leisure time. The fact that their customers ate ham and bacon, believed in Jesus, celebrated Christmas and Easter, and bought religious goods from them did not impede human interactions and the blossoming of mutual religious respect.

The immigrant peddlers and their immediate descendants left their mark on the religious life of the new world. Pious Christians, believers in their obligation to convert the Jews to Christianity and share the Gospel's truth, hosted Jewish men in their homes, men who covered their heads, eschewed most food served, donned prayer shawls, and wound leather straps on their foreheads and arms for their early morning prayers before they set out on the roads. The Christian Dakotans who implored the Jewish peddler to lead their worship services when they lacked a clergyman took a step toward what the mid-twentieth century would call interfaith dialogue or ecumenicalism. When small southern churches turned to local Jewish men, peddlers and former peddlers, to teach Bible in their Sunday schools, they opened the door for Jewish-Christian exchange. Circumstance compelled them to reach out to the Jews, but doing so made a powerful statement.

Peddler autobiographies, Jewish communal documents of the time, and oral histories looking backward make nearly no mention of customers or local community people trying to convert these Jewish men to Christianity. The silence in the peddler accounts speaks volumes about how peddling smoothed out Jewish-Christian antipathy in the new world. The Jewish men who went in and out of small towns, suburbs of big cities, mill and mining camps, and farmlands did not endure pleas—or harangues—from those whose homes they entered, to see the light and accept Jesus. This contrasts starkly with the vigorous activities of missionary societies during the great century of Jewish migration, particularly in England and the United States, to convert the Jews. The fact that peddlers did not refer to evangelicalism in their own writings deviated from the worry expressed by Jewish communal leaders over the great threat to Judaism posed by evangelicals. A gap exists between the vast frantic outpouring by rabbis and Jewish newspaper editors about the threat posed by missionaries and the reality of the poor immigrant Jews who spent time on the road and discussed the Bible and matters of faith with customers who had no interest in making them over from Jews into Christians.[3]

Former peddlers also had nearly nothing to say about anti-Semitism, most claiming when asked that they never experienced it, or that it cropped up so rarely and innocuously as not to shape their encounters with the new world. They had no reason to deny its existence other than that they remembered their lives that way. In interviews conducted with them and their children, they recalled many rich details about peddling, mincing no words about the misery of their years carrying their backpacks, trudging the roads, always uncomfortable, and usually lonely. They did not hesitate to talk about robberies and customers who refused to pay them. But they claimed that they met no anti-Jewish hostility, or so little as to render it meaningless.

Yet historians have rightly pointed out the degree of anti-Jewish prejudice and discrimination around the world during the century of migration. The peddlers, mostly active and engaged Jews, probably read the Jewish press and attended meetings of Jewish societies, but they made no connection between anti-Semitism and the relationships they forged in their own small sphere with customers and other non-Jews, those who invited them to join their service organizations and hailed them in their local press as pillars of civic respectability. The customers who welcomed peddlers into their homes, offering places to sleep and food to eat, who bought from the peddlers and welcomed them as settled merchants in their midst, did not see these men as operatives in some international Jewish conspiracy. Nor, if asked, would they have been likely to suggest that Jews corrupted their communities.

When, starting in the late nineteenth century, Jewish elites, particularly in the United States, attempted to defend the Jews against defamation, verbal attack, and discrimination, they capitalized on the goodwill broadly forged between peddlers and customers. They constructed a rhetoric celebrating the peddler as a pioneer, a man of courage, as among the founding fathers of new-world societies. Israel Abrahams made this point in his 1895 rejoinder to

Anatole Leroy-Beaulieu; Abrahams was writing a year into the Dreyfus affair in France and two years after some elite New Englanders founded the Immigration Restriction League, dedicated to ending free, open, and unrestricted immigration to the United States. From the Israel Abrahams days well into the 1940s, Jewish communal leaders, writers, rabbis, and other public figures pleaded for the Jews, particularly for access to immigration rights, through the heroic peddler who contributed so much to his new home. Rabbi Joseph Hertz, the chief rabbi of South Africa, declaimed in 1905 that "Jews should be taught the truth; that they themselves should no longer look upon themselves as interlopers, as exploiters; but rather as active participants in the upbuilding of the national life." He pointed to the thousands of smous who serviced the hinterland folks to prove his claim.[4]

Year after year Jews around the new world told this story to themselves and their non-Jewish fellow citizens. Jewish communities published compendia of outstanding Jews, pointing with pride to those who began as peddlers. The *American Jewish Yearbook* highlighted in its biographical sketches and necrologies the former immigrant peddlers who had benefited the nation. Irish and South African Jewish yearbooks and other outlets of the new-world Jewish press told the same story. M. I. Cohen, minister of the Bulawayo Hebrew Congregation of Rhodesia, narrated his community's history through the tale of the pioneer Jews, "mostly young men without means, ready to rough it," who "did their share in the opening up of the country." Selling from packs on their backs, they had come from Lithuania, and their story, according to Cohen, "is a vindication of the 'Russian Jew' . . . [who] stuck to the country through all its vicissitudes and [has] made good."[5] The 1918 *Prominent Jews of America* packed its pages with tributes to former peddlers and accounts of how they had enriched America. Elias Beren, from the province of Vitebsk in Belarus, came to the United States in 1870, peddled in Ohio, and within three years settled in Marietta, where he opened the Buckeye Supply Company. Amid straightforward biographical details, entries like that on Beren echoed with deeply political notes: "The exalted position which America holds among the nations today is largely attributable to the fine class of immigrants who have sought her shores. Oppressed by tyrannies and traditions of the old world, these free, progressive spirits have come under the protection of Liberty's banner, bringing with them a priceless heritage of self-reliance, and love for the land of their adoption." Compiled at a moment in time when Congress and the public debated immigration restriction, *Prominent American Jews* implied, with little subtlety, that, faced with an America that limited European immigration, Beren would have stayed in the

Ukraine; America thus would have been deprived of his contribution, and he would have faced the unbridled violence that was sweeping that region at that precise moment.[6]

After the mid-1920s, when the United States finally bolted the door to mass European immigration, the peddler became cemented in modern Jewish history, a figure increasingly invested with political meaning by authors and community leaders. Stephen Wise emphasized that in his eulogy for Sigmund Eisner. George Cohen wrote a book on the Jews in 1924, part of the Racial Contribution Series sponsored by the Knights of Columbus. The appearance of Cohen's *The Jews in the Making of America*, a work that praised those who had begun as "peddlers and shopkeepers," coincided with the passage of the National Origins Act. Cohen celebrated the Jews' "restlessness which impelled the race to seek newer realms and better climes." That restlessness, he told his readers, endowed the Jews with an "adaptability and a readiness that are useful in the life struggle. What is so potent a factor in mental development as travel, and Israel has been the most traveled of peoples." That "most traveled of peoples," it seemed, would no longer be seeking homes in the United States.[7]

In the increasingly desperate days after the end of easy immigration to the United States, Jewish communal leaders praised peddling as they tried to persuade countries in Latin America to encourage Jewish immigration. Ironically, the Jewish elite had for much of the modern period wanted to wean Jews from peddling, believing that Jewish men on the road with their bags slung over their shoulders made matters worse for the Jews, impeding meaningful emancipation and civic integration. But despite their historic aversion to peddling, in the 1920s Jewish notables started to recognize it as the engine that had propelled new-world Jews on a path toward mobility and respectability.

This rhetorical trope continued into the 1930s in the writings, oratory, and political action of western Jewry. Keep immigration open, they argued. Jews may come as peddlers, but people and their governments need not worry. Those peddlers will, as they had over the course of the long century of migration, become solid and contributing citizens. Cecil Roth published *Jewish Contribution to Civilization* in 1938, the year of Kristallnacht, of the mass pogrom perpetrated on the Jews of Vienna, and the worsening violence and discrimination against Poland's Jews. Roth was writing about the United States, but he could have described any new-world society to which Jewish peddlers immigrated when he declared, "It was the travelling pedlar who brought the amenities of life" to the "pioneers from the Atlantic coast or the European immigrant who took up a holding." The peddlers, "refugees from the intolerant policies of Central Europe," opened a new chapter in Jewish history, while improving the lives of Americans spreading across the continent.[8]

Roth's paean to the Jewish peddlers in America also fit for those who went to England in the late eighteenth century and extended to those who arrived in other parts of North America, the Caribbean, South America, southern Africa, Australia, Sweden, and the Celtic fringe. These millions of men who took up the peddlers' pack and sat down on the seats of their wagons left the world a different place from the one they had found, changing themselves and making those places and Jewish history modern.

Notes

1. Let me offer one example here. Western historians Patricia Nelson Limerick, Clyde A. Milner II, and Charles Rankin, in a photo essay in *Trails: Toward a New Western History* (Lawrence: University Press of Kansas, 1991), before page 160, include a photo of two Native Americans seated on a bottom row and three white men above. The caption reads, "English, Cornish, Welsh, Irish, Portuguese, Italian, Greek, French, Flemish, German, Austrian, Polish, Slovenian, Czech, Danish, Swedish, Finnish, Norwegian, Russian, Serbian, Spanish, and Basque" made their way to American West. The racialized mythmaking of the West hid the "region's complexity." Yet all three of the white men were Jews—Bernard Seligman, Zadoc Staab, and Lehman Spiegelberg—and all had come to New Mexico as peddlers. The authors thus in telling the story of the complexity of the American West handily obliterate the Jewish presence.
2. Walter A. Friedman, *The Birth of a Salesman: The Transformation of Selling in America* (Cambridge: Harvard University Press, 2004).

ROAD MAPS

1. Israel Abrahams, *Jewish Life in the Middle Ages* (London: Macmillan, 1896), 231.
2. German Jewish refugees fleeing Nazism also took up peddling in the Americas. Their story will not be covered here, but the topic deserves to be written about.
3. Jewish peddling continued in many places after the 1920s, and there is a book to be written about German and Polish Jews in the 1930s who went to a variety of new-world settings as peddlers. So, too, in the aftermath of the Holocaust, survivors coming to Cuba, Australia, and elsewhere also turned to peddling to get started.

4. Arthur Ruppin, *The Jews of To-Day* (New York: Henry Holt), 85.
5. The subjection of the Irish population by England does not quite follow the colonial pattern, although Irish nationalists might argue with my assertion here.
6. Jews from eastern Europe went to Germany in the late nineteenth century and peddled there. They fall outside of my story here, however, inasmuch as German customers knew Jews, and the immigrant Jews had some degree of familiarity with the German language. The presence of a sizable native-born German Jewish population with long roots in the country also made their experience different from that of those who migrated to and peddled in the new world.
7. There is no history of Jewish peddling as either a pre- or postmigration phenomenon.
8. Jane Tai Landa, *Trust, Ethnicity, and Identity: Beyond the New Institutional Economics of Ethnic Trading Networks, Contract Law, and Gift-Exchange* (Ann Arbor: University of Michigan Press, 2001).
9. There is an enormous literature on middlemen and middleman theory. See, for example, Walter P. Zenner, *Minorities in the Middle: A Cross-Cultural Analysis* (Albany: State University of New York Press, 1991).
10. The literature on the history of consumption is enormous and cannot be succinctly cited. See John Brewer and Roy Porter, eds., *Consumption and the World of Goods* (New York: Routledge, 1993), 1; Much of this literature goes back to the work of Fernand Braudel and such works as *Capitalism and Material Life, 1400–1800* (New York: Harper and Row, 1967); Neil McKendrick, John Brewer, and J. H. Plumb, eds., *The Birth of Consumer Society* (Bloomington: Indiana University Press, 1982); Peter Stearns, *Consumerism in World History: The Global Transformation of Desire* (New York: Routledge, 2006); Martin Daunton and Matthew Hilton, *The Politics of Consumption: Material Culture and Citizenship in Europe and America* (Oxford: Berg, 2001); Susan Strasser, Charles McGovern, and Matthias Judt, eds., *Getting and Spending: European and American Consumer Societies in the Twentieth Century* (New York: Cambridge University Press, 1998).
11. On women and pawning see Melanie Tebbutt, *Making Ends Meet: Pawnbroking and Working-Class Credit* (New York: St. Martin's, 1983); Wendy Wolosson, *In Hock: Pawning in America from Independence Through the Great Depression* (Chicago: University of Chicago Press, 2009).
12. No scholar has yet written a history of Jewish peddling anyplace, let alone in the entirety of the premigration Jewish world.
13. This is not just a European story. See Clifford Geertz, *Peddlers and Princes: Social Change and Economic Modernization in Two Indonesian Towns* (Chicago: University of Chicago Press, 1963), or T. G. McGee, *Hawkers in Selected Asian Cities* (Hong Kong: Centre of Asian Studies, University of Hong Kong, 1970).
14. Klaus J. Bade, *Migrations in European History* (Malden, Mass.: Blackwell, 2003), 20–30.
15. Laurence Fontaine, *History of Pedlars in Europe*, trans. Vicki Whittaker (Cambridge: Polity, 1996), 6.
16. Quoted in Charles Lemert, *Social Theory: The Multicultural and Class Readings*, 4th ed. (Boulder, Colo.: Westview, 2009), 184–189.

17. The literature on Yankee peddling is fairly robust, and enough material exists to allow us to compare their experiences with those of Jews. See "The Persistent Fringe of House to House Selling in American History," *Bulletin of the Business Historical Society* 9, no. 2 (1935), 24–28; Fred Mitchell Jones, *Middlemen in the Domestic Trade of the United States, 1800–1860* (Urbana: University of Illinois Press, 1937); Thomas D. Clark, *The Rampaging Frontier: Manners and Humors of the Pioneer Days in the South and the Middle West* (Bloomington: Indiana University Press, 1939), 301–320; Lewis E. Atherton, "The Pioneer Merchant in Mid-America," *University of Missouri Studies: A Quarterly of Research* 14, no. 2 (1939), 7–37; Richardson Wright, *Hawkers and Walkers in Early America* (Philadelphia: Lippincott, 1927); Theodore F. Marburg, "Manufacturer's Drummer, 1852, with Comments in Western and Southern Markets," *Bulletin of the Business Historical Society* 22, no. 3 (1948), 106–114; Lee M. Freedman, "The Drummer in Early American Merchandise Distribution," *Bulletin of the Business Historical Society* 21, no. 2 (1947), 39–44; Lewis E. Atherton, "Itinerant Merchandising in the Ante-Bellum South," *Bulletin of the Business Historical Society* 19, no. 2 (1945), 35–59; J. R. Dolan, *The Yankee Peddlers of Early America* (New York: Clarkson N. Potter, 1964); Penrose Scull, *From Peddlers to Merchant Princes: A History of Selling in America* (Chicago: Follett, 1967); Paul J. Uselding, "Peddling in the Antebellum Economy: Precursors of Mass-Marketing or a Start in Life?" *American Journal of Economics and Sociology* 34 (1975), 55–67; David Jaffee, "Peddlers of Progress and the Transformation of the Rural North, 1760–1860," *Journal of American History* 78 (1991), 511–535; Joseph T. Rainer, "The Honorable Fraternity of Moving Merchants: Yankee Peddlers in the Old South, 1800–1860," Ph.D. diss., College of William and Mary, 2000.

18. Charles Hindley, ed., *The Life and Adventures of A Cheap Jack. By One of the Fraternity* (London: Tinseley Brothers, 1876), 2.

19. Sven Dahl, "Travelling Pedlars in Nineteenth Century Sweden," *Scandinavian Economic History Review* 7 (1959), 167–178.

20. Ameen Rihani, *The Book of Khalid and Arab Life in Lower Manhattan* (New York: Dodd Mead, 1911); Sarah Gualtieri, *Between Arab and White: Race and Ethnicity in the Early Syrian American Diaspora* (Berkeley: University of California Press, 2009).

21. Quoted in Theresa Alfaro-Velacamp, *So Far from Allah, So Close to Mexico: Middle Eastern Immigrants to Modern Mexico* (Austin: University of Texas Press, 2007), 35.

22. The literature on Arab peddling in Latin America and the United States is extensive, and some makes the comparison with Jewish peddlers. Notably literature on Jewish peddlers makes no attempt to compare or link their subjects with other immigrant peddlers. See Philip K. Hitti, *The Syrians in America* (Piscataway, N.J.: Gorgias, 2005); Stewart G. McHenry, "The Syrian Movement into Upstate New York," *Ethnicity* 6 (1979), 327–345; Afif I. Tannous, "Acculturation of an Arab-Syrian Community in the Deep South," *American Sociological Review* 8 (1943), 264–271; Albert Harouni and Nadim Shehadi, *The Lebanese in the World: A*

Century of Emigration (London: Center for Lebanese Studies in Association with I. B. Tauris, 1992); Aaron D. Jesch, "A Peddler's Progress: Assimilation and Americanization in Kearney, Nebraska, 1890–1924," Ph.D. diss., University of Nebraska, 2008; Oswaldo Truzzi, "The Right Place at the Right Time: Syrians and Lebanese in Brazil and the United States, a Comparative Approach," *Journal of American Ethnic History* 16, no. 2 (1997), 3–34; Adele L. Younis, *The Coming of the Arabic-Speaking People to the United States* (New York: Center for Migration Studies, 1995); Louise Fawcett, "Arabs and Jews in the Development of the Colombian Caribbean, 1850–1950," *Boletin Cultural y Bibliografico* 35 1998), 57–79; William Sherman, Paul Whitney, and John Guerrero, *Prairie Peddlers* (Bismarck: University of North Dakota Press, 2002); Philip M. Kayal and Joseph Kayal, *The Syrian-Lebanese in America: A Study in Religion and Assimilation* (Boston: Twayne, 1975); Alixa Naff, *Becoming American: The Early Arab Immigrant Experience* (Carbondale: Southern Illinois University Press, 1985); Eric J. Hooglund, ed., *Crossing the Waters: Arabic-Speaking Immigrants to the United States Before 1940* (Washington, D.C.: Smithsonian Institution Press, 1987); John Tofik Karam, "A Cultural Politics of Entrepreneurship in Nation-Making: Phoenicians, Turks, and the Arab Commercial Essence in Brazil," *Journal of Latin American Anthropology* 9 (2004), 319–351.

1. ROAD WARRIORS

1. Aryeh Tartakower, *In Search of Home and Freedom* (London: World Jewish Congress, British Section, 1958), 27.
2. See, for example, Paula Hyman, *The Emancipation of the Jews of Alsace: Acculturation and Tradition in the Nineteenth Century* (New Haven: Yale University Press, 1991), 90–92.
3. England had expelled its Jews in 1290, only to readmit them in limited numbers in 1655.
4. Garment making tended to require relatively little capital, certainly compared with other heavier industries. It took place in small spaces and operated with a much more simple organizational structure than did steel, tool, textile, rubber, or other industries.
5. Quoted in Mark Wischnitzer, *To Dwell in Safety: The Story of Jewish Migration Since 1800* (Philadelphia: Jewish Publication Society, 1948), 34–35.
6. Ibid.
7. I will not be dealing with the migration of eastern European Jews into Germany and France who peddled throughout the late nineteenth century. These Jewish peddlers took the place of those who left the rural areas and peddled in areas that had long had Jewish populations, particularly a population of peddlers. For information on these east-to-west peddlers see Moses A. Shulvass, *From East to West: The Westward Migration of Jews from Eastern Europe During the Seventeenth and Eighteenth Centuries* (Detroit: Wayne State University Press, 1971); Vicki

Caron, *Between France and Germany: The Jews of Alsace-Lorraine, 1871–1918* (Stanford: Stanford University Press, 1988), 167.

8. Simon Kuznets, "Immigration of Russian Jews to the United States: Background and Structure," *Perspectives in American History* 9 (1975), 35–161, is the most thorough and elaborate analysis of that migration, and Kuznets played a crucial role in disproving the narrative of flight from pogrom, which has dominated the historiography and the culture of communal memory.

9. Lothar Kahn, "Early German-Jewish Writers and the Image of America (1820–1840)," *Leo Baeck International Yearbook* 31 (1986), 407–439.

10. Jacob Lestschinsky, "Jewish Migrations, 1840–1956," in *The Jews: Their History, Culture, and Religion*, ed. Louis Finkelstein (Philadelphia: Jewish Publication Society of America, 1949), 1536–1596, quotations on 1547.

11. Ibid., 1562.

12. Quoted in Lloyd P. Gartner, *American and British Jews in the Age of the Great Migration* (London: Vallentine Mitchell, 2009), 45.

13. E. Abraham–van der Mark, "The Ashkenazi Jews of Curaçao: A Trading Minority," *New West Indian Guide* 74 (2000), 257–280, http://www.kitlv-journals .nl, 259–261.

14. Norman Salsitz, *A Jewish Boyhood in Poland: Remembering Kolbuszowa* (Syracuse: Syracuse University Press, 1992), xiv, 201–202.

15. *Autobiography of Julius Weiss* (New Orleans: Goldman's Printing Office, 1903), 1, 5, 7.

16. "Joseph Austrian's Autobiographical and Historical Sketches. Dedicated to My Wife and Members of My Family," American Jewish Archives, SC-598, box 228s.

17. Kuznets, "Immigration of Russian Jews," provides a convincing portrait of those who left for the United States and in the process demolishes the pogrom narrative.

18. Quoted in Steven Aschheim, *Brothers and Strangers: The East European Jew in German and German Jewish Consciousness, 1800–1923* (Madison: University of Wisconsin Press, 1982), 107.

19. See Esther Schor, *Emma Lazarus* (New York: Next Book, 2006).

20. Yuri Slezkine, *The Jewish Century* (Princeton: Princeton University Press, 2004), 1.

21. Arab migrants provide the example of a group similar to Jews in terms of the importance of peddling, and they too had long commercial histories.

22. For a general statement on this matter see Jose Moya and Adam McKeown, *World Migration in the Long Twentieth Century: Essays on Global and Comparative History* (Washington, D.C.: American Historical Association, 2011), 23–25.

23. Benedict Anderson, *Imagined Communities: Reflections on the Origin and Spread of Nationalism* (London: Verso, 1983).

24. Walter Nugent, *Crossings: The Great Transatlantic Migrations, 1870–1914* (Bloomington: Indiana University Press, 1992); Leslie Page Moch, *Moving Europeans: Migration in Western Europe Since 1650* (Bloomington: Indiana University Press, 2003).

25. Avraham Barkai, "The German Jews at the Start of Industrialisation: Structural Change and Mobility, 1835–1860," in *Revolution and Evolution: 1848 in German-Jewish History*, ed. Werner E. Mosse, Arnold Paucker, and Reinhard Rürup (Tübingen: J. D. C. Mohr, 1981), 123–156.
26. See Glenn R. Sharfman, "Bavarians and Jews: A Study in Integration and Exclusion During the Nineteenth Century," *Journal of Religious History* 19, no. 2 (1995), 125–140.
27. Avigdor Levi, *The Sepharadim in the Ottoman Empire* (Princeton: Princeton University Press, 1992).
28. Victor A. Mirelman, "Sephardim in Latin America After Independence," in *Sepharadim in the Americas: Studies in Culture and History*, ed. Martin Cohen and Abraham Peck (Tuscaloosa: University of Alabama Press, 1993), 235–265.
29. Hermann Schwab, *Jewish Rural Communities in Germany* (London: Cooper, n.d.), 16–17.
30. Quoted in Jacob Lestschintsky, "The Economic Struggle of the Jews in Independent Lithuania," *Jewish Social Studies* 3, no. 4 (1946), 267–296.
31. Quoted in Gustav Saron, "The Making of South African Jewry: An Essay in Historical Interpretation," in *South African Jewry* (Johannesburg: Fieldhill, 1965), 9–49.
32. Edgar Samuel, "Jewish Settlement in Victoria, 1850–1914," in *Patterns of Jewish Migration, 1850–1914*, Proceedings of the International Academic Conference of the Jewish Historical Society of England and the Institute of Jewish Studies, University College London, ed. Aubrey Newman and Stephen Massil (London: Jewish Historical Society of England and the Institute of Jewish Studies, University College London, 1996), 330–345.
33. Leslie G. Kelen and Eileen Hallet Stone, *Missing Stories: An Oral History of Ethnic and Minority Groups in Utah* (Salt Lake City: University of Utah Press, 1996), 273.
34. Sheryl Gay Stolberg, "Arlen Specter, Pennsylvania Senator, Is Dead at 82," *New York Times*, October 15, 2012.
35. On the lack of entrepreneurial activity among Jewish immigrants to England in the late nineteenth century, see Andrew Godley, *Jewish Immigrant Entrepreneurship in London and New York: Enterprise and Culture* (Basingstoke: Palgrave, 2001).
36. Mark Wischnitzer, *To Dwell in Safety: The Story of Jewish Migration Since 1800* (Philadelphia: Jewish Publication Society, 1948), 118, 132, 101.
37. Judith Laikin Elkin, *Jews of the Latin American Republics* (Chapel Hill: University of North Carolina Press, 1980).
38. Mirelman, "Sephardim in Latin America After Independence"; Walter F. Weiker, *Ottomans, Turks, and the Jewish Polity: A History of the Jews of Turkey* (Lanham, Md.: University Press of America, 1992), 126–127.
39. For the phrase see Harold Pollins, "Hopeful Travellers: Jewish Migrants and Settlers in Nineteenth Century Britain," *London Museum of Jewish Life Series*, ed. Aubrey Newman, vol. 2 (n.d.), 14.

40. Harry A. Ezratty, *500 Years in the Jewish Caribbean* (Baltimore: Omni Arts, 2002), 117.
41. Walter F. Weiker, *Ottomans, Turks, and the Jewish Polity: A History of the Jews of Turkey* (Lanham, Md.: University Press of America, 1992), 268.
42. Ariel Segal, *Jews of the Amazon: Self-Exile in Earthly Paradise* (Philadelphia: Jewish Publication Society, 1999), 51–52.
43. Walter Zenner, *A Global Community: The Jews from Aleppo* (Detroit: Wayne State University Press, 2000), 109–114.
44. Notably, until the second decade of the twentieth century, Lithuania sent out the largest number of Jewish emigrants of any place in eastern Europe, including to the United States.
45. B. A. Kosmin, *Majuta: A History of the Jewish Community of Zimbabwe* (Gwelo: Mambo, 1980), 26.
46. Quoted in Leon Feldberg, *South African Jewry* (Johannesburg: Fieldhill, 1976), 25.
47. Hannah Berman and Melisande Zlotover, *Zlotover Story* (Dublin: Hely Thom, 1966); Cormac O'Grada, *Jewish Ireland in the Age of Joyce: A Socioeconomic History* (Princeton: Princeton University Press, 2006), 17–22.
48. Sven Dahl, "Traveling Pedlars in Nineteenth Century Sweden," *Scandinavian Economic History Review* 7 (1959), 455–506.
49. John Simon Levi, *The Forefathers: A Dictionary of Biography of the Jews of Australia, 1788–1830* (Sydney: Australian Jewish Historical Society, 1976).
50. This is the convincing thesis of Roger Daniels, *Coming to America: A History of Immigration and Ethnicity in American Life* (New York: HarperCollins, 1990).
51. Edward Cohen, *The Peddler's Grandson: Growing Up Jewish in Mississippi* (Jackson: University of Mississippi Press, 1999), 50.
52. Elliott Ashkenazi, *The Business Jews of Louisiana, 1840–1875* (Tuscaloosa: University of Alabama Press, 1988); Ewa Morawska, *Insecure Prosperity: Small-Town Jews in Industrial America, 1890–1940* (Princeton: Princeton University Press, 1996).
53. Robert H. Babcock, "A Jewish Immigrant in the Maritimes: The Memoirs of Max Vanger," *Arcadiensis: Journal of the History of the Atlantic Region* 16, no. 1 (1986), 136–148.
54. On the unsuitability of the Southwest for peddling, see Floyd S. Fierman, "Peddlers and Merchants on the Southwest Frontier, 1850–1880," *Western States Jewish History* 37, no. 1 (2004), 56–71.
55. Jewish peddlers may also have gone to the Far East and around the Pacific Rim. See David White, "Prayers Before Business in Singapore," *Southern Israelite*, April 1933, which makes reference to Jewish peddlers in that predominantly Muslim city on the Malay Peninsula.
56. Morawska, *Insecure Prosperity;* Deborah Weiner, *Coal Field Jews: An Appalachian History* (Urbana: University of Illinois Press, 2006).
57. Arnold Levy, *History of the Sunderland Jewish Community* (London: Macdonald, 1956), 23–30.

58. There is an enormous and somewhat contentious literature about the rise in the desire for material goods in the late nineteenth century. See Timothy Guinnane, *Households, Migration, and the Rural Economy in Ireland, 1850–1914* (Princeton: Princeton University Press, 1997), 196–197, as one example; for the quotation, Conrad Arensberg, *The Irish Countryman: An Anthropological Study* (Garden City, N.Y.: Natural History Press, 1937), 39.

59. Richard Bushman, *The Refinement of America: Persons, Houses, Cities* (New York: Random House, 1992), xii, 264–265.

60. On the material level of rural Americans through much of the nineteenth century see David Danborn, *Born in the Country: A History of Rural America* (Baltimore: Johns Hopkins University Press, 1995).

61. Marcus Arkin, "In the Footsteps of Nathaniel Isaacs: A Bird's Eye Overview of the Economic History of KwaZulu-Natal Jewry," *Jewish Affairs* 56, no. 3 (2001), 24–35.

62. On the material level of American slaves see, for example, Charles L. Perdue, Jr., Thomas Barden, and Robert K. Phillips, *Weevils in the Wheat: Interviews with Virginia Ex-Slaves* (Charlottesville: University of Virginia Press, 1976), 82, 96–97, 103, 107, 139–140, 229.

63. Darío Euraque, "The Arab-Jewish Economic Presence in San Pedro Sula, the Industrial Capital of Honduras: Formative Years, 1880s–1930," *Immigrants and Minorities* 16, nos. 1–2 (1997), 94–124.

64. Barbara Weinstein, *The Amazon Rubber Boom, 1850–1920* (Stanford: Stanford University Press, 1983), 51.

65. Regina Igel, "Haquitiaas Spoken in the Brazilian Amazon," in *From Iberia to Diaspora: Studies in Sephardic History and Culture*, ed. Yedida Stillman and Norman Stillman (Leiden: Brill, 1999), 446–450; *Autobiography of Julius Weis*, 7.

66. See, for example, Benjamin Schlesinger, "The Jews of Jamaica: A Historical View," *Caribbean Quarterly* 13, no. 1 (1967), 46–53, and Jacob Levitz, "The Acculturation of the East European Jews in Mexico City (1920–1946)," M.A. thesis, Wayne State University, 1946, p. 61.

67. See, for example, Corinne Azen Krause, "The Jews in Mexico: A History with Special Emphasis on the Period from 1857 to 1930," Ph.D. diss., University of Pittsburgh, 1907.

68. Karen Falk and Avi Decter, *We Call This Place Home: Jewish Life in Maryland's Small Towns* (Baltimore: Jewish Museum of Maryland, 2002).

69. Hecht, Simeon, Memoir 21, Typed version of handwritten document, Jewish Museum of Maryland.

70. Quoted in Richard Mendelsohn and Milton Shain, *The Jews in South Africa: An Illustrated History* (Johannesburg: Jonathan Ball, 2011), 38.

71. Tobias Brinkmann, "Between Vision and Reality: Reassessing Jewish Agricultural Colony Projects in Nineteenth Century America," *Jewish History* 21 (2007), 305–324.

72. Levi, *The Forefathers*, 6.

2. ROAD RUNNERS

1. As is often the case, most of these works use "Jews" to mean Jewish men.
2. Isaac Factor, "The Jewish Communities of South Wales Port Talbot," *Cajex: The Magazine of the Association of Jewish Ex-Service Men and Women (Cardiff)* 11, no. 4 (1961), 65–67.
3. "Los Hebreos in Peru," *Oyfgang* 5 (1934), 32.
4. Boris Rubenstein, "How Jews Live in Honduras," *Havaner Lebn* 1, no. 9 (1933), 15.
5. Lee Shai Weissbach, *Jewish Life in Small-Town America: A History* (New Haven: Yale University Press, 2005).
6. Jewish peddling got a bit of a revival in the late 1940s and 1950s in individual locations like Australia with the arrival of Holocaust survivors, a story worth telling on its own.
7. Quoted in Ross L. Muir and Carl J. White, *Over the Long Term . . . The Story of J. and W. Seligman & Co.* (New York: J. and W. Seligman, 1964), 33.
8. Linda Schloff, "Jewish Religious Life in Four Market Towns," in *Minnesota History* 51 (1988), 3–14.
9. Louis Schmier, *Reflections of Southern Jewry: The Letters of Charles Wessolowsky, 1878–1879* (Albany, Ga.: Mercer University Press, 1982), 6–7.
10. "Singer, Louis E. Autobiography, No Date," Miscellaneous file, SC-11557, Small Collection, American Jewish Archives.
11. Elliott Ashkenazi, *The Business Jews of Louisiana, 1840–1875* (Tuscaloosa: University of Alabama Press, 1988), 38.
12. Liz Hamui-Halabe, "Re-Creating Community: Christians from Lebanon and Jews from Syria in Mexico, 1900–1938." *Immigrants and Minorities* 16, nos. 1–2 (1997), 125–145; Ariel Segal, *Jews of the Amazon: Self-Exile in Earthly Paradise* (Philadelphia: Jewish Publication Society, 1999), 45.
13. Weissbach, *Jewish Life in Small-Town America.*
14. "Jewish Life in Aiken, S.C.: Childhood Memories of Esther Surasky Pinck," ed. Arnold Shankman, *Southern Jewish History Newsletter* 4, no. 13 (1982), 2–3.
15. Jordan S. Alpert, *The Alperts and Cohens of Bangor, Maine* (San Francisco: privately published, 1990), 45.
16. *Jewish Chronicle*, December 20, 1918, p. 11.
17. Reginald Wright Kauffman, *Jesse Isidor Straus: A Biographical Portrait* (New York: privately published, 1973); Saul Viener, "The Political Career of Isidor Straus," M.A. thesis, West Virginia University, 1947.
18. Phillip Applebaum, "The Jews of Luce County, Michigan," *Michigan History* 21, no. 1 (1980), 3–9.
19. "The Immigration of Levantine Jews into the United States," *Jewish Charities* 4, no. 11 (1914), 12–27.
20. Hasia Diner, *A Time for Gathering: The Second Migration, 1820–1880*, The Jewish People in America, vol. 2 (Baltimore: Johns Hopkins University Press, 1992), 80–81.

21. On Jews and scrap see Jonathan Z. Pollack, "Success from Scrap and Second-Hand Goods: Jewish Businessmen in the Midwest, 1890–1930," in *Chosen Capital: The Jewish Encounter with American Capitalism*, ed. Rebecca Kobrin (New Brunswick, N.J.: Rutgers University Press, 2012), 93–112.

22. Devera S. Stocker, Bess Alper Deutsch, and Naomi Buchhalter Floch, "History of the Traverse City Jewish Community, Part Two," *Michigan Jewish History* 20, no. 1 (1980), 4–19.

23. Baila Shargel and Harold L. Drimmer, *The Jews of Westchester: A Social History* (Fleischmanns, N.Y.: Purple Mountain, 1994), 34.

24. Quoted in Bella Rosenbaum, "In My Lifetime," *American Jewish Archives* 19, no. 1 (1967), 8.

25. Judith Levin Cantor, *Jews in Michigan* (East Lansing: Michigan State University Press, 2001), 17.

26. Gerald Tulchinsky, *Canada's Jews: A People's Journey* (Toronto: University of Toronto Press, 2008), 96.

27. Simon Belkin, *Through Narrow Gates: A Review of Jewish Immigration, Colonization, and Immigrant Aid Work in Canada, 1840–1940* (Montreal: Eagle, 1966), 43.

28. Jeffrey Lesser, "The Immigration of Polish Jews in Brazil, 1924–1934," *The Americas* 51, no. 2 (1994), 173–191; Jacob Levitz, "The Jewish Community in Mexico: Its Life and Education, 1900–1954," Ph.D. diss, Dropsie College for Hebrew and Cognate Learning, 1954, p. 20.

29. Rosa Perla Raicher, *Uruguay, La Comunidad Israelita y el Pueblo Judio* (Montevideo: Universidad de la República, 2003), 75; Jacob X. Cohen, *Jewish Life in South America* (New York: Bloch, 1941), 45–46.

30. Israel Solomon, "Records of My Family," Susser Archive, www.jewishgen.org/jcr-uk/susser/israelsolomonstory.htm.

31. Lester S. Levy, *Jacob Epstein* (Baltimore: Maran, 1978); see dozens of references to the Baltimore Bargain House in the *Encyclopedia of Southern Jewish Communities*, http://www.isjl.org/encyclopedia-of-southern-jewish-communities.html.

32. Elaine Crowley, *A Dublin Girl: Growing Up in the 1930s* (New York: Soho, 1996), 42.

33. Philip Doherty, "The Last Pawnshops of Dublin City," *Dublin Historical Record* 47, no. 1 (1994), 87–94.

34. Milton Lomask, *Seed Money: The Guggenheim Story* (New York: Farrar Straus, 1964), 16.

35. District Grand Lodge No. 7 of B'nai Brith, Floyd S. Fierman Papers, Box 13, Folder 10, Coll. 649, American Jewish Archives.

36. Bella W. Rosenbaum, "In My Lifetime," *American Jewish Archives* 19, no. 1 (1967), 3–33.

37. "Memoir Abe Gellman," Memoir 13, Jewish Museum of Maryland.

38. Adolf Kraus, *Reminiscences and Comments: The Immigrant, The Citizen, A Public Office, The Jew* (Chicago: Adolf Kraus, 1925), n.p.

39. "Yud Shin," p. 11, RG 102, box 6, no. 53 YIVO.
40. "B. M. Laikin (Ben-Moyshe)," RG 106, box 6, no. 144, YIVO.
41. Quoted in Esther J. Panitz, *Simon Wolf: Private Conscience and Public Image* (Rutherford, N.J.: Fairleigh Dickinson University Press, 1987), 19.
42. *New York Times*, May 18, 1902.
43. Elizabeth K. Berman, "M. S. Polack's Circumcision Record Book: A Record of 911 Jewish Families from 1836–1862, Compiled by a Rural Peddler and Mohel," *Generations: The Magazine of the Jewish Historical Society of Maryland*, Fall 1989, pp. 10–11.
44. Irving Katz, *Max and Rebecca Katz* (privately published, 1979), 26, available at Jewish Museum of Maryland.
45. See, as one small example, Linda Mack Schloff, *And Prairie Dogs Weren't Kosher: Jewish Women in the Upper Midwest Since 1855* (Saint Paul: Minnesota Historical Society, 1996), 123–124.
46. Ibid., 159–160; Wendy Besman, *A Separate Circle: Jewish Life in Knoxville, Tennessee* (Knoxville: University of Tennessee Press, 2001), 34; Lance Sussman, *Beyond the Catskills: Jewish Life in Binghamton, New York, 1850–1975* (Binghamton: Southern Tier Jewish History Project, State University of New York, 1989), 18.
47. Quoted in Schloff, *And Prairie Dogs Weren't Kosher*, 71.
48. Sandra McGee Deutsch, *Crossing Borders, Claiming a Nation: A History of Argentine Jewish Women, 1880–1955* (Durham: Duke University Press, 2010), 45.
49. Frank L. Byrne and Jean Powers Soman, *Your True Marcus: The Civil War Letters of a Jewish Colonel* (Kent, Ohio: Kent State University Press, 1985), 4–6.
50. Quoted in Judith Laiken Elkin, *Jews in Latin American Republics* (Chapel Hill: University of North Carolina Press, 1980), 105.
51. Quoted in Clyde Webb, "Jewish Merchants and Black Customers in the Age of Jim Crow," *Southern Jewish History* 2 (1999), 55–80.
52. Abram Vossen Goodman, "A Jewish Peddler's Diary, 1842–1843," *American Jewish Archives* 3, no. 3 (1951), 81–111; Abraham Kohn, "Diary of His Life in Chicago, Ill and New England, 1842–1845," American Jewish Archives, Small Collection, 6384.
53. Bernard Horwich, *My First Eighty Years* (Chicago: Argus, 1939), 120.
54. Mark H. Elovitz, *A Century of Jewish Life in Dixie: The Birmingham Experience* (University: University of Alabama Press, 1974), 60.
55. Sylvia Sprigge, *Berenson: A Biography* (Boston: Houghton Mifflin, 1960), 29–30.
56. Isaac Mayer Wise, *Reminiscences* (Cincinnati: L. Wise and Son, 1901), 37–38.
57. *Atlanta Constitution*, July 29, 1882, ProQuest Historical Newspapers, *Atlanta Constitution* (1868–1945), 5.
58. Clipping, Lucy Dawidowicz Collection, 11, 2, American Jewish Historical Society.
59. David Geffen, "Delaware Jewry: The Formative Years, 1872–1889," *Delaware History* 16, no. 4 (1975), 269–297.

60. I. J. Schwartz, *Kentucky*, trans. Gertrude Dubrovsky (Tuscaloosa: University of Alabama Press, 1990), 30–31, 36–37.

3. ALONG THE ROAD

1. J. Ida Jiggetts, *Religion, Diet, and Health of Jews* (New York: Bloch, 1949), 1–2.
2. Quoted in Gideon Shimoni, *Jews and Zionism: The South African Experience* (Cape Town: Oxford University Press, 1980), 11.
3. R. G. Dunn and Company Collection, Maine, vol. 3, pp. 3, 57; vol. 4, p. 512.
4. I. J. Schwartz, *Kentucky*, trans. Gertrude Dubrovsky (Tuscaloosa: University of Alabama Press, 199).
5. Louis Schmier, "For Him the 'Schwartzers' Couldn't Do Enough: A Jewish Peddler and His Black Customers Look at Each Other," in *Strangers and Neighbors: Relations between Blacks and Jews in the United States*, ed. Maurianne Adams and John Bracey (Amherst: University of Massachusetts Press, 1999), 234–236.
6. Thank you to Shayne Smulyan for this reference. See http://www2.canada.com/montrealgazette/news/archives/story.html?id=cdbd9a23-f9c5-41d5-8f76-5f22oab8e315.
7. Quoted in Bertram Wallace Korn, *Jews and Negro Slavery in the Old South, 1789–1865* (Elkins Park, Pa.: Reform Congregation Keneseth Israel, 1961), 68.
8. Quoted in Ruth D. Sheinberg, "The Pekl: Folk/Histories of Jewish Peddlers in the South, 1890–1914," manuscript in possession of the author, 14, n.p.
9. M. L. Marks, *Jews Among Indians: Tales of Adventure and Conflict in the Old West* (Chicago: Benison, 1992), 53.
10. Abraham Peck, "That Other 'Peculiar Institution': Jews and Judaism in the Nineteenth Century South," *Modern Judaism* 7, no. 1 (1987), 99–114.
11. Eliot R. Davis, *A Link with the Past* (Auckland: Unity, 1948), 18.
12. Casper [Kasirel] Sober, *The Story of My Life, 1876–1956*, p. 37, unpublished memoir in possession of the author. My thanks to Dara Pefit for sharing this with me.
13. Abe Schapera, "The Jews of Namaqualand," *Jewish Affairs* 35, no. 12 (1980), 23–29.
14. Quoted in Robin McGrath, *Salt Fish and Shmattes: The History of Jews in Newfoundland and Labrador from 1770* (St. John's, Newfoundland: Creative Book Publishing, 1989), 52.
15. Eli Goldstein, "Litvaks in the Rural South African Economy," *Jewish Affairs* 57, no. 2 (2002), 9–13.
16. "Segal, Robert Ephraim," American Jewish Archive Autobiographical Questionnaire, Small Collections SC11149, American Jewish Archives.
17. Beryl Berman [Mrs. Theodore H.] Gordon, "Zieve, Moses Menahem: Holy Moses," Biographies File, SC-13364, Small Collection, American Jewish Archives.

18. Quoted in Sheinberg, "The Pekl," 5–6.
19. Hollace A. Weiner, "The Misers: The Role of Rabbis Deep in the Heart of Texas," in *Dixie Diaspora: An Anthology of Southern Jewish History*, ed. Mark K. Bauman (Tuscaloosa: University of Alabama Press, 2006), 55–101.
20. Eva Abraham–van der Mark, "The Ashkenazi Jews of Curaçao: A Trading Minority," *New West Indian Guide/Nieuwe West-IndischeGids* 74, nos. 3–4 (2000), 257–280.
21. B. A. Kosmin, *Majuta: A History of the Jewish Community of Zimbabwe* (Salisbury: Mambo, 1980), 11.
22. Montagu Frank Modder, *The Jew in the Literature of England to the End of the 19th Century* (Philadelphia: Jewish Publication Society of America, 1944), 80.
23. American Life Histories: Manuscripts from the Federal Writers' Project, 1936–1940, http://www.loc.gov/item/wpalh0000081.
24. Arnold R. Pilling and Patricia L. Pilling, "Cloth, Clothes, Hose, and Bowes: Nonsedentary Merchants Among the Indians of Northwestern California," *Migration and Anthropology: Proceedings of the 1970 Annual Spring Meeting of the American Ethnological Society*, ed. Robert F. Spencer (Seattle: University of Washington Press, 1970), 97–119.
25. Marks, *Jews Among Indians*, 50.
26. Korn, *Jews and Negro Slavery*, 63.
27. Melissa Walker and James C. Cobb, eds. *The New Encyclopedia of Southern Culture*, vol. 11, *Agriculture and Industry* (Chapel Hill: University of North Carolina Press, 2008), 50–51.
28. Rosaline Levenson, "Chico's Jewish Community in the Twentieth Century, Part One," *Western States Jewish Historical Quarterly* 20, no. 3 (1988), 187–198.
29. "Benzely, Mrs. Marion," 1982, 54-C, Upper Midwest Jewish Archives.
30. Watson Parker, *Deadwood: The Golden Years* (Lincoln: University of Nebraska Press, 1981), 141.
31. Catherine Kenney, "Dragging Main with Esther Bindursky," *Arkansas Times* 13, no. 7 (1987), 40–44.
32. "Rubin, Philip: Jewish Country Boy: An Autobiography, 1897–1957," SC-10533, Small Collections, box 1277, American Jewish Archives.
33. Ewa Morawska, "A Replica of the 'Old Country' Relationship in the Ethnic Niche: East European Jews and Gentiles in Small-Town Western Pennsylvania, 1880s–1930," *American Jewish History* 77, no. 1 (1987), 87–105.
34. Quoted in Levitz, "The Acculturation of the East European Jews," 49.
35. Harry Golden, "The Jewish People of North Carolina," *North Carolina Historical Review* 32, no. 2 (1955), 194–216.
36. "Memoirs: Julius F. Solomon, Lima, Ohio, 1971," SC 11731, Small Collection, American Jewish Archives.
37. Transcript, Interview Re: Louis Silverman, Danville, Va., by Mrs. Feagin of Royal Palm Beach, Florida, May 6, 1980, Emory University, p. 22.
38. Thank you to Leonard Rogoff for this reference.

39. Kenney, "Dragging Main," 41.
40. Quoted in Marcus Arkin, *Aspects of Jewish Economic History* (Philadelphia: Jewish Publication Society, 1975), 218.
41. Rudolf Glanz, *Jew and Mormon: Historic Group Relations and Religious Outlook* (New York: Waldron, 1963), 163–164.
42. L. A. Casper, "A Short History of the Jews of Middletown," SC-8518, "Histories File," Small Collection, American Jewish Archives.
43. Sarah Gertrude Millin, *The South Africans* (New York: Boni and Liveright, 1927), 187.
44. See, for example, Esther Regina Largman and Robert M. Levine, "Jews in the Tropics: Bahian Jews in the Early Twentieth Century," *The Americas* 43, no. 2 (1986), 159–170.
45. Ariel Segal, *Jews of the Amazon: Self-Exile in Earthly Paradise* (Philadelphia: Jewish Publication Society, 1999), 52–54; Katherine A. Benton, "The Border Jews: Border Marriages, Border Lives: Mexican-Jewish Intermarriage in the Arizona Territory, 1850–1900," M.A. thesis, University of Wisconsin–Madison, 1997, pp. 1–2; Hilary L. Rubinstein, *The Jews in Victoria, 1835–1985* (Sydney: George Allen and Unwin, 1986), 24–25.
46. See David Rome, *Through the Eyes of the Eagle: The Early Montreal Yiddish Press, 1907–1916* (Montreal: Véhicule, 2001), 146, on families living in rural Quebec with such last names as Levy, Vosberg, Flashman, and the like.
47. Nell Irvin Painter, *The Narrative of Hosea Hudson: The Life and Times of a Black Radical* (New York: Norton, 1994), 95.
48. Louis E. Schmier, "Hellooo! Peddlerman! Helloo!" in *Ethnic Minorities in Gulf Coast Society*, ed. Jerrell H. Shofner and Linda V. Ellsworth (Pensacola, Fla.: Historic Pensacola Preservation Board, 1979), 75–88.
49. Thomas D. Clark, *My Century in History: Memoirs* (Lexington: University of Kentucky Press, 2006), 37–38.
50. Harry Crews, *Childhood: The Biography of a Place* (New York: Harper and Row, 1978), 73–74.
51. Elizabeth Jane Dietz, "As We Lived a Long Time Ago," *Goldenseal* 7, no. 3 (1981), 12–18.
52. Quoted in W. Gunther Plaut, *The Jews in Minnesota: The First Seventy-Five Years* (New York: American Jewish Historical Society, 1959), 128.
53. Quoted in Louise Fawcett, "Arabs and Jews in the Development of the Colombian Caribbean 1850–1950," *Immigrants and Minorities* 16, no. 1 (1997), 57–79.
54. Jack Arons Collection 703, Vol. 2, p. 4, Tulane University, Louisiana Research Collection.

4. ROAD RAGE

1. *American Jewish Yearbook: 5665 (1904–1905)* (Philadelphia: Jewish Publication Society of America, 1905), 19–24.

2. Dermot Keogh, *Jews in Twentieth-Century Ireland* (Cork: Cork University Press, 1998).
3. See Kerby Miller, *Emigrants and Exiles: Ireland and the Irish Exodus to North America* (New York: Oxford University Press, 1985), 464–465.
4. Quoted in David Englander, ed., *A Documentary History of Jewish Immigrants in Britain, 1840–1920* (Leicester: Leicester University Press, 1994), 281–288.
5. Seán Spellissy, *The History of Limerick City* (Limerick: Celtic Bookshop, 1998), 81–82.
6. Joseph Lee, "Reflections on the Study of Irish Values," in *Irish Values and Attitudes: The Irish Report of the European Value System Study* (Dublin: Dominican Publications, 1984), 113; K. H. Connell, *Irish Peasant Society: Four Historical Essays* (Dublin: Irish Academic Press, 1996), 135.
7. Quoted in Keogh, *Jews in Twentieth-Century Ireland*, 45.
8. For earlier episodes see Cormac O'Grada, *Jewish Ireland in the Age of Joyce: A Socioeconomic History* (Princeton: Princeton University Press, 2006); Louis Hyman, *The Jews of Ireland: From Earliest Times to the Year 1910* (Shannon: Irish University Press, 1972).
9. Alfred R. Schumann, *No Peddlers Allowed* (Appleton, Wis.: C. C. Nelson, 1948).
10. Jacques Langlais and David Rome, *Jews and French Quebecers: Two Hundred Years of Shared History* (Waterloo, Ont.: Wilfrid Laurier University Press, 1991), 42, 53–54; Erna Paris, *Jews: An Account of their Experience in Canada* (Toronto: Macmillan of Canada, 1980), 50; J. Spievak, YIVO Oral History, no. 35, 1; Michael Brown, "From Stereotype to Scapegoat: Anti-Jewish Sentiment in French Canada from Confederation to World War I," in *Anti-Semitism in Canada: History and Interpretation*, ed. Alan Davies (Waterloo, Ont.: Wilfrid Laurier University Press, 1992), 39–66; Gerald Tulchinsky, *Taking Root: The Origins of the Canadian Jewish Community* (Toronto: Lester, 1992), 242–243.
11. See León Trahtemberg Siederer, *La Vida Judia en Lima y en las Provincias del Peru* (Lima, 1989), 13–15; Judith Laikin Elkin, *The Jews of Latin America* (New York: Holmes and Meier, 1998). There is a wealth of literature on individual countries as well.
12. Jeffrey Alderman, "The Anti-Jewish Riots of August 1911 in South Wales," *Welsh History Review/Cylchgrawn Hanes Cymru* 6 (1971–1972), 190–200.
13. W. D. Rubenstein, "The Anti-Jewish Riots of 1911 in South Wales: A Re-Examination," *Welsh History Review/Cylchgrawn Hanes Cymru* 18, no. 4 (1997), 667–699.
14. Carol Henrick Carlson, *Naturalisation and Discrimination: Eastern Jews and Other Immigrants to Sweden, 1860–1920: Summary* (Uppsala: Uppsala Universitet, 2004), 8; Sven Dahl, "Travelling Pedlars in Nineteenth Century Sweden," *Scandinavian Economic History Review* 7, no. 2 (1959), 167–178. Special thanks to Pontus Rudburg of Uppsala University for drawing my attention to this issue.

15. House of Assembly, *Report of the Select Committee on Asiatic Grievances, September, 1908* (Cape Town: Cape Times, ltd., Government Printers, 1908), 102–104.

16. Quoted in Milton Shain, *The Roots of Antisemitism in South Africa* (Charlottesville: University of Virginia Press, 1994), 26.

17. Alexis de Tocqueville, *Democracy in America*, ed. Harvey Mansfield and Delba Winthrop (Chicago: University of Chicago Press, 2000), 511–512.

18. Quoted in Steven Hertzberg, *Strangers Within the Gate City: The Jews of Atlanta, 1845–1915* (Philadelphia: Jewish Publication Society of America, 1978), 125.

19. *Jewish Messenger*, January 19, 1858, pp. 108–109; William Hagy, *This Happy Land: The Jews of Colonial and Ante-Bellum South Carolina* (Tuscaloosa: University of Alabama Press, 1993), 195; John Foster Carr, *Guide to the United States for the Jewish Immigrant: Second Yiddish Edition* (New York: Immigrant Publication Society, 1916), 38.

20. Quoted in Robert Rosen, *The Jewish Confederates* (Columbia: University of South Carolina Press, 2000), 265; Jonathan Sarna, *When Grant Expelled the Jews* (New York: Next Books, Schocken, 2012).

21. Louis Schmier, "Notes and Documents on the 1862 Expulsion of Jews from Thomasville, Georgia," *American Jewish Archives* 32, no. 1 (1980), 9–22.

22. Betty Naggar, *Jewish Pedlars and Hawkers, 1740–1940* (Camberley, Surrey: Porphyrogenotis, 1992), 37.

23. Isaac Frank, "Memoir," Small Collections, SC-14538, American Jewish Archives, 15.

24. Hilary L. Rubenstein, *The Jews in Victoria, 1835–1985* (Sydney: George Allen and Unwin, 1986), 36.

25. "Transcript of Irving M. Engel Oral Memoir, New York, N.Y., 1969–1970," Small Collections 3213, American Jewish Archives.

26. *The Particulars of the Murder of Nathan Adler on the Night of November Sixth, 1849, Venice, Cayuga County, N.Y., Including the Whole Testimony Taken by the Coroner and the Inquisition and Arrest of the Three Bahams* (Auburn, N.Y.: Finn and Rockwell, 1850); see also Richard Brown, "Nathan Adler Stops at the Bahams," *New York Folklore Quarterly* 24, no. 1 (1968), 27–43.

27. My thanks to Leonard Rogoff for this clipping.

28. David Brener, *The Jews of Lancaster, Pennsylvania: A Story with Two Beginnings* (Lancaster, Pa.: Congregation Shaarai Shomayim, 1979), 30.

29. See Charles E. Jones, *Life and Confessions of Charles E. Jones Convicted of the Murder of Isaac Jackson, A Jew Peddler, at Springfield, Mass., December 7, 1857* (Montpelier, Vt.: Ballou, Loveland, 1860).

30. Frank Felsteiner, *Anti-Semitic Stereotypes: A Paradigm of Otherness in English Popular Culture, 1660–1830* (Baltimore: Johns Hopkins University Press, 1995).

31. Walter Zenner, *Minorities in the Middle: A Cross-Cultural Analysis* (Albany: SUNY Press, 1991), 50–51.

32. Rudolph Glanz, "Jew and Yankee: A Historic Comparison," *Jewish Social Studies* 6 (1944), 3–30.

33. For one example of the murder of an Irish peddler in the American South, see Lu Ann Jones, *Mama Learned Us to Work: Farm Women in the New South* (Chapel Hill: University of North Carolina Press, 2002), 31.

34. Dario A. Euraque, "The Arab-Jewish Economic Presence in San Pedro Sula, the Industrial Capital of Honduras: Formative Years, 1880s–1930s," *Immigrants and Minorities* 16, no. 1 (1997), 94–124.

35. Quoted in Julius Carlebach, *The Jews of Nairobi, 1903–1962* (Nairobi: Hebrew Congregation, 1962), 18.

36. Quoted in Tony Kushner, *Anglo-Jewry Since 1066: Place, Locality, and Memory* (Manchester: Manchester University Press, 2009), 136.

37. See Walter Nugent, *Crossings: The Great Transatlantic Migration, 1820–1914* (Bloomington: Indiana University Press, 1992).

38. "Poison in the Spring," *New York Times*, April 18, 1886.

39. "Cholera at St. Louis," *Chicago Daily Tribune*, January 22, 1895.

40. Karen Falk and Avi Y. Decter, eds., *We Call This Place Home: Jewish Life in Maryland's Small Towns* (Baltimore: Jewish Museum of Maryland, 2002), 53.

41. "The Growing Menace of the Use of Cocaine," *New York Times*, August 2, 1908.

42. William T. Parsons, *Tramps and Peddlers* (Collegeville, Pa.: Chestnut, 1988), 74.

43. "McKeesport, Pa. The Early History of the McKeesport Jewish Community by Sarah Landesman," History Files, SC-7982, Small Collections, American Jewish Archives.

44. L. M. Montgomery, *Anne of Green Gables* (Boston: L. C. Page, 1908).

45. Quoted in Lowell Gudmundson, "Costa Rican Jewry: An Economic and Political Outline," in *The Jewish Presence in Latin America*, ed. Judith Laikin Elkin and Gilbert W. Merk (Boston: Allen and Unwin, 1986), 219–231.

46. James O. Breeden, ed., *Advice Among Masters: The Ideal in Slave Management in the Old South* (Westport, Conn: Greenwood, 1980), 270.

47. Quoted in B. A. Kosmin, *Majuta: A History of the Jewish Community of Zimbabwe* (Gwelo: Mambo, 1980), 42.

48. Quoted in Marilyn Delevante and Anthony Alberga, *The Island of One People: An Account of the History of the Jews of Jamaica* (Kingston: Ian Randle, 2005), 32.

49. See Jones, *Mama Learned Us to Work*, 30–32.

50. *Havaner Lebn*, November 3, 1933, p. 4.

51. W. Lee Provol, *The Pack Peddler* (Greenville, Pa.: Beaver, 1933), 59–60.

52. Baila Shargel and Harold L. Drimmer, *The Jews of Westchester: A Social History* (Fleschmanns, N.Y.: Purple Mountain, 1994), 35–36.

53. Gerald Tulchinsky, *Canada's Jews: A People's Journey* (Toronto: University of Toronto Press, 2008), 141.

54. Marcus Arkin, *Aspects of Jewish Economic History* (Philadelphia: Jewish Publication Society, 1975), 218.

55. "Key West Florida Family Anecdotes and Chapters of a History of the Jewish Community of Key West Collected and Written by Mrs. Goldie Schuster and Misc. Correspondence, St. Petersburg, Fla, Je 18 and 29, 1979," Small Collections, 6292, American Jewish Archives.

56. Jay Levinson, *Jewish Community of Cuba: The Golden Age, 1906–1958* (Nashville: Westview, 2006), 73.

57. *Southern Israelite*, November 16, 1934, p. 1.

58. "The Jewish Community of Rhodesia and the North," 1926, RH/BYO/I-I-1, Central Archives for the History of the Jewish People, Jerusalem.

59. "Austrian, Joseph, Autobiographical and Historical Sketches, Chicago, Ill., 1904," box 2282, SC-598, Small Collections American Jewish Archives, 69.

60. Quoted in "Early Anti-Semitism: The Imprint of Drumont," David Rome, compiler, *Canadian Jewish Archives* (Montreal: National Archives, Canadian Jewish Congress, 1985), 56.

61. Quoted in Milton Shain, "Representations of the Jew in Cape Colony c. 1850–1885: Confirmation of the Interactionist Model of Antisemitism?" in *Patterns of Migration, 1850–1914* (London: Jewish Historical Society of England, 1996), 207–219.

62. Quoted in Suzanne D. Rutland, *Edge of the Diaspora: Two Centuries of Jewish Settlement in Australia* (New York: Holmes and Meier, 1997), 95.

63. William Faulkner, *The Sound and the Fury* (New York: Vintage, 1954), 237, 239.

64. W. D. Robinson, *Memoir Addressed to Persons of the Jewish Religion in Europe on the Subject of Emigration to, and Settlement in, One of the Most Eligible Parts of the United States of North America* (London: H. Hay, 1819), 8, 13, 24.

65. Mark Wischnitzer, "The Historical Background of the Settlement of Jewish Refugees in Santo Domingo," *Jewish Social Studies* 4, no. 1 (1942), 49–58.

66. Michael Davitt, *Within the Pale: The True Story of Anti-Semitic Persecutions in Russia* (London: Hurst and Blackett, 1903), 88–89, 246.

67. *Jewish Chronicle*, September 20, 1907, p. 10.

68. Quoted in Jacob Levitz, "The Jewish Community in Mexico: Its Life and Education, 1900–1954," Ph.D. diss., Dropsie College for Hebrew and Cognate Studies, 1954, p. 10.

69. Quoted in Corinne Azen Krause, "The Jews in Mexico: A History with Special Emphasis on the Period from 1857 to 1930," Ph.D. diss., University of Pittsburgh, 1970, p. 281.

70. Maurice B. Hexter, *The Jews in Mexico* (New York: Emergency Committee on Jewish Refugees, 1926), 7.

71. Quoted in Victor A. Mirelman, "Sephardic Immigration to Argentina Prior to the Nazi Period," in Elkin and Merk, *Jewish Presence in Latin America*, 12–32.

72. Quoted in Jeffrey Lesser, *Welcoming the Undesirables: Brazil and the Jewish Question* (Berkeley: University of California Press, 1995), 32–33.

73. *Occident*, February–March, 1863.

74. *Jewish Chronicle*, June 23, 1882, p. 12.

75. *Jewish Chronicle*, January 1855, p. 568.

76. *Brooklyn Eagle*, February 16, 1891, p. 4.

77. Quoted in Hilary L. Rubinstein, *Chosen: The Jews in Australia* (Sydney: Allen and Unwin, 1987), 79.

78. Quoted in J. Sanford Rikoon, "The Jewish Agriculturalists' Aid Society of America: Philanthropy, Ethnicity, and Agriculture in the Heartland," *Agricultural History* 72, no. 1 (1998), 1–32.

79. *Jewish Criterion*, October 28, 1898, p. 1.

80. *Jewish Chronicle*, July 6, 1906, p. 8.

81. Quoted in Rubenstein, *Jews in Victoria*, 125.

82. Quoted in Michael Brown, "The Empire's Best Known Jew and Little Known Jewry," in *The Canadian Jewish Studies Reader*, ed. Richard Menkis and Norman Ravvin (Calgary: Red Deer, 2004), 73–89.

83. Reprinted in Janet E. Schulte, "'Proving Up and Moving Up': Jewish Homesteading Activity in North Dakota, 1900–1920," *Great Plains Quarterly* 10 (1990), 228–244.

84. *Jewish Criterion*, August 31, 1906, p. 12.

85. *Jewish Chronicle*, June 28, 1850, p. 303.

86. A. R. Rollin, "Russo-Jewish Immigrants in England Before 1881," *Transactions of the Jewish Historical Society of England* 21 (1968), 202–213.

5. THE END OF THE ROAD

1. "In Memory of Sigmund Eisner: February 14, 1859"; January 5, 1925, privately published, available at New-York Historical Society.

2. Gustav Saron and Louis Hotz, *The Jews in South Africa: A History* (Cape Town: Oxford University Press, 1955), 126–127.

3. Quoted in Corinne Azen Krause, "The Jews in Mexico: A History with Special Emphasis on the Period from 1857 to 1930," Ph.D. diss., University of Pittsburgh, 1970, pp. 312–313.

4. Letter to David Bressler, February 28, 1906, IRO papers, box 83, I-91, American Jewish Historical Society.

5. "In Memory of Sigmund Eisner."

6. See Judith Laikin Elkin, *The Jews of the Latin American Republics* (Chapel Hill: University of North Carolina Press, 1980), for a country-by-country rundown of the process of Jewish migration, peddling, economic mobility, and integration.

7. On Sammy Marks, see Eli Goldstein, "Litvaks in the Rural Economy," *Jewish Affairs* 57, no. 2 (2002), 9–13.

8. Maritz Corrales Capestany, *La Island Elegida: Los Judios en Cuba* (Havana: Editorial de Ciencias Sociales, 2007), 8.

9. Courtney Randolph, "Otto Mears, Pathfinder of San Juan," *Westways* 4, no. 1 (1948), 18–19.

10. Brenda Gayle Plummer, "Between Privilege and Opprobrium: The Arabs and Jews of Haiti," in *Arab and Jewish Immigrants in Latin America: Images and Realities*, ed. Ignacio Klich and Jeffrey Lesser (London: Frank Cass, 1998), 80–93.

11. See the reference to Pine Bluff, Arkansas, in the online *Encyclopedia of Southern Jewish Communities*, Goldring/Woldenberg Institute of Southern Jewish Life, http://www.isjl.org/encyclopedia-of-southern-jewish-communities .html.

12. Laura R. Westbrook, "Common Roots: The Godchaux Family in Louisiana History, Literature and Public Folklore," Ph.D. diss., University of Louisiana at Lafayette, 2001.

13. Judith Stix, "Some Notes on the Early Jewish Communal History of Noble County, Indiana, and Solomon Meir, Pioneer and Patriarch," SC-13663, Small Collections, American Jewish Archives.

14. Allen Breck, *The Centennial History of the Jews of Colorado* (Denver: University of Denver, 1960), 46–47.

15. Isaac Wolfe Bernheim, *The Closing Chapters of a Busy Life* (Denver: Welch-Haffner, 1929).

16. William Lee Provol, *The Pack Peddler* (New York: John C. Winston, 1937).

17. Quoted in Gwynn Schrive, "Mostly Smouse?—South African Jews and Their Occupations a Century Ago," *Jewish Affairs* 55, no. 1 (2000), 9–15.

18. Cormac O'Grada, "Settling In: Dublin's Jewish Immigrants of a Century Ago," *Field Day Review* 1 (2005), 87–99; Kenneth Collin, *Be Well! Jewish Immigrant Health and Welfare in Glasgow, 1860–1914* (East Lothian, Scotland: Tuckwell, 2001), 37.

19. Jessie Bloom, "The Good Old Days in Dublin: Some Girlhood Recollections of the 1890s," *Commentary*, July 1952, pp. 21–32.

20. "Singer, Louis E., Autobiography," n.d., SC-11557, Small Collections, American Jewish Archives.

21. Maxwell Whiteman, "Notions, Dry Goods and Clothing," *Jewish Quarterly Review* 53, no. 4 (1963), 306–321.

22. Quoted in Lucien Wolf, ed., *Essays in Jewish History* (London: Jewish Historical Society of England, 1914), 137–138.

23. Israel J. Solomon, *Records of My Life* (New York, 1887), 80.

24. Abraham Flexner, *I Remember: The Autobiography of Abraham Flexner* (New York: Simon and Schuster, 1940), 12.

25. Morris R. Werner, *The Life of a Practical Humanitarian* (New York: Harper and Brothers, 1939), 4.

26. "Sophia Goldsmith: The Story of a Courtship," in *Memoirs of American Jews, 1775–1865*, 3 vols., vol. 2, ed. Jacob R. Marcus (Philadelphia: Jewish Publication Society of America, 1955), 279.

27. Quoted in David Brener, *The Jews of Lancaster, Pennsylvania: A Story With Two Beginnings* (Lancaster, Pa.: Congregation Shaarai Shomayim, 1979), 43.

28. Quoted in Hasia R. Diner, *A Time for Gathering: The Second Migration, 1820–1880* (Baltimore: Johns Hopkins University Press, 1992), 83–84.

29. Julius H. Kretzmer, "Shtetl Life in the Swartland in the Twenties: Nostalgic Memories of Malmesburg," *Jewish Affairs* 41, no. 4 (1986), 17–23.

30. Foster Hirsch, *The Boys from Syracuse: The Shubert's Theatrical Empire* (Carbondale: Southern Illinois University Press, 1998), 11–13.

31. Capestany, *La Isla Elegida*, 97–98.

32. Lee K. Frankel, "Self-Respect Funds," *Jewish Charities* 5, no. 1 (1914), 19–23.

33. David da Sola Pool, "The Immigration of Levantine Jews into the United States," *Jewish Charities* 4, no. 11 (1914), 12–27.

34. Rosa Perla Raicher, *Uruguay, La Comunidad Israelita y el Pueblo Judio* (Jerusalem: Avraham Harman Institute of Contemporary Jewry, 2003), 75.

35. On Sweden see Sture Hammarström, "The Stepchildren of the Nation: Jewish Integration into the Society in Some Cities of Northern Sweden, 1870–1940," Ph.D. diss., University of Uppsala, 2007.

36. Capestany, *La Isla Elegida*, 151, 213.

37. Quoted in Joseph Abraham Poliva, *Biography of Nehemia Dov Hoffman: Founder of the Jewish Press in South Africa. Its First Editor and Printer (1860–1928)* (Johannesburg: privately published, 1968).

38. Lazarus Morris Goldman, *The History of the Jews in New Zealand* (Wellington: A. H. and A. W. Reed, 1958), 109.

39. E. Abraham–van der Mark, "The Ashkenazi Jews of Curaçao, a Trading Minority," *New West Indian Guide/Nieuwe West-Indische Gids* 74, nos. 3–4 (2000), 257–280.

40. Quoted in Jeffrey Lesser, "The Immigration and Integration of Polish Jews in Brazil, 1924–1934," *Americas* 51, no. 2 (1994), 173–191.

41. Quoted in Arnold Shankman, "Friend or Foe? Southern Blacks View the Jew, 1880–1935," in *"Turn to the South": Essays in Southern Jewish History*, ed. Nathan M. Kaganoff and Melvin Urofsky (Charlottesville: University of Virginia Press, 1979), 105–123.

42. "Preserving a Culture: Growing Up in the Shetland Islands," November 1, 2007, http://www.scotland.org/about-history-tradition-and-roots/features/culture/Jewish-in-shetlands, accessed May 9, 2013.

43. Harry Golden, "The Jewish People of North Carolina," *North Carolina Historical Review* 32, no. 2 (1955), 194–216.

44. E. Merton Coulter, *The South During Reconstruction* (Baton Rouge: Louisiana State University Press, 1947), 202–203.

45. Irving Katz, Memoir 28, Max and Rebecca Katz, Jewish Museum of Maryland.

46. On the Steinbach brothers and the Temple of Fashion, see Alan S. Pine, Jean C. Hershenov, and Aaron Lefkowitz, *Peddler to Suburbanite: The History of the Jews of Monmouth County, New Jersey: From the Colonial Period to 1980* (Deal Park, N.J.: Monmouth Jewish Community Council, 1981), 55.

47. On the racial aspect see Beth Kreydatus, "'You Are a Part of All of Us': Black Department Store Employees in Jim Crow Richmond," *Journal of Historical Research in Marketing* 2, no. 1 (2010), 108–129.
48. "Dumas, Arkansas," *Encyclopedia of Southern Jewish Communities*, http://www .isjl.org/arkansas-dumas-encyclopedia.html.
49. Clive Webb, "Jewish Merchants and Black Customers in the Age of Jim Crow," *Southern Jewish History* 2 (1999), 55–80.
50. Hilary L. Rubenstein, *Chosen: The Jews of Australia* (Sydney: Allen and Unwin, 1987), 121; Suzanne Rutland, *Edge of the Diaspora: Two Centuries of Jewish Settlement in Australia* (New York: Holmes and Meier, 1997), 124.
51. Bill Williams, *The Making of Manchester Jewry, 1740–1875* (Manchester: Manchester University Press, 1976), 127.
52. Nathan Ginter, "How the Jews Live in Lima, Peru," *Havaner Lebn*, June 1935, p. 9.
53. Leon Birbraher, "Two Experiences in Identity: Colombia and the United States of America," in *Identity in Dispersion: Selected Memoirs from Latin American Jews*, ed. Leon Klenicki (Cincinnati: Hebrew Union College Press, n.d.), 12–16.
54. Victor Perera, "Growing Up Jewish in Guatemala," in *Echad: An Anthology of Latin American Jewish Writings*, ed. Robert Kalechofsky and Roberta Kalechofsky (Marblehead, Mass.: Micah, 1980), 70–73.
55. Lloyd P. Gartner, *The Jewish Immigrant in England, 1870–1914* (London: Vallentine Mitchell, 1960), 59.
56. Margaret Walsh, "Industrial Opportunity on the Urban Frontier: 'Rags to Riches' and Milwaukee Clothing Manufacturers, 1840–1880," *Wisconsin Magazine of History* 57, no. 3 (1974), 175–194.
57. On the more obscure of these references see Robin McGrath, *Salt Fish and Shmattes: A History of the Jews in Newfoundland and Labrador From 1770* (St. Johns, Newfoundland: Creative, 2006), 64; Harold L. Laroff, "The Rockland Jewish Community," unpublished paper, Historical Society of Rockland County, n.d., p. 5; Michael W. Rich, "Henry Mack: An Important Figure in Nineteenth-Century American Jewish History," *American Jewish Archives* 47, no. 2 (1995), 261–279.
58. H. L. Meitis, *History of the Jews of Chicago* (Chicago: Jewish Historical Society of Chicago, 1924), 114.
59. Hugh Macmillan and Frank Shapiro, *Zion in Africa: The Jews of Zambia* (London: I. B. Tauris, 1999), 13.
60. Arthur Daniel Hart, *The Jew in Canada: A Complete Record of Canadian Jewry from the Days of the French Regime to the Present Time* (Toronto: Jewish Publishing Ltd., 1926), 567.
61. Interview with Rose Olds, November 25, 2002, and December 2, 2002, Oregon Jewish Museum, Oral History Transcripts.
62. "Toronto Jewry 60 Years Ago," Toronto, Canadian Jewish Congress, Central Region, December 1958.

63. Carl Zimring, "Dirty Work: How Hygiene and Xenophobia Marginalized the American Waste Trades, 1870–1930," *Environmental History* 9 (2004), 90–124.

64. Cormac O'Grada, *Jewish Ireland in the Age of Joyce: A Socioeconomic History* (Princeton: Princeton University Press, 2006), 61–62.

65. "Perlstine Distributors: A Brief History," *Jewish Historical Society of South Carolina* 11, no. 2 (2006), 9.

66. Abraham–van der Mark, "Ashkenazi Jews of Curaçao."

67. For Friedman's store see "Tuscaloosa" in the online *Encyclopedia of Southern Jewish Communities,* http://www.isjl.org/alabama-tuscaloosa-encyclopedia.html.

68. See John S. Levi and G. F. J. Bergman, *Australian Genesis: Jewish Convicts and Settlers, 1788–1860* (Melbourne: Melbourne University Press, 1974), 297.

69. Ray Rivlin, *Shalom Ireland: A Social History of Jews in Modern Ireland* (Dublin: Gill and Macmillan, 2003), 178–179.

70. Devera Stocker, "When Grandfather Julius Came to Michigan," *Michigan Jewish History* 6, no. 1 (1965), 11–14.

71. Alfred R. Schumann, *No Peddlers Allowed* (Appleton, Wis.: C. C. Nelson, 1948).

72. Carl Henrick Carlsson, *Naturalisation and Discrimination: Eastern Jews and Other Immigrants in Sweden, 1860–1920* (Uppsala, Sweden: Uppsala University Library, 2004), 12.

73. Simon Guberek, *Yo Vi Crecer un País* (Bogotá: Departmento Administritavo Nacional de Estadistica, 1974).

74. Edgar Samuel, "Jewish Settlement in Victoria, 1850–1914," *Patterns of Migration, 1850–1914: Proceedings of the International Academic Conference of the Jewish Historical Society of England and the Institute of Jewish Studies, University College London,* ed. Aubrey Newman and Stephen W. Massil (London: Jewish Historical Society of England/Institute of Jewish Studies, 1996), 330–345.

75. Jonathan V. Plaut, *The Jews of Windsor, 1790–1990: A Historical Chronicle* (Toronto: Dundurn, 2007), 43–46.

76. Morris Silverman, *Hartford Jews, 1659–1970* (Hartford: Connecticut Historical Society, 1970), 173; Frank L. Byrne, ed., *Your True Marcus: The Civil War Letters of a Jewish Colonel* (Kent, Ohio: Kent State University Press, 1985), 8; Benjamin Band, *Portland Jewry: Its Growth and Development* (Portland, Maine: Jewish Historical Society, 1955), 16; Wendy Lowe Besman, *A Separate Circle: Jewish Life in Knoxville, Tennessee* (Knoxville: University of Tennessee Press, 2001), 11; Abraham Shinedling, *West Virginia Jewry: Origins and History, 1850–1958* (Philadelphia: Maurice Jacobs, 1963), 867; *The Jewish Texans* (San Antonio: University of Texas at San Antonio Institute of Texan Cultures, 1974), 7.

77. Emanuel Hertz, *Lincoln's Contacts: Delivered at the Jewish Club, October 1, 1929* (Tarrytown, N.Y.: Magazine of History with Notes and Queries, 1930), 113.

78. Selma Lewis, *A Biblical People in the Bible Belt: The Jewish Community of Memphis, Tennessee, 1840s–1960s* (Macon, Ga.: Mercer University Press, 1998), 15.

79. "Pine Bluff, Arkansas," *Encyclopedia of Southern Jewish Communities;* Phillip Applebaum, "The Jews of Kalkaska County, Michigan," *Michigan Jewish History* 19, no. 1 (1979), 4–11.

80. Charles Risen, *Some Jewels of Maine: Jewish Maine Pioneers* (Pittsburgh: Dorrance, 1997), 2.

81. Henry K. Freedman, *The Jewish Congregations of Plattsburgh, New York* (no publication data, 1975), 4, 9.

82. M. Lissack, *Jewish Perseverance, or The Jew, at Home and Abroad: An Autobiography* (London: Hamilton, Adams, 1851), 80–88.

83. Robert Lynd and Helen Lynd, *Middletown: A Study in Contemporary American Culture* (New York: Harcourt Brace, 1929), 407–408.

84. "The Story of Gustav and Bella Kussy of Newark, New Jersey: A Family Chronicle," SC 6529, American Jewish Archives.

85. Israel Rosen interview, 15, 1, RG 102/3A, YIVO.

86. Morris A. Galatzan, "The Galatzans of El Paso, Texas," ms. 649, box 13, 12, American Jewish Archives.

87. Rubey Edgar Harlan, *The Narrative History of the People of Iowa* (Chicago: American Historical Society, 1931), 4: 51–52, 469–470.

88. J. A. A. Burnquist, *Minnesota and Its People* (Chicago: S. J. Clarke, 1924).

89. My thanks to Leonard Rogoff for providing me with this clipping.

90. Harry Hall, *America's Successful Men of Affairs: An Encyclopedia of Contemporaneous Biography* (New York: New York Tribune, 1895–1896).

91. Jim Gould, ed., *Rooted in Rock: New Adirondack Writing, 1975–2000* (Blue Mountain Lake, N.Y.: Adirondack Museum, 2001), 99.

92. "Woolf Ruta Cohen . . . by Mrs. Beillie Einfeld, His Grand-Niece," *Australian Jewish Historical Society Newsletter* 77 (October 2007), 2.

93. Isaac Factor, "The Jewish Communities of South Wales: Port Talbot," *CAJEX* 11, no. 4 (1961), 65–67.

94. "The Story of Gustav and Bella Kussy," 132–133.

95. Y. A. Pinis, "Jewish Life in the Cuban Provinces: Its Present and Future," *Havaner Lebn*, June 1935, pp. 10–11.

96. Kretzmer, "Shtetl Life in the Swartland," 19.

97. Brochure, Historic Beth Joseph Synagogue; Judith E. Endelman, *The Jewish Community of Indianapolis, 1849 to the Present* (Bloomington: Indiana University Press, 1984), 66.

98. D. H. L. Fleishaker, "The Illinois-Iowa Jewish Community on the Banks of the Mississippi River," Ph.D. diss., Yeshiva University, 1957, p. 21.

99. Lawrence A. Rubin, "William Saulson—Michigan Pioneer," *Michigan Jewish History* 4, no. 1 (1963), 3–9.

100. Tobias Brinkmann, *Sundays at Sinai: A Jewish Congregation in Chicago* (Chicago: University of Chicago Press, 2012), demonstrates the concentration of former peddlers among the founders of this Reform congregation.

LEGACIES OF THE ROAD

1. León Trahtemberg Siederer, *La Vida Judia en Lima y en las Provincias del Peru* (Lima, 1989), 122–124.

2. Quoted in Steven Hertzberg, *Strangers in the Gate City: The Jews of Atlanta, 1845–1915* (Philadelphia: Jewish Publication Society, 1978), 103.

3. On the evangelical effort toward the Jews in America, see Yaakov Ariel, *Evangelizing the Chosen People: Missions to the Jews in America, 1880–2000* (Chapel Hill: University of North Carolina Press, 2000).

4. Quoted in Gwynne Schire, "Mostly Smouse?—South African Jews and Their Occupations a Century Ago," *Jewish Affairs* 55, no. 1 (2000), 9–15.

5. M. I. Cohen, "The Jewish Communities of Rhodesia and the North," in *The South African Jewish Year Book and Who's Who in South African Jewry, 1929, 5689–90* (Johannesburg: South African Jewish Historical Society, 1929), 131–136.

6. S. B. Goodkind, *Prominent Jews of America: A Collection of Biographical Sketches of Jews Who Have Distinguished Themselves in Commercial, Professional, and Religious Endeavor* (Toledo, Ohio: American Hebrew Publishing, 1918), 17–18.

7. George Cohen, *The Jews in the Making of America* (Boston: Stratford, 1924), 120, 243–244.

8. Cecil Roth, *The Jewish Contribution to Civilization* (London: Macmillan, 1938), 247.

Index

Abrams, Henry, 37
Adler, Nathan, 128–129
African Standard (newspaper), 132–133
Alabama, 80, 94, 103, 128, 179
Aliens Act, 30
Allgemeine Zeitung des Judentums
   (newspaper), 18
Alliance Israélite Universelle, 29, 35,
   110, 149, 150, 160
Alpert, Fruma (Zlata), 63
Alpert, Nathan, 63
Alsatian Jews, 29, 38, 46, 113, 162, 186;
   violence against 28, 146, 188
Amazon, 35, 44, 46, 57, 110, 194
American Jewish Congress, 148, 156
American Jewish Yearbook, 115, 116,
   118, 210
Anne of Green Gables, 136
Argentina, 34, 35, 36, 75, 103
Arizona, 40, 110, 168
Arkansas, 162, 174
Assa, Moisés Nae, 170
Association catholique de la jeunesse
   canadienne, 121
Atlanta Constitution, 81
Australia, 23, 42–43, 106, 110, 145, 159,

174, 180; gold rush, 32, 49; Jewish
   migration, 37, 49; Melbourne, 32,
   150; New South Wales, 173;
   Queensland, 147; Sydney, 193;
   Victoria, 128, 180, 183

Baevski, Elcon, 174
Baevski, Sidney, 174
Balkan Jews, 35, 49
Baltimore Bargain House, 47–48, 66,
   176
Baron de Hirsch Fund, 60, 64, 151, 152
Baron de Hirsch Institute, 64
Bavarian Jews: Midwest, 20–21, 76;
   New England, 79, 182; South, 92,
   179; United States, 29, 55, 109, 144,
   162; violence against, 28, 146, 188
Belarusian Jews, 38, 39, 63, 169, 210
Benavides, Óscar, 122
Benguigui, Moyses, 46
Bentwich, Norman, 163
Beren, Elias, 210
Berenson, Bernard, 80, 163
Berenson, Senda, 80, 163
Bernheim, Isaac, 162
Bernstein, Hyman, 101–102

239